The Longest Psalm

*Day-by-Day Responses
to Divine Self-Revelation*

Michael Casey, OCSO

LITURGICAL PRESS

Collegeville, Minnesota

www.litpress.org

Imprimi potest:
Abbot Steele Hartmann OCSO
October 27, 2022

Cover design by Savanah N. Landerholm

Cover photo by Ivana Cajina on Unsplash

2   3   4   5   6   7   8   9

Library of Congress Cataloging-in-Publication Data

Names: Casey, Michael, author.
Title: The longest psalm : day-by-day responses to divine self-revelation / Michael Casey, OCSO.
Description: Collegeville, Minnesota : Liturgical Press, [2023] | Includes bibliographical references. | Summary: "As the longest Psalm in the Bible, Psalm 119 comprises 176 verses. In The Longest Psalm, Michael Casey offers a meditative reading of each verse of the psalm to facilitate a truly personal expression of prayer and reflection. Each verse stands alone, intended to be read slowly, like the litanies familiar to Catholic devotion. Through this reflection, readers will discover the text is not merely a psalm to be sung but also a path to be followed"— Provided by publisher.
Identifiers: LCCN 2023009268 (print) | LCCN 2023009269 (ebook) | ISBN 9798400800009 (paperback) | ISBN 9798400800016 (epub) | ISBN 9798400800016 (pdf) | ISBN 9798400800344 (pdf)
Subjects: LCSH: Bible. Psalms, CXIX—Meditations.
Classification: LCC BS1450 119th .C37 2023 (print) | LCC BS1450 119th (ebook) | DDC 223/.206—dc23/eng/20230504
LC record available at https://lccn.loc.gov/2023009268
LC ebook record available at https://lccn.loc.gov/2023009269

"Michael Casey's insightful meditations on Psalm 119, the longest psalm of the Psalter, are to be read slowly and savored. By reflecting on the meaning of each of the Psalm's 176 verses, he shows us how God's Torah can form and renew our lives today. Here is a volume to which you can turn for spiritual nourishment and guidance."

—Frank J. Matera, professor emeritus, The Catholic University of America

"How to joyfully fulfil the Law of the Lord in all the varied circumstances emerging from one's life? Who else but Michael Casey could weave together 176 answers to this question using the 176 verses of Psalm 118 (119)? With his usual laser-sharp gaze on the text, his comprehensive exploration and penetrating acumen we have all come to expect from his work, Casey draws us into the profound riches and purpose of this otherwise repetitive and predictable text."

—Carmel Posa, SGS, University of Divinity, Australia

"God's self-revelation in Scripture can be known by us through *lectio*. Fr. Michael Casey has done the homework. All we have to do is turn the page. This book is an example of how we can hold and grasp the whole of Hebrew Scripture."

—Meg Funk, OSB, Our Lady of Grace Monastery, Beech Grove, Indiana

"The long, repetitive Psalm 119, like an apparently barren landscape, yields surprising variety and abundance to the practiced, patient gaze. Thanks to Michael Casey's well-trained eye and long experience, this neglected psalm now receives the attention it deserves. To read this commentary is both to appreciate the psalm and to assimilate rewarding habits of close reading."

—Elias Dietz, OCSO, Abbey of Gethsemani

"Psalm 119 occurs more frequently in the Liturgy of the Hours than any other psalm, but it has long been neglected in commentary because it doesn't seem to be going anywhere. Michael Casey executes here a successful rescue mission, showing that the very point of the Psalm is that it is staying where it is, celebrating the word of God by turning it over and over like a diamond so that we can appreciate all its facets."

—Jerome Kodell, OSB, Subiaco Abbey

"From the author who gave us *Sacred Reading*, the finest introduction to *lectio divina* that I know, comes this volume in which Michael Casey leads us through a *lectio divina* for Psalm 119. With each biblical verse, Casey plumbs concrete questions of daily life, such as our experience of longing, evil, vanity, and stumbling. Each of the 176 verses of this psalm is given a two-page reflection, perfect for a brief meditation before beginning the day."

—Craig E. Morrison, OCarm, Pontifical Biblical Institute, Rome

"If you find Psalm 119 tedious and suppose that its main virtue must lie in its acrostic cleverness, appreciated only in the original Hebrew, this book will make you think again. In a meditative, practical, and sometimes even playful reading of each of the psalm's 176 verses, Michael Casey shows how the law celebrated in this psalm, far from being something harsh and coercive, is a source of joy and delight, nothing less than the divine self-revelation offering us a pathway to fullness of life. The law, understood in this way, encompasses not only the written word, but the assimilated word, active in our hearts, shaping our outlook and values. The fruit of a Cistercian monk's long exposure to the psalms, singing them, as verse 146 says, 'seven times in the day,' this book is a gift to all who treasure them, both Jewish and Christian."

—Margaret Daly-Denton, PhD, Trinity College Dublin

For
B² J/R G C

Contents

Introduction

Psalm 119 runs to 176 verses. It is, by far, the longest of all the psalms in the Bible. For that reason, commentators generally dismiss it, at best with faint praise.[1] Its message is deemed both straightforward and repetitive: it sings the praise of Israel's Law. Its form is an attempt to create and sustain an alphabetic acrostic in which the word "Law" or one of its near-synonyms is used in almost every verse.[2] Instead of regarding each couplet as a self-standing unit, many commentators try to group several verses together so that their content can be conveniently summarized and left behind. Meanwhile the purpose of such a curious composition is not considered.

My belief is that the psalm is to be approached in a spirit more devotional than doctrinal. The psalm is a means of reflecting on God's gift of self-revelation encapsulated in the gift of the Torah. The progression of thought is circular rather than linear, using the intuitive right hemisphere of the brain rather than its rational counterpart. The psalm functions in a way similar to the litanies familiar to Catholic devotion of a former time: a steady drone intended to facilitate personal reflection. A similar practice exists in Islam with the use of the *misbahah* beads to pass through the ninety-nine attributes or names of God. In both cases, what is involved is a meditative *tour d'horizon*, not an exploration of dogma.

To speed through the text of Psalm 119 will result only in a state of mental befuddlement. What is needed is a slow, meditative reading of each verse of the psalm, using the technique of close reading, letting no word pass unexamined. Perhaps a spirit of playfulness is also needed. A dour academic analysis will not achieve much. Some commentators qualify the psalm as a celebration, and that is an apt description. Our reading of Psalm 119 will be most profitable if it is suffused with the same quiet spirit of glad familiarity.

This post-exilic psalm circles around the gift of God's self-revelation. I use the term "self-revelation" deliberately. What is revealed is not primarily a selection of theological or philosophical facts intended for mental processing. It is the first step in the beginning of a life-enhancing relationship. The self-revelation of God allows us to make deeper contact with ultimate reality and, in the process, come to a more comprehensive self-knowledge.

Building on the experience of Israel, formed over centuries and crystallized in the giving and living of the covenant, during the period in which this psalm was compiled, the people's faith was obliged, to cope with radically changed circumstances. The kingdom of Israel had been divided and then destroyed, the population had been scattered. The Ark of the Covenant was lost. The Jerusalem Temple, considered to be God's dwelling on earth had been defiled and destroyed. And even though a Second Temple was built, it seemed merely a pale imitation of what had preceded it (Haggai 2:3). The routine of animal sacrifices was restored but during the decades of interruption it had ceased to be central. Likewise, the priestly caste still existed but with reduced moral authority, perhaps due to their involvement in aspects of secular administration.

The upshot was that, as communities re-formed after the period of exile, popular religion came to be expressed less through pilgrimages to Jerusalem and participation in the rituals of the Temple, and more through local gatherings (or synagogues), in which the faithful could immerse themselves in the traditional writings of their faith, as these were compiled and made available. The Torah came to replace the Temple as the central element in Jewish faith. Unlike the Temple it could not be destroyed since, even if the scrolls were obliterated (1 Macc 1:56), the word of God continued to live in the hearts of the faithful.

The fundamental response to God's self-revelation was embodied in such terms as *shama'* (hear/heed/obey), *shamar* (keep/

observe), and *'ashah* (do). However, these external expressions of covenantal fidelity relied on an accurate interpretation and application of the ancient texts. Since there was no formal institutional authority to issue an authentic interpretation, the field was open for discussion and argument. This meant that devotion to the Torah often took the form of prolonged debate, as is evidenced in the *Mishnah*. Those who demonstrated a dexterity in the interpretation of texts exercised influence, but there was always scope for new ways of combining the multiple injunctions of the sacred text and the traditions arising from the opinions of revered scholars.

Reading the Torah and discussing it were intended as a means to ensuring that it was observed. There is, however, a significant knot to be untied as far as most contemporary readers are concerned. Usually the Hebrew word *torah* is translated as "Law." Even though it is graced with an initial capital, the word has a harsh and coercive sense to our ears. We tend to think of laws as regulations which inhibit our freedom and confine our choices to a narrow band of approved options. We tolerate laws as necessary for the common good but, whenever there is an element of intrusion into our own plans, resentment follows. To appreciate this psalm, we need a more complete understanding of the word *torah* and its associated terms.

In Semitic languages, the meaning of a particular word is nuanced not only by the foundational etymology of the word itself, but also by the extended family of related terms which surrounds it. This can result in a certain breadth and fluidity of meaning that does not always correspond to the official equivalent assigned to it in other languages. In addition, every language imbues words with emotional connotations that do not necessarily carry over into even the most rigorous translations. Idiom is idiomatic precisely because it is particular and distinctive. No doubt this is why there is an Italian maxim: *Traduttore traditore*. The translator is also a betrayer.

The foundation of the term *torah* is the verb *yarah*, which means to throw something or send it forth. For example, it is used of the shooting of arrows or the falling of rain. What is implied is movement from one place to another. It can be used of the action of pointing the way. Thence derives its meaning as giving direction, instructing, and teaching. The agent of this action is termed *moreh*, a teacher.[3] The feminine noun *torah* means "teaching" or "instruction," perhaps originally associated with the use of the verb to describe the action of "casting" lots in order to receive divine guidance. This instruction is always something that moves from the teacher to the learner. It is not a static reality. In the book of Proverbs the term is applied to familial instruction but, progressively, especially in the Deuteronomic tradition, it is used mainly of divine teaching whether by priests, prophets or codified norms. In rabbinic circles, the word was used specifically but not exclusively of the Pentateuch. In common usage, the term *torah* referred to the first five books of the Bible.

It is, perhaps, worth reminding ourselves that in pre-modern times the notion of teaching involved more than the communication of knowledge. There was a moral dimension involved. Beyond the communication of information and skills, the relationship of teacher and pupil involved an apprenticeship in living. It contributed to the existential formation of good character. This is why a certain rigor was required so that the learner would begin to reduce inappropriate attitudes and habits. The learner was thought to be under discipline—remembering that the Latin term *disciplina* is derived from the verb "to learn" *discere*. Often this relationship was governed by behaviorist principles. There were sanctions involved: rewards for "good" behavior, punishments or the withholding of rewards for "bad" behavior. In addition, we may point out that such formation was more concerned with pragmatic wisdom rather than abstract knowledge. The Hebrew term, usually translated as "wisdom," often means "cleverness and skill for the purpose of practical action," rather than any intellectual attainment.[4]

This wisdom was reinforced by the narrative portions of the Pentateuch. The great stories of Genesis and Exodus were more than information or entertainment. They communicated a sense of historical identity along with a mandate for living. Moses and the patriarchs were meant to inspire and so to serve as models of appropriate conduct before God. The people learned how to behave by becoming familiar with how they lived.

All of this sets the stage for the narrowing down of *torah* to designate practical norms for behavior. The code of conduct included not only the Decalogue in its three forms[5] but, since the third century, some 613 additional regulations that were distinguished in the sacred text.[6] The purpose of these additional rules of behavior was to erect a safety barrier around the fundamental requirements of Israelite religion.[7] The Pharisees seem to have expanded the ambit of the Law initially as an expression of devotion, but progressively—consciously or not—these customary norms became a means of micromanaging social life. Saint Paul, especially, rejected this approach by insisting on the freedom that follows grace. To his way of thinking, the Law had become a burden.

When the Hebrew text of the Bible was translated into Greek in the third and second centuries before the present era, *torah* was habitually (some 200 times out of 220 occurrences) rendered by *nomos*, the Greek term for legal enactments. Originally "law" was understood somewhat informally as referring to existing norms or customs but, around the fifth century, when these began to be codified in writing, the element of obligation was reinforced.[8] The word thus drifted away from any sense of "instruction" and adopted the connotation of external "obligation" to be imposed coercively, if necessary. This process continued through the centuries, notably with the emergence of legal positivism. For many, today, any law is an expression of heteronomy, the enemy of autonomy, something whose influence must be minimized as much as possible.[9] It is important not to import such attitudes into our interpretation of the biblical use of *torah* and its associated terms.

Even when ritual worship in the Temple was discontinued the psalms continued to be used to embody the community's prayer. In a certain sense, Psalm 119 may be regarded as a kind of post-exilic compendium of the entire Psalter.[10] Poetry has moved further from Canaanite models. The norms and customs of social life have changed. Torah has replaced the Temple as the center of the people's religion. Kingship is no more than a distant memory.

The memory of the covenant and the Patriarchs no longer plays a central role. It is almost as though themes of more universal relevance have been extracted from the Psalter and given more contemporary expression. By my count, in the marginal notes to the New International Version translation of Psalm 119, there are, in addition to cross-references within the psalm itself, 219 references to other psalms—an indication that much of the psalm is in harmony with the rest of the Psalter. It is as though familiar sentiments from throughout the Psalter were artfully collected to form a new psalm which could provide the starting point for meditation on the gift of divine self-revelation and on its significance for providing a pathway for the faithful. It has been suggested that the psalm as "a constant and repeated meditation on the theme of the teaching of Yahweh"[11] was "primarily intended to be read and reflected on outside of the worship situation."[12]

Psalm 119 brings together elements from all over the Psalter. It is celebration and lament, sometimes expressing praise and thanksgiving and at other times crying out for help. The psalm challenges, but it also comforts and consoles. The self-revelation of God brings joy and delight; it is a source of comfort and confidence and peace. At the same time, it provides the possibility for ardent prayer in difficult times. Each verse stands alone, and for each there is a situation in life for which it is apt. This is why it is important to move through the psalm in a leisurely fashion, pausing at every verse in an effort to allow the words of the text to interact with our situation, so that the psalm is not just a sacred text, but a truly personal expression of prayer. The reflections in this book are meant to facilitate this process. They are intended to be read one at a time over an extended period since, like the psalm itself, their message is repetitive.

The version of Psalm 119 that I offer has not been made with any literary aspirations. In attempting to make some of the important terms visible it mostly translates literally. This preserves some of the awkwardness of the original—awkwardness caused by its acrostic form and by its constant repetition of the eight near-synonyms denoting the self-revelation of God. In an effort to be faithful to the reflective genre of the psalm, the singability of the text was not my first priority. The translation is intended primarily for personal reflection.

I have tried to be consistent in my renderings, even at the expense of rhythm. The term *chesed* is translated as "kindness" rather than "mercy" to make the point that its action is not limited to forgiveness or determined by the condition of the recipient, but flows forth from the nature of God. The word *sedaqah* is translated as "righteousness" even though this is only one of several English terms that convey elements of this aspect of divine reality. The choice of translations for the eight key words of the psalm is as follows.

> **Instruction**: *torah* (25 times). As we have explained above, the word should be interpreted more in an educational or formational context than regarded as legal prescription. This context includes some notion of relationship between instructor and disciples. The psalmist expresses an affective bond with the Torah. This instruction is a source of delight; it is to be loved more than silver and gold. As a result, it is to be kept and held fast and not forgotten.

> **Utterance**: *'imrah* (19 times). This term belongs to a word family which is very common in the Old Testament. It is usually associated with the content of what is said rather than with the act of speaking. As with *torah*, the divine utterances are cherished, desired, kept and not forgotten. They are a source of sweetness and joy. The term can include the notion of promise, but its range of meanings is far broader than that.

> **Word**: *davar* (22 times). This also is a common term, with a wider range of meanings, perhaps with the suggestion that the usual emphasis is on the fact of speaking more than on its content. It was used over 200 times in the phrase "the word of the Lord" given currency by the Deuteronomist and used with reference to the prophetic message of revelation. God's word is, according to the psalmist, a source of

life, support, hope, light and understanding; it is to be kept and not forgotten.

Judgment: *mishpat* (23 times). The term is much broader than the translation indicates and can often be paraphrased as "judicious intervention" since it includes executive and legislative as well as judicial acts. "Judgment" could well be understood as the proposal of norms of behavior appropriate in particular circumstances. In the psalm, God's judgments are said to be good, righteous and upright, standing firm and giving life. They are to be feared, learned, remembered and put into practice.

Commandment: *mitsvah* (22 times). This should be translated "commandment" rather than "command," the latter usually being oral rather than written. The term can cover both a particular ordinance and the totality of laws. The body of commandments is something to be gazed on as a source of delight and joy. They are a pathway to love from which we may not hide or stray.

The final three terms are usually more narrowly legal than the others, although they can be used in a transposed sense.

Testimony: *'edut* (23 times). Based on the idea of giving witness or making a formal attestation, this term is sometimes translated as referring to the "will" of God. Although the divine ordinances undoubtedly indicate what God wills, this term is a more definitive than that. According to the psalm, the testimonies are righteous and a source of love, knowledge and delight. They are to be pondered, understood and kept.

Statute: *choq* (22 times). Another word for formal prescription: its etymology evoking the idea of engraving. Most often the psalm affirms that the statutes are to be taught and learned so as to be put into practice, but they are also to be sought as a cause for delight and celebration.

Precept: *piqqud* (21 times). This is probably a relatively later term than the others. Precepts are to be loved, desired, sought, chosen, pondered, understood and observed; not forgotten or forsaken.

As is evident, all the terms share the same group of qualifiers. The psalmist's attitude toward the Torah is unambiguously positive. Although obligations and duties are involved, these are viewed as a means toward a greater level of conformity with the divine plan and, according, a source of increased happiness and delight. The general opinion that the various terms are, for all practical purposes, near-synonyms is probably correct.

Although Psalm 119 is a unique creation it draws its strength from its relationship with the Bible as a whole. Its aim is to describe how the faithful should respond to the gift of God's self-revelation—how to live in the context of their relationship with God. The psalm is descriptive rather than prescriptive, focusing on particular aspects of the people's response as objects for reflection. There is, moreover, an element of celebration inherent in the psalm, even though it recognizes that difficulties will be encountered in the service of God. Its message is predominantly joyful. In this it echoes and expands the sentiments expressed in the post-exilic portion of Psalm 19 (vv. 7-13).

> The instruction of the LORD is perfect,
> reviving the soul.
> The testimony of the LORD is worthy of trust,
> making the simple wise.
> The precepts of the LORD are upright,
> rejoicing the heart.
> The commandments of the LORD are brilliant,
> giving light to the eyes.
> The fear of the LORD is pure,
> enduring for ever.
> The judgments of the LORD are faithful,
> all of them righteous.
> They are more precious than gold,
> much gold.
> They are sweeter than honey,
> honey from honeycomb.
> By them is your servant admonished;
> there is a great reward for observing them.

Far from being a burden, the cherishing and observance of God's Law brings human beings to a level of joyous fulfilment that is impossible on the basis of their own meagre resources. Having the divine Law as our mentor helps us to become more fully alive and more fully ourselves. Living in the presence of God is not a duty, it is humanity's ultimate benefit.

In using Psalm 119 devotionally, it is important not to limit our understanding of God's self-revelation to the sacred texts contained in the books of the Bible. The inspired words of the Scriptures are externalizations of the enlightenment received by prophets and sages and filtered by their reception in succeeding generations. The mystery of the divinity can be expressed verbally only through approximations. This is why poetry and graphic imagery play such a large part in Scripture. The full meaning is not accessible to merely rational investigation of the words—useful though this may be. Scripture is an element in God's ongoing dialogue with humanity. For it to be understood we need to share a common language with the text—I don't mean Hebrew and Greek, but the language of faith, which is the only means of communication between us and God. Texts speak to us because they generate a resonance within us, a kind of pre-existent echo that embodies something of what the text contains. Understanding the message of Scripture requires of us a kind of *Sprachgefühl*—an intuitive sense of the total content of what is said, along with some awareness of its vast range of affective connotations. The gift of faith gives us an affinity with God that enables us to receive more from a text than its logical content. This is why revelation may appear to be foolish or scandalous to unbelievers. Without the gift of faith there are only words; their power to move is radically diminished. But, by faith, God's word becomes living and active for us, showing us the way forward, giving us the strength to follow that path, and consoling us in the inevitable challenges that lie ahead.

As we celebrate in this psalm the gift of God's self-revelation we may find it useful to do so in the context of God's word within us: internalized, assimilated, and endlessly active. When we profess our love and our willingness to obey the word, we are committing ourselves not primarily to live according to the practical regulations that Scripture contains but, more especially, to follow the guidance of this inner voice, the conscience formed and re-formed by long exposure to divine self-revelation. This is what Saint Paul indicates when he distinguishes between the "spirit" and the "letter" of revelation.

God's self-revelation makes its home within us; it is not something foreign or exotic. Deuteronomy reminds us of this.

> The commandment that I give you this day is not difficult, nor is it beyond your reach. It is not up in the sky that you should say, "Who will go up into the sky and fetch it for us that we may hear it and keep it?" Nor is it across the seas that you should say, "Who will cross the seas and fetch it for us that we may hear it and keep it?" No. The word is very near to you; it is in your mouth and in your heart, ready to be kept. (Deut 30:11-14)

There is constant interplay between the exterior word embodied in texts, and the interior word cherished by the believer. Between the word common to the community and the word received by the faith-filled heart. There is an inherent harmony between outer and inner so that sometimes there is much that simple souls can teach learned commentators.

Even in the most desolating experiences, God's word does not desert us.

> O people of Zion, who live in Jerusalem, you will weep no more. [God] will show favor when you cry for help. As soon as God hears, there will be an answer for you. Although the

> Lord has given you the bread of adversity and the water of
> affliction, your Teacher will be hidden no longer; with your
> own eyes you will see your Teacher. Whether you turn to the
> right or to the left, your ears will hear a voice behind you,
> saying: This is the way; walk in it. (Isa 30:19-21)

An interior voice that teaches us the way to a fuller life, a Teacher that is not silenced by external disaster, but continues to instruct us. This is the "implanted word" of which Saint James writes (Jas 1:21). This is the inner anointing which teaches us everything (1 John 2:27).

In reflecting on this psalm in the context of prayer we may find it helpful to interpret the various terms by which God's self-revelation is designated as applying also to this interior source of guidance that grows strong as faith flowers. We acknowledge God's voice speaking within us, we ponder its implications and we give thanks because it opens to us a future in which we may move toward loving God with all our heart, with all our soul and with all our strength.

Psalm 119

ALEPH

1 Blessed are they whose way is innocent
who walk according to the Lord's instruction.
2 Blessed those who observe [God's] testimonies,
and seek [God] wholeheartedly.
3 Indeed, they do not do what is evil,
but they walk in the Lord's ways.
4 You have instituted your precepts
to be kept well.
5 Oh, may my ways be made firm
in keeping your statutes.
6 Then I shall not be shamed
when I gaze on your commandments.
7 I will praise you with an upright heart
as I learn the judgments of your justice.
8 I shall keep your statutes,
do not ever forsake me.

BETH

9 How shall youth remain pure in their path?
By keeping your word.
10 With all my heart I seek you,
do not let me wander from your commandments.
11 In my heart I cherish your utterances,
so that I do not sin against you.
12 Blessed be you, O Lord,
Teach me your statutes.

13   With my lips have I narrated
      all the judgments of your mouth.
14   In the way of your testimonies I rejoiced
      as over all riches.
15   On your precepts I shall ponder,
      I shall gaze upon your paths.
16   I delight in your statutes,
      I will not forget your word.

GIMEL

17   Deal kindly with your servant that I may live
      and may keep your word.
18   Open my eyes that I may perceive
      the wonderful things in your instruction.
19   I am a sojourner in the land,
      do not hide your commandments from me.
20   My soul is consumed with desire
      for your judgments, at all times.
21   You rebuke the proud, the accursed,
      who have strayed from your commandments.
22   Take away from me scorn and contempt,
      for I have carefully kept your testimonies.
23   Though the powerful sit to conspire against me,
      your servant muses on your statutes.
24   Indeed, your testimonies are my delight;
      they are my counsellors.

DALETH

25   My soul clings to the dust;
      by your word, give me life.
26   I narrated my ways and you responded;
      teach me your statutes.
27   Make me understand the ways of your precepts
      and I shall ponder your wonders.
28   My soul faints through anguish;
      By your word sustain me.

29 Keep me from the way of falsehood,
    by your instruction show me favor.
30 I have chosen the way of faith,
    Your judgments I have upheld.
31 I cling to your testimonies, Lord,
    Let me not be put to shame.
32 I will run on the way of your commandments,
    since you have enlarged my heart.

HE

33 Lord, teach me the way of your statutes,
    and I will keep it until the end.
34 Give me understanding that I may hold fast to your
        instruction
    and keep it with all my heart.
35 Make a way for me on the path of your commandments,
    for I take delight in it.
36 Incline my heart to your testimonies,
    and not to wrongful gain.
37 Avert my eyes from seeing what is worthless,
    in your way, give me life.
38 Bring your utterances to completion for your servant
    who fears you.
39 Avert the reproach that I dread
    for your judgments are good.
40 Behold, I have desired your precepts;
    in your righteousness, give me life.

VAU

41 Lord, let your kindness come to me,
    salvation according to your utterance.
42 I have a word to respond to those who reproach me,
    for I have trusted in your word.
43 Never take the word of truth from my mouth
    for I have hoped in your judgements.
44 May I always keep your instruction
    for ever and ever.

45   May I walk in an open space
        for I have sought your precepts.
46   I will speak of your testimonies before kings
        and not be ashamed.
47   I have delighted in your commandments,
        and I have loved them.
48   I lift up my hands to your commandments, which I love;
        and I ponder your statutes.

ZAYIN

49   Remember the word to your servant;
        on it I have waited.
50   This comforts me in my affliction;
        your utterances give me life.
51   The arrogant mocked me greatly;
        I did not turn from your teaching.
52   I remember your judgments from long ago,
        Lord, and I am consoled.
53   Rage seized me because of the wicked;
        they forsake your instruction.
54   Your statutes are my songs
        in the house of exile.
55   I remember your name in the night, Lord,
        and I keep your instruction.
56   This has been what befell me,
        because I have observed your precepts.

HETH

57   I have said: You are my portion, Lord,
        and so I keep your words.
58   I have sought your favor with all my heart,
        be gracious to me according to your utterance.
59   I considered my ways
        and I turned my steps back to your testimonies.
60   I hurried and did not dawdle
        to keep your commandments.

61   The cords of the wicked ensnared me
     but I did not forget your instruction.
62   At midnight I will rise and thank you
     for the judgments of your righteousness.
63   I am a companion to all who fear you,
     to those who keep your precepts.
64   Your kindness, Lord, fills the earth;
     teach me your statutes.

TETH

65   You have done what is good for your servant, O Lord,
     according to your word.
66   Teach me good discretion and knowledge,
     for I have faith in your commandments.
67   Before I was afflicted I went astray,
     but now I keep your utterance.
68   You are good and you do what is good;
     teach me your statutes.
69   The arrogant smear me with lies,
     with all my heart I observe your precepts.
70   Their hearts are gross like fat,
     but I delight in your instruction.
71   It was good for me to be afflicted,
     so that I may learn your statutes.
72   The instruction from your mouth is better for me
     than thousands in silver and gold.

YOD

73   Your hands made me and established me;
     give me understanding so that I may learn your
          commandments.
74   Those who fear you will see me and rejoice,
     because I hope for your word.
75   I know, Lord, that your judgements are righteous,
     and that it was in faithfulness that you afflicted me.
76   Please, may your kindness console me,
     according to your utterance to your servant.

77   Let your compassion come and I shall live
       for your instruction is my delight.
78   Let the arrogant be shamed who afflict me with falsehood,
       I will muse on your decrees.
79   Let those who fear you turn to me,
       those who know your testimonies.
80   Let my heart be upright in your statutes,
       that I may not be put to shame.

CAPH

81   My soul longs for your salvation,
       I hope in your word.
82   My eyes yearn for your utterances,
       saying: When will you console me?
83   Though I am like a wineskin shriveled by smoke,
       I did not forget your statutes.
84   How many are the days of your servant?
       When will you do justice to those who persecute me?
85   The arrogant dig pitfalls for me;
       this is not according to your instruction.
86   All your commandments are faithful;
       help me; they persecute me without cause.
87   They almost brought me to an end on earth,
       but I did not forsake your precepts.
88   Give me life, according to your kindness,
       and I will keep the testimony of your mouth.

LAMED

89   For ever, O Lord,
       your word stands firm in heaven.
90   Your faithfulness is from generation to generation
       like the earth you made, it stands firm.
91   Until today your judgments have stood firm,
       for all things are your servants.
92   If your instruction were not my delight,
       I would have perished in my affliction.

93 I will not ever forget your precepts,
    because in them you give me life.
94 I am yours; save me;
    for I am searching your precepts.
95 While the wicked hope to bring me to nothing,
    I gained insight from your testimonies.
96 I have seen that there is a limit to every achievement,
    but your commandment is exceedingly wide.

MEM

97 How I love your instruction!
    I ponder it all day long.
98 Your commandment makes me wiser than my enemies,
    for it is always with me.
99 I understand better than those who would teach me,
    because I ponder your testimonies.
100 I have gained more understanding than the elders
    since I have observed your precepts.
101 I hold back my feet from every evil path,
    because I keep your word.
102 I have not swerved from your judgments
    since you yourself have instructed me.
103 How sweet to my tongue is your utterance,
    more than honey in the mouth.
104 From your precepts I gain understanding,
    therefore I shun every way of falsehood.

NUN

105 Your word is a lamp for my feet
    and a light for my path.
106 I have sworn an oath and will fulfil it,
    to keep your righteous judgments.
107 Lord, I am badly afflicted;
    by your word give me life.
108 Accept, I pray O Lord, the freewill offering of my mouth,
    and teach me your judgments.

109   My soul is continually in the palm of my hand,
         but I do not forget your instruction.
110   The wicked set a trap for me,
         but I have not wandered from your precepts.
111   Your testimonies are my inheritance for ever;
         they are the joy of my heart.
112   I turn my heart to do your statutes,
         for ever, to the end.

SAMECH

113   The divided I hate,
         but I love your instruction.
114   You are my shelter and my shield,
         in your word I have hoped.
115   Depart from me, you doers of evil;
         I will observe the commandments of God.
116   Sustain me by your utterance and I shall live;
         let my hopes not be abashed.
117   Uphold me so that I will be saved,
         and I shall continually gaze on your statutes.
118   You make light of all who wander from your statutes;
         their deceitfulness yields no result.
119   You treat all the wicked of the earth like dross;
         therefore I love your testimonies.
120   My flesh bristles in fear of you,
         I fear your judgments.

AYIN

121   I have practiced judgment and righteousness;
         do not abandon me to my enemies.
122   Promise good for your servant;
         do not let the arrogant oppress me.
123   My eyes long for your saving help
         and your righteous utterance.
124   Act for your servant according to your kindness
         that I may learn your statutes.

125 I am your servant, give me understanding
    that I may know your testimonies.
126 It is time for the Lord to act
    for your instruction has been contravened.
127 That is why I love your commandments,
    more than finest gold.
128 Thus all your precepts are for me a straight line;
    I have hated the paths of falsehood.

PE

129 Your testimonies are wondrous:
    My soul practices them.
130 The opening of your word illumines
    and gives understanding to the simple.
131 I opened my mouth, panting,
    I yearn for your commandments.
132 Turn to me and show me favor;
    according to your judgment for those who love your name.
133 Confirm my steps through your utterances;
    let evil not be my master.
134 Ransom me from human oppression,
    and I will keep your precepts.
135 Let your face shine on your servant,
    and teach me your testimonies.
136 My eyes shed streams of water,
    because people did not keep your instruction.

TSADE

137 You are righteous, Lord,
    and your judgments are upright.
138 Righteous you declared your testimonies,
    with great faithfulness.
139 My passion consumes me,
    for my enemies forget your words.
140 Your utterance is most pure
    and your servant loves it.

141   I am small and despised,
         but I am not forgetful of your precepts.
142   Your righteousness is forever righteous
         and your instruction is truth.
143   Anguish and distress have found me,
         but your commandments are my delight.
144   Your testimonies are forever righteous,
         grant me understanding and I shall live.

KOPH

145   I have cried out with all my heart, answer me, O Lord;
         I will observe your statutes.
146   I call you: Save me
         and I will keep your testimonies.
147   I anticipated the changing of the light and cried out:
         Your word is my hope.
148   My eyes anticipated the watches of the night
         as I pondered your utterances.
149   Hear my voice, in accordance with your kindness,
         give me life in accordance with your judgment.
150   Schemers are near,
         but they are far from your instruction.
151   You are near, O Lord,
         and all your commandments are truth.
152   From antiquity I have known from your testimonies
         that they are established for ever.

RESH

153   See my affliction and rescue me,
         for I have not forgotten your instruction.
154   Be an advocate in my case and act as my kinsman,
         for I have not forgotten your utterances.
155   The wicked are far from salvation,
         for they have not sought your statutes.
156   Great is your compassion, Lord,
         according to your judgments, give me life.

157   Many are my pursuers and enemies,
      but I have not turned aside from your testimonies.
158   I look with disgust on those who break faith,
      for they do not keep your utterance.
159   See how I love your precepts,
      Lord, in your kindness give me life.
160   Truth is the foundation of your word,
      and all your judgments are forever righteous.

SHIN

161   Princes oppressed me without cause,
      yet my heart is in awe of your word.
162   I rejoiced over your utterances,
      like one finding great plunder.
163   I hate and abhor falsehood,
      but I love your instruction.
164   Seven times in the day I have praised you
      for your righteous judgments.
165   There is much peace for those who love your instruction
      and no occasion for stumbling.
166   O Lord I looked forward to your salvation
      and I fulfilled your commandments.
167   My soul keeps your testimonies
      and loves them very much.
168   I keep your precepts and your testimonies
      since all my ways are before you.

TAU

169   May my cry come before you O Lord,
      by your word give me understanding.
170   Let my supplication come before your face;
      deliver me according to your utterance.
171   Let my lips utter praise
      because you teach me your statutes.
172   My tongue sings of your utterances,
      because all your commandments are righteous.

173   Let your hand be my help,
       for I have chosen your precepts.
174   Lord, I long for your salvation;
       your instruction is my delight.
175   My soul lives and praises you,
       for your judgments are my help.
176   I wandered like a lost sheep, seek your servant
       for I have not forgotten your commandments.

1   Blessed are they whose way is innocent
     who walk according to the Lord's instruction.

INTEGRITY

The opening verse of the longest psalm announces that it belongs to the *genre* of wisdom literature. Its purpose is to invite us to reflect about our life with God in all its practicality. To go round and round in circles, pondering how to respond to God's self-revelation. The reader may draw some delight not only from the text but also from the manner in which the text educates us in spiritual literacy, teaching us to read what is happening in the deepest regions of our being.

The psalm offers us the key to a blessed life. The blessedness to which it refers is not the kind of happiness that comes to us from the outside, but the deep contentment that is the result of interior harmony. A person whose heart is undivided, who is not constantly being torn apart by contrary desires, lives in peace. It is not a static condition, akin to stagnation, but an ongoing state of growth than interacts with its evolving environment and is constantly changing in response to it.

The life of the blessed is characterized by integrity. Integrity is so rare a quality that we do not have an adjective that corresponds to it. In most of us there is a certain dissonance between what we are interiorly and how we present ourselves to the outside world. Others may know the external facts of our life but our intimate identity remains a secret. The Latin version of Isaiah 24:16, "My secret is my own," was used by both Bernard of Clairvaux and Edith Stein to block the entrance of outsiders to this sacred space. It is only through our visible behavior that, eventually, some external indication is given of what transpires within. For those of high integrity what you see is what you get. For the rest of us there is often ambiguity.

The way by which we arrive at this better space is through our willingness to be instructed by God's self-revelation. Because we are made in God's image there is an innate compatibility between us and God. And this dynamic affinity means that the closer we come to God the more fully human we become. To allow ourselves to be instructed by God is to place ourselves in the way that leads to human fulfilment and, thereby, to ultimate happiness. We become what we were created to be.

The *torah* or instruction of God is less about religion than we are inclined to think. It is the way to a more abundant human life. The self-revelation of God is also a revelation of who and what we are. Modelling ourselves on God leads to a profoundly satisfying life. Conversely, to depart from this path is a guarantee of a miserable existence. Someone once remarked to me after watching a drama on television: "They wouldn't have got into so much trouble if they had just kept the Ten Commandments." A fair enough judgement! Think of what the world would be like if there was no killing or stealing or adultery or telling lies or coveting what others have. Not much drama and little bad news for the media to trumpet. But, to heed God's instruction and to follow it to the end is the sure road to a happy life.

2   Blessed those who observe [God's] testimonies,
       and seek [God] wholeheartedly.

SEEKING

The self-revelation of God, in whatever form it takes, profoundly changes a person's life. Moses, Isaiah, Jeremiah and Jonah all bear witness to this. Even the shadowiest glimpse of God undermines our facile certainties and calls on us to re-assess our priorities. Something new has been introduced into our lives and we can no longer be content with what previously satisfied us. We feel the need to make room for the unexpected change of perspective. We are being summoned to a conversion. Our happiness is dependent on our wholehearted assent to this challenge.

The momentary experience needs to be translated into a lifestyle. The witness of what God is, provides us with the ultimate indication of what we should aspire to become. It is an indication of the road on which we should travel. When the psalm speaks of God's testimonies in the plural, there is question of multiple signposts along the way which nudge us into choosing the path that is more likely to lead to life.

The written law of the commandments is not the whole revelation of God, or of God's plan for us. Ideally the commandments serve as reminders of what we have experienced and of the subsequent choices that we made. They hark back to our hopes of a better self, and show us how these aspirations may be brought to fulfilment. To come closer to God is largely a matter of following the yearnings that God has implanted in our soul—which sometimes need to be disentangled from other desires triggered by alternative attractions. Our desire to encounter God needs to be buttressed by a certain sobriety in our manner of life.

Saint Ambrose knew well that responding to God's call involves the struggle to live a good life. "The eye of the mind becomes blind and is darkened through a lack of discipline and is unable to plumb deep mysteries. First we need to engage in the warfare of living by upgrading our lifestyle . . . First, therefore, comes morality; then mysticism."[13] It is not just a matter of obeying external impositions. It is more a recognition that for the seed that God has planted within us to blossom, care must be taken that it is not stifled by submitting ourselves to unruly tendencies.

This is why we must undertake a wholehearted search to comprehend the plan of God for us in the here-and-now. In the Scriptures, "seeking God" often means asking for an oracle from God, trying to determine what we must do in these present circumstances. Seeking direction from God. In simplicity of heart and with an open mind. Willing to have our future actions conform to the great mystery that has opened out before us.

❧❧❧

3   Indeed, they do not do what is evil,
     but they walk in the Lord's ways.

EVIL

The psalm now says negatively what has already been positively affirmed; the ones who are blessed with fulfilment are those who follow the Lord's instruction and abstain from evil deeds. A parallel sentiment is expressed in Ps 34:15: "Turn from what is bad and do what is good." The key word is "and." Some people are accomplished at avoiding what is bad, others are expert in doing what is good; few people manage both to avoid evil and to be active in doing good. True blessedness demands both innocence and practical virtue. It is only when good deeds flow from within that they have the power to make life happier.

The word "evil" is a strong translation; the word could also be rendered by "bad" or "wicked" or, more playfully, by "naughty." The important thing to note about the word is that it is referring to a disposition as well as to the actions that derive from it. Evil is intrinsically negative, ultimately it has harmful effects. What is condemned by external regulation refers only to external actions. The law may suggest certain attitudes, but it cannot enforce them. We can be required to observe royal protocol, but we cannot be compelled to think highly of those enthroned on high. The law tells us what to do; underneath, our attitudes may well remain unchanged.

Enforced virtue is not a source of happiness; it probably makes us miserable. This is why some people respond negatively to any direction that comes from outside themselves. It is an attitude expected of adolescents, but a sign of immaturity in adults. A mellower wisdom often demands that we negotiate an *entente* between interior promptings and exterior demands, so that we are able simultaneously to live with ourselves and to live with others.

As societal animals, any attempt to go it alone distorts our nature, and is more likely to make us unhappy than any external exactions.

Walking in God's ways is more than being law-abiding. What alienates us from God is deeper than our morals, and cannot be remedied by the performance of prescribed actions. It requires radical change at the very center of our being. For this to happen the Ego has to be dislocated, removed from its role as the determinant of our choices and made subject to the discernment that derives from our relationship with God. We will discover for ourselves that when we choose to walk in God's ways habitually, our narcissistic tendencies are gently blocked, and what is finest in us flourishes and grows.

True goodness is more than window-dressing. Evil is so powerful that it is able to inject its toxins into otherwise good actions. As T. S. Eliot's Becket exclaims: "The last temptation is the greatest treason: / To do the right deed for the wrong reason."[14] This is why purity of heart is a quality to be greatly cherished. To walk God's paths in simplicity and sincerity, avoiding even the semblance of evil, is a certain means of a joyful life for ourselves and the kindest gift we can offer others.

✦

4   You have instituted your precepts
     to be kept well.

YOU

There is an important change in tone in this verse. The author moves away from the third-person statement of general principles to a direct address to God. Perhaps we do not appreciate sufficiently the boldness found in the psalms which allows us to address ourselves directly to God from whatever situation we find ourselves. The psalms are not just celebrations of the qualities of an abstract God. They are expressions of an I-Thou relationship. More than that, they are invitations to us to enter into dialogue with God.

The precepts that come from God must be understood within the context of this interpersonal dialogue. They are not hard-edged enactments imposed from on high without any appreciation of the situation in which we find ourselves. The many precepts that come from God are not lightly given; they have been instituted with due diligence and deliberation and, therefore, are not lightly to be dismissed.

We are admonished to keep God's commandments well. This is not to be understood as an incitement to obsessive punctiliousness. In this context, Saint Augustine invokes the moderating principle: *ne quid nimis*: Don't go to extremes.[15] God understands that we are human. We are not machines. As a result, our acceptance, our understanding, and our implementation of divine precepts will be stamped with the particularities of who we are and in what situation we find ourselves. Keeping the precepts well is not merely scrupulous observance, but it involves the use of our intelligence. As Saint Bernard writes, "With a tranquil mind, [the obedient person] *will match the level of care to the weight of the matter in hand*, both in fulfilling what is commanded and in avoiding what is prohibited."[16] Seeing God as a stern master can only have the effect of inhibiting our loving response.

The precepts of God are given in the context of a loving relationship. This means we receive them as gifts of love, even though we do not always understand them immediately. Sometimes we have to grapple with them, as Jacob wrestled all night with the angel before he obtained the blessing God intended to give him. But first we have to receive the precepts and hold onto them until they begin to make sense to us.

Mostly divine precepts are given us to hold onto so that they begin to have a formative effect on our beliefs and values. It is only when they have been successful in bringing about a change of heart that they begin to influence our choices and our actions. To use the terminology of the book of Deuteronomy, we begin to "remember" what has been enjoined on us. It becomes part of our outlook on life. It begins to shape who we are. This is the meaning of keeping God's precepts well. As Saint Augustine notes, "It is useless keeping them in memory if we do not also keep them in life."[17]

5   Oh, may my ways be made firm
        in keeping your statutes.

JOURNEY

Here we have a prayer that the good intentions that currently guide me may continue to exercise an influence over my actions. Although there are times when the practice of virtue seems natural and easy, we all know from experience that there will also be occasions when we are under siege to change our options and pursue an alternative path. Job was a good man, innocent, upright and fearing God. Yet he was led to conclude that human life was a continuing warfare (Job 7:1). We are constantly faced with a variety of challenges that test how realistic is our commitment to living in accordance with the plan of God.

One of the enduring images of human life is that of the journey. We are in a state of continual movement and the conditions around us are constantly changing. What was suitable yesterday may not be the best course for today. A path that seemed safe can quickly become slippery and treacherous. This is why we pray in another psalm: "May your good spirit lead me on level ground" (Ps 143:10). Our experience as we travel teaches us how to handle many different situations but, if we are wise, we do not forget that the future does not necessarily follow the familiar routines of the past.

If we live long enough we will experience different kinds of variation in our daily lives. Some, but not all of it, may be trivial and easily dealt with or, at least, endured. There will be seasonal changes during which our lives are painted in different hues and our levels of vitality surge and then sag. And it may well happen that at some stage we will be precipitated into life-threatening disasters which are far beyond our capabilities to cope. Maintaining our course during these fluctuations is not easy unless we have some point of reference from which we can take our bearing.

The psalm suggests that the best means of arriving at a good level of constancy is to take our cue from God's self-revelation. Our adherence to the divine statutes is a matter of choice. We decide that automatically following the promptings of our Ego is likely to lead to eventual disaster. We need something outside ourselves to put a check on these tendencies which claim to be self-enhancing but which are often self-destructive. Allowing ourselves to be assessed by objective criteria opens the possibility of progress. We are less likely to wander off the track and find ourselves in a situation which, even if it is not dangerous, involves the expenditure of energy which could have been more profitably invested in nobler pursuits.

To open our hearts and our lives to God's word and to allow it to influence the choices we make is to arrive at a higher level of freedom, which permits us to go forward with greater security. If we have a guide, we are less likely to go astray—supposing we pay attention to the advice that is given us.

But there is more. A companion on the journey not only offers guidance but also encourages us to keep moving ahead. "Many want to walk on the road, but not [all the way] to the end."[18] God's word is a source not only of guidance but also of hope. Our footsteps are firm when our heart is strong and our eyes see clearly.

6   Then I shall not be shamed
     when I gaze on your commandments.

ASSURANCE

The penalty imposed on Adam and Eve for their disobedience was shame. Shame is far deeper than guilt. Guilt means feeling bad about what we have done. Shame means feeling bad about what we are. Guilt can be assuaged by undoing, shame is a semi-permanent condition. Because of the shame our first ancestors felt, they were alienated from their Creator and, so, they hid from God, and from themselves.

To welcome God's self-revelation into our purview and to live responsive to it is the primary means of overcoming our ontological shame. Our sense of self-rejection is cancelled as we meditate on what God is revealed to be—a proactive source of recovery and wholeness. A context in which our many failures do not poison the innate nobility that is ours, created as we are in God's image and likeness. We can reclaim our own sense of dignity and self-honor to the extent that we open ourselves to perceive the broadness of God's mercy.

The commandments of God are not tyrannical impositions that inhibit our freedom, but they are kindly indicators of how we may regain the freedom that we have lost. Meditating on God's word we begin to see more clearly the road ahead that leads to a more abundant life. If you have ever been lost and bewildered, or even mildly disorientated, you may remember that the kindliest word your heard was that which directed you how to get to the place you wanted to be. God's word is a beacon by which we can re-orient ourselves to continue our journey. And, as we progress, we begin to be happier in ourselves, more self-accepting—even with our evident liabilities—and more assured.

The great foolishness to which most of us are, at least sometimes, prone is to claim a false autonomy and to ignore God's revelation and try to make our own way. Our failure to make much progress leads us, in moments of self-honesty, to conclude that we are of little worth and, in small increments, we begin to abandon the journey which had initially inspired so much joy. We set our sights on a lesser goal.

Gazing upon God's commandments is more than merely knowing what God recommends as the ideal for human behavior. That laudable outcome is, in fact, secondary. What gazing upon God's commandments really means is that we enter more fully into a relationship with God, allowing ourselves to be drawn into the divine reality, feeling ourselves drawn beyond mundane preoccupations into the burning bush of divine mystery. Perhaps we are too ready to interpret religion mainly in terms of morality, with the result that we underestimate the attractive power of God. In such a case, God becomes for us a stern master instead of being the inherent focus of all our desire and striving, the only reality in which our restless hearts find deep repose.

Religion that is based on revelation is fundamentally contemplative. By gazing upon what has been revealed we are deeply transformed, and it is no wonder that the shape of our life becomes both more human and more divine. And we feel no shame.

7   I will praise you with an upright heart
     as I learn the judgments of your justice.

LEARNING

The benefits that accrue from opening our lives to God's self-revelation are not experienced immediately. They require a long intermediate period during which we are gradually changed so that we can receive the full benefit of our correspondence with God's plans. We have to pass through an extended stage of discipleship; we must be willing to learn, and to keep relearning. God's self-revelation transcends human categories so that we can never receive it whole and entire, once and for all. We are lifelong learners. The *torah* is our teacher.

The "law" of God is more than ten brief sentences carved into stone; it is the revelation of a Thou, it is an invitation to an encounter and to an ongoing relationship. This relationship is not frozen at the moment it begins, but continues to evolve as we ourselves pass through the different seasons of our life. This means that we have to remain learners; responsive to the changes that human life involves. God is unchanging, but our relationship with God is never static; it keeps pace with us as we grow and develop.

This means that we have to remain mentally alert so that we can discern the movement of both tides and eddies in our relationship with God. Saint Augustine reminds us of this when he writes: "We realize that God's word cannot be kept through mere obedience unless it has been first grasped by intelligence."[19] This involves giving ourselves to the study of God's word, not as an intellectual exercise, but reading it in the context of our ever-changing experience. "If today you hear God's voice, harden not your hearts" (Ps 95:7). We have to listen with "an awakened ear" (Isa 50:4). The translation of the *torah* into norms for living does not happen without our cooperation.

The object of this learning is God's *mishpat* and *sedaqah*: "the judgments of your justice."[20] The two words are grammatically combined to express a single reality: God's goodness becomes for us a norm, a criterion for assessing the moral value of our lives. It is not that we measure ourselves against God, but our encounter with God has opened our eyes to what really constitutes human goodness or righteousness. Our progress is not primarily due to conformity to a written code, but it is a matter of being formed and re-formed through our evolving relationship with God.

Catching sight of something of the reality of God is a vision of our own future. This is why a simple and upright heart is spontaneously drawn to praise the Revealer. God's self-revelation not only instructs us about the reality of God, it also reveals to us our own deepest reality—what we may become if we are assiduous disciples at the school of *torah*. "The reality of God discloses the truth about mankind."[21]

8   I shall keep your statutes,
     do not ever forsake me.

COVENANT

Our relationship with God is reciprocal. Both parties are bound by covenantal loyalty. For our part, we express this relationship by keeping the statutes in mind and embodying them in the choices we make, and in the actions we perform. This is more than wooden conformity with external rules and regulations. Doing recommended actions in a spirit of mindfulness is a way of reiterating our fundamental commitment to God and to our side of the covenant.

This prayer rises from our hearts when we are fearful that God will not reciprocate. This rises either because of the general shallowness of our faith or because of the seriousness of the troubles which afflict us and have left us bereft of comfort, so that we feel abandoned and alone. Conscious of the precariousness of our existence and of our absolute dependence on God, we plead with God not to withdraw from us.

This verse reminds us of the psalms of lament, which cry out to God from a sense of absence. You will remember Psalm 22. "My God, my God, why have you forsaken me?" and "Do not remain far from me." How often in these psalms we hear the complaint that God's face is hidden. The relationship has been broken and we are left alone. When God departs from our awareness there is not much prospect of consolation.

When religion is reduced to morality, the primary emphasis is on what we do—or fail to do. This is ultimately a depressing and dispiriting stance. Authentic religion is primarily about what God does. In chapters 40–55 of Isaiah, the part commonly ascribed to Second Isaiah, the prophetic words are addressed to a remnant of the people deported to Babylon, seemingly with nothing left to them but a life of servitude and dishonor. The prophet offers words of consolation to the exiles, assuring them that, despite appearances, God is still with them. This is the key to the consolation he offers: they are not alone. God is with them. As God is with us: *Immanu-el.*

In a mysterious way, our sense of the absence of God is changed when we begin to put more energy in observing our side of the covenant. When we consciously and freely choose to order our lives according to the word of God, glimmers appear in the darkness. What is happening is that the power of faith, rising from the depths of our being, is contending against all the arguments of false reason which tell us that everything is lost. Our conscious observance of the statutes—whatever this may involve—is sending a signal that we have not given up on God. The action itself may be relatively trivial; what matters is the sentiment behind it. We are sending a message. I am here. I have not lost faith. I await your saving presence. Do not leave me stranded. Do not leave me alone. Do not ever forsake me. We are reminded of the lines penned by Gerard Manley Hopkins in one of his sonnets: "And my lament / Is cries countless, cries like dead letters sent / To dearest him that lives alas! away."

9   How shall youth remain pure in their path?
    By keeping your word.

UNADULTERATED

The question is asked: How can a young person maintain their innocence in a world full of allurements to evil? How can youth remain un**adult**erated? The word itself seems to indicate that reaching adulthood involves some loss of simple goodness. Those who travel in the world soon become aware that moving around and dealing with different situations often involve a threat to cleanliness. This was especially true in the ancient world which was less sanitized than our own. Similarly, our way through life almost inevitably renders us less pure than we were when we began. Our vices multiply and our virtues are compromised. As Ecclesiastes notes: "Surely there is no person who is just on the earth, who does good and does not sin" (Eccl 7:20).

Especially in rabbinic Judaism, there was a strong emphasis on the avoidance of ritual impurity; provision for multiple occasions of purification attested to the ease with which a person could be defiled through ordinary daily living. If we transpose this insight into the moral sphere we can see how the beautiful innocence of the very young will be under threat as they grow to maturity. The question about safeguarding this level of simple goodness is answered by reference to God's self-revelation. Innocence will be maintained and even restored by opening our lives to God's self-revelation.

You will notice that in this place God's word is spoken of in the singular; it is not a question of the different manifestations of God, but the fact that God is speaking to us. God has begun a dialogue with us, and for this to be possible, God has become in some way present to us. Not only through the *torah* but also through our own inner sense of the divine, our conscience. God is present to us but, as Saint Augustine frequently laments, we are not present to God. We are inattentive and forgetful; we allow ourselves to be more concerned with things that do not matter. And so we become progressively more insensitive to God's voice. As Saint Bernard notes: "An appetite for vanity bespeaks a contempt for truth; contempt for truth makes us blind."[22] By becoming strangers to God's word we become ever more alienated from God and it is not surprising that, in this state, integrity of life is lost.

Applying ourselves to hearing God's word, to receiving it with meekness, to remembering it, to putting it into practice, all these are involved in keeping God's word. We will find by experience that it is a sure way of ensuring that our life is more virtuous and less adulterated. We will retain some of the purity of our first youth. Attachment to God's word is an ongoing source of energy and vitality. "Those who wait upon the Lord will renew their strength; they shall lift up their wings like the eagle's; they shall run and not be weary; they shall walk and not be faint" (Isa 40:31).

10   With all my heart I seek you,
        do not let me wander from your commandments.

WANDERING

This verse begins with a strong statement that as soon as it is made, generates a sense of trepidation. Yes, I seek God wholeheartedly, but I am also fearful that my inward gaze may be distracted and, as a result, my feet will wander from the path I have chosen. Such duality is a commonplace feature of the human condition. We are filled with a desire for the highest realities, yet find ourselves being drawn aside to things that matter less. The question arises: How do we deal with these contrary inclinations?

As a first step, we might ask ourselves whether the first part of this verse is really true in our case. Are we really seeking God? If the answer is affirmative, then another question presents itself: Are we seeking God wholeheartedly. So, we have to try to find indications within our behavior that throw light on what might be the fundamental orientation of our existence. In those people whom we unkindly name as "narcissists," it is clear that all their choices, in one way or another, are directed toward self-enrichment. Others come into the picture only as acolytes to this. "Whatever they think or choose, this they call holy; what they do not want they reject as unlawful."[23]

If we are truly seeking God, then two complementary attitudes are necessary. The first is a habitual tendency to look beyond the here-and-now, to seek the better gifts, the things that are above, and to define our interaction with the world in the light of eternity.

The second is a certain self-forgetfulness, a willingness to let go of our preferences; not to assert ourselves but to make room for others in our immediate environment—even if they have priorities different from ours.

That this is no easy task any who have tried it know. Although there may be a certain degree of enthusiasm at the beginning, as time goes by, it is easy to become slack in our efforts and disoriented in our thinking. The fading of fervor is not deliberate; it often happens without our being fully aware of what is happening. If I allow myself to develop a taste for junk food, I will unthinkingly eat more of it and less of what is nourishing. Eventually, I may be surprised when I become aware of problems with my health. To avoid wandering from the life-giving commandments of God we need to be fairly disciplined in ensuring that contact with them is maintained through all the different circumstances of our life. God's word must become "a lamp for my steps and a light for my paths" (Ps 119:105).

Our hope is that, even when we fail in seeking God, God will search for us. We hope that God will be the proactive agent in the relationship, recognizing that we are prone to wander and need to be rescued. And so, in the last verse of this psalm, we pray: "I have wandered like a sheep, seek your servant, for I have not forgotten your commandments" (Ps 119:176).

11   In my heart I cherish your utterances,
        so that I do not sin against you.

TREASURE

Sometimes media pundits speak about religion as though it were a burden—something that reduces the level of contentment and personal freedom. In contrast, multiple verses of this psalm celebrate the reality that the acceptance of God's revelation—that is to say, the gift of faith—is a source of joy and delight. It brightens every aspect of human existence, heightening the experience of happiness and also giving strength to bear with the inevitable sufferings inherent in our mortal condition. This was brought home to me when an acquaintance was diagnosed with aggressive and terminal cancer and had not long to live. When I approached the topic with her, she burst out: "I am just so grateful for the gift of faith. Without it I could never have coped." Knowing God does not make life more difficult; it is the simultaneous source of both comfort and creative challenge.

The psalmist cherishes the words that carry God's self-revelation; the verb means to "hide," or to "treasure" or to "put away safely." Revelation is not something to be trumpeted in the public arena for our own gratification, but something intimate to be mulled over, with a view to extracting every fragment contained within its rich and complex totality. What we receive from the indwelling word is conditioned by our situation at a particular time. We are gifted with what will be most life-giving in the here-and-now. In a sense, yesterday's word has expired; every day we need to re-discover the newness and aptness of what has been given to us. "If today you hear God's voice, harden not your hearts" (Ps 95:7).

The cherishing of God's word both as indwelling and as expressed in the Scriptures is a principal means of remaining in contact with God throughout the vicissitudes of daily life. It becomes a kind of anchor that secures us to an unmoving point amid the swirling uncertainties of a changing world. It is a simple enough exercise that does not demand great resources of us; it is open even to those who have little. "The commandment that I give you this day is not difficult, nor is it beyond your reach. It is not up in the sky that you should say, 'Who will go up into the sky and fetch it for us that we may hear it and keep it?' Nor is it across the seas that you should say, 'Who will cross the seas and fetch it for us that we may hear it and keep it?' No. The word is very near to you; it is in your mouth and in your heart, ready to be kept" (Deut 30:11-14).

The cherishing of God's word allows us to live in the context of God. This means that we are not alienated from God. This outcome is not achieved through iron willpower or the meticulous observance of rigorous moral precepts. Attachment to God comes about through allowing our attitudes to be slowly formed by ongoing attention to God's word. This is our strongest bulwark against sin.

12   Blessed be you, O Lord,
          Teach me your statutes.

GRATITUDE

The simple words "Thank you" begin life as a grateful response to some benefit received. When someone does me a favor I respond: 'Thank you. May you be blessed for doing such a thing for me." It was a concrete act that inspired this expression of gratitude. A similar benediction can also be directed to God for favors received. An easy form of prayer flows from the recognition of gifts received and the offering of thanks to our divine benefactor. Later the form became more general and was institutionalized. We see this in Psalms 103 and 104, which begin "Bless the Lord, my soul," and then go on to narrate the favors for which God is to be blessed. There is a certain reverent solemnity about the word "bless" in such contexts, even when its use multiplies.

This verse prompts me to ask myself to what extent my attitude towards God is colored by gratitude. Many see God as a demanding taskmaster, who imposes moral burdens on them and judges their failures harshly. Others live in everyday forgetfulness of God until some disaster occurs and then they cry out for help. And there are some who appreciate God as a source of comfort and consolation, but are immune from any sense of the challenge that the relationship implies.

Gratitude provides us with a solid foundation for both faith and hope: gratitude for my own creation, gratitude for the beauty that surrounds me and the friends that light up my life, gratitude for the gift of faith and for those who have passed it on to me. "I acclaim you for the wonder of what I am; for the wonder of your work" (Ps 139:14). I am not my own artefact, I am the creation of God's loving wisdom. Therefore, it is from God that I will learn the authentic path to fulfilment. The connection between our acknowledgement of God's creation of us and our learning the way to fuller life is often made in this psalm. For example: "Your kindness, Lord, fills the earth; teach me your statutes" (v. 64). "You are good and you do what is good; teach me your statutes" (v. 68). "Your hands made me and formed me, give me understanding to learn your commandments" (v. 83).

Eagerness to learn is strengthened by a sense of gratitude towards the one from whom learning is acquired. If we really cherish what we are receiving, we will be appreciative of the giver. And vice versa. Being mindful of my own worth as a unique and original artefact of God's hands makes me conscious of my responsibility to arrive at my "omega point"—the ultimate realization of my potential. Since this future is hidden from me I have to entrust myself to the guidance of the One whose deep knowledge of me exceeds my own.

I willingly submit myself to the discipline of learning about God because I know that, in the process, I will begin to learn something about myself, and this new knowledge will serve me well in the choices that I make in determining my future. For this I am grateful.

"Heavenly Master, you know all things without a teacher, and you teach all things without any labor. Illumine my heart, Lord, teach me your statutes."[24]

13   With my lips have I narrated
      all the judgments of your mouth.

ECHO

What God has spoken is not allowed to remain without effect. I cherish every utterance that comes from the mouth of God and make it my own. The word of God does not remain foreign to me. I welcome it into my heart. The typical biblical way of internalizing God's word was by repeating it softly to oneself. The verb used is *hagah*, which is often translated "meditate," but it is more an oral than a mental exercise. I familiarize myself with the word through repetition.

This was the practice enjoined by Deuteronomy: "These words which I command you this day are to be taken to heart. Repeat them to your children when you are at rest in your house or when you are walking on the road; when you lie down and when you rise" (Deut 6:6-7). It is by viewing divine revelation in the context of our changing life-situations that we begin to understand its richness and its ever-changing relevance. We allow God's word to address all the elements of our evolving life.

It seems to me that today's educational and devotional methods underestimate the value of repetition and memorization, and place much more emphasis on originality and spontaneity. There is no need for these processes to be mutually exclusive since they involve different parts of the brain. But maybe we need to discover for ourselves that there is a value in having a private library of scriptural texts which we can chew over at will. This is the ancient practice known as rumination. Like a cow chewing its cud, we regurgitate what we have read and continue to extract nourishment from it. If we do this we will often experience that, at the first surgings of prayer, a text will often spring to mind to embody what is rising from the heart. Our intimate prayer will be an echo of the word we have welcomed, now enriched by our own responsiveness.

If there is a word that summarizes the book of Deuteronomy, it is surely "Remember." We are called on to make the judgments and determinations that are expressed in the Scriptures part of our own outlook on life. Not only do they animate our prayer, but they become dynamic determinants of the choices that we make in living. This will have on ongoing effect on the quality of our life. Many sins are committed through forgetfulness. We don't look too closely at an option in order to discern its moral quality, but simply close our eyes and follow the promptings of passion and prejudice. We don't evaluate possibilities in the light of God's word but, by exercising a false autonomy, decide independently to do something or leave it undone. Wisdom, by contrast, involves taking a step back from present reality to allow the light of God's word to shine on it so that its true colors are revealed.

Faithful to revelation we allow it to possess our minds and hearts so that when we speak our words are an echo of what we have received, and when we act, our actions mirror the gentle power of the Creator. When we receive the word, it stamps itself on all we do. "How I love your instruction, all day it is my meditation" (Ps 119:97).

14   In the way of your testimonies I rejoiced
      as over all riches.

ENRICHMENT

The self-revelation of God is an enrichment of human life; it opens the door to allow access to the spiritual world and, thus, gives a wider context to the events that occur in the here-and-now. To view this gift primarily in terms of burdensome obligations is to miss the point. It is true that where there are rights, there also are responsibilities, but the imposition of duties is not the primary focus in revelation. It is the opening of a relationship—and a binding relationship at that. God's glory is made manifest in the establishment of a covenant with humanity, an enduring relationship that transcends the vagaries of human behavior, a relationship that is stabilized in the unchanging eternity of God.

God's self-revelation enriches human life. This is not to proclaim some kind of prosperity gospel whereby religion gives us the entitlement to expect that material wealth will come our way. Such wealth is not a source of happiness, as Saint Bernard notes. We are disgruntled if we do not have it; if we have it we are fearful lest we lose it, if we lose it we grieve over our misfortune. All in all, money is the source of much misery.

The enrichment that comes through our attachment to God is the fruit of a real (as distinct from a notional) assent to God's promises. Our faith that all will be well gives us a confidence that reduces the level of anxiety and releases in us our most creative energies. To the extent that we are fearful for our survival, we will live in a state of trepidation and accomplish little. If we live somewhat conscious of the loving benevolence of God we will likely be bolder, more original and more productive. And this is the fundamental source of our joy.

Léon Bloy once wrote that "joy is the most infallible sign of the presence of God." God's presence in our life is the ongoing source of our rejoicing, presupposing that we have allowed it to influence the choices that we make. Revelation is not only a source of guidance in the ever-changing situations in which we find ourselves, it is also a great wealth of affirmation and encouragement which overpowers our native timidity. And, even more mysteriously, through the gift of forgiveness, it repairs some of the damage we have inflicted on ourselves in the past. And "that is why I love your commandments, more than finest gold" (Ps 119:127).

On the feast of *Simchat Torah*, Jewish congregations dance with the scrolls of the Torah as an expression of joy and gratitude for the gift of the revelation. The *Shacharit* prayer which follows the reading of the Torah begins: "Rejoice and exult on *Simchat Torah* and pay homage to the Torah, for its goods are superior to all other goods, more precious than fine gold and gems. Let us delight and rejoice with this Torah, for it is our life, our strength and our light."[25]

15 On your precepts I shall ponder,
   I shall gaze upon your paths.

DEPTHING

The great mistake made by many fundamentalists is thinking that the biblical text will yield its complete meaning immediately, at a first reading. Just as it takes years of interaction before we really get to know another person, so understanding the Scriptures requires of us a lot of diligence and perseverance. Yes, something is evident at a first glance, but understanding the full richness that underlies the text means that we have to spend a lot of time in studying it not only in isolation but in the context of the whole of God's self-revelation. For a text really to speak to our life, we have to engage in the back-and-forth of dialogue until both elements in the conversation are on the same wave length. The text needs to be translated into an idiom that our heart understands.

In many religious traditions there is a practice of repetitive prayer, with the form often counted off on beads. Not only does the repetition have a soothing effect by reducing anxieties, but it also serves to keep distractions at bay. When the mouth is consciously saying words, it is hard for the brain to think of anything else. However, there is more to the practice than this. As we move forward in recitation, as in life, the context in which the words are received slowly changes, and we hear new accents in the familiar formulas.

The same rule applies more generally. Living with God's word allows it to interact with the ever-evolving situations through which we pass. God's word becomes for us something living and active, addressing the issues that we face and providing us with guidance and strength. We may sometimes have the experience that a word of the Scripture that has struck us during our reading, floats around our thoughts in the course of the day and then, providentially, provides us with light and the energy to respond creatively to something that happens or to an issue that is presented to us.

The precepts of God are not military-style commands to which we are expected to give immediate response. Their effect is cumulative over the course of a lifetime. Once, when I was in India, I was shown a rock that had been placed under the outlet of a large water storage tank. When, during the monsoon, the tank overflowed, a spout of water hit the rock before being dispersed. When I looked closely at the rock there was a hole at the center, where the water had hit. Over the years the water had worn away the rock. It didn't happen in a single day, or a single year, but happen it did, over the course of many years.

When we are committed to the practice of pondering God's word it changes us. Not in a single day, or a single year, but over the course of a lifetime. God's word is both formative and transformative. The fact that we are unaware that we are being changed is an indication that we are not the agents of change. It is the living and active word reforming us in its own likeness. This is what salvation involves.

16   I delight in your statutes,
       I will not forget your word.

DELIGHT

To many on the margins of religion it may come as a surprise that delight is an essential component of all authentic religious practice. This is not to say that religious people exist in a state of continual exaltation, but to make the point that unless there is some experience of uplift, people will not persevere for long in adherence to their faith. This was a viewpoint embraced particularly by Saint Augustine who saw the experience of delight as the means by which our attention is seized and directed beyond the sphere of immediate gratification. Particularly at the beginning of the spiritual journey, there is often a strong feeling of inward pleasure that supports and motivates a person to change their ways.

The self-revelation of God is a delight to human beings because, made in God's image, we have a strong sense of incompleteness unless at least some of our inward space is filled by God. In the process of receiving and accepting and expressing God's word, our spiritual faculties are expanded and, as a result, our outlook on life is gradually modified. As Saint Augustine notes: "When the heart expands, there is a delight in goodness. This is a gift of God that, in his precepts, we are not made anxious by the fear of punishment, but we are expanded by love and delight in goodness."[26]

Our sense of joy in our attachment to the spiritual world is not static. Like many other aspects of life, it is marked by seasonal variation. In springtime, there is the excitement of new discovery and the sense that we are moving into areas that we have not hitherto explored. In summer, we experience the full impact of what we have embraced and feel that we are growing. Autumn is a time of fruitfulness, so much so that we are often left weary and empty as we pour ourselves out and generate new life. And then there is the emptiness and coldness of winter, when we seem to have become resourceless. Bare and cold, we struggle to observe even the minimum elements of practice. But then, by a miracle of grace, new buds emerge and the cycle begins again.

What is important is that we recognize that these changing seasons are normal; they are not indications that something is wrong with our life. Amid the ups and downs of experience we strive not to become forgetful of God's word, but to realize that the beneficent providence of God is educating us, bringing forth different qualities in us through different challenges.

If we are wise, we open ourselves to find delight in all the changes that we encounter in our journey. God's word speaks to us every day and accommodates itself to the situation through which we are passing. If we do not forget God's faithful word, it will be our companion on the journey, helping us to find meaning even in the unlikeliest of places, and offering us the prospect of spiritual delight even when things seem to be going badly.

17   Deal kindly with your servant that I may live
       and may keep your word.

RECOMPENSE

The psalmist anticipates that those who freely offer themselves in service to God will draw from God a kindly response. The verb used here is not easy to interpret, but it seems to contain some sense of reciprocity. To worshippers who lift up their hands and hearts to God in prayer, God responds by descending to provide them with whatever assistance they need. Without the term being used, the idea of covenant is evoked: freely assumed mutual relationships and responsibilities. To our way of thinking this is a bold concept. God has undertaken the obligations of a covenant-partner. These include deliverance from death or serious illness, protection from attackers and from oppression by enemies. Anything that threatens my life is due to become the target of God's wrath. God's dealing kindly with me makes it possible for me to remain living.

In the Scriptures God is often named as the *go'el* of the chosen people. When this robust term is translated "redeemer" its concrete meaning is weakened. The basic context of *go'el* is blood relationship; it denotes kinship and the consequent responsibility to avenge any harm done to a member of the group. To declare that God is inside this ring of solidarity is to affirm that God is obliged to pay back any who inflict hardship on me. This attitude is expressed very often in the psalms, sometimes in terms so bloodthirsty that pious souls are embarrassed. But it is truth worth pondering. This title is given to God nine times in Second Isaiah and is related to the epithet "savior." God is proactive in protecting us from possible sources of harm, and ready to wage war to reverse any damage inflicted by enemies. In consequence, we are told: "Do not be afraid."

When God deals kindly with us, it opens up the way for us to advance toward a more abundant life. We are no longer diminished by concentrating our efforts on minimizing the impact of hostile forces, but can devote ourselves more fully to making progress on our journey. With God's help, we will keep moving toward the goal.

It is sometimes said that virtue is its own reward. Whatever is good and wholesome will benefit us whether we are directly aware of its impact or not. When we keep God's word in our hearts and on our lips, it changes the context of our daily living. No life is without its troubles, but for the one who remembers God's self-revelation, who understands that God is our protector and defense, no threat is absolute. Situations may challenge us, they may cause us to suffer, they may sow the seeds of desperation in our minds but, ultimately, through God's intervention, the threats will be undone and, instead, they will work for our good. "You are my King, O God, who command victories for Jacob. Through you we repel our enemies, through your name we trample on our foes" (Ps 43:5-6). As the prophet Elisha declaimed: "Do not be afraid. Those who are for us are more than those who are against us" (2 Kgs 6:16).

18   Open my eyes that I may perceive
        the wonderful things in your instruction.

PERCEPTION

It is clear that there is more than one level of vision. It often happens that our brains can be fully receptive to sensory data without our being able to perceive the significance of what is happening before our eyes. As the prophets lamented, faithless people have eyes that cannot see (Isa 6:10, Jer 5:21; Ezek 17:2; Ps 135:16). In this verse we are asking for the gift of a deeper penetration, so that God's instruction, or *torah*, may communicate its message more powerfully to us. Not just the letter, but the spirit inherent in the text.

If we are serious about exposing our lives to the word of God, we will often find that a particular passage through which we have already passed many times, suddenly comes alive for us. It may be because of a technicality of the language, or the newly noticed elegance of its style, or the emotional impact that it delivers. We read the text as though for the first time. It seems to be directed to us personally, to have a relevance to what is happening in our lives at this time. The text has been wondrously transformed to speak directly to us—or, perhaps, we have been transformed to see more in the text than was previously evident. Our eyes have been opened.

We see what we see but there is no guarantee that we see everything. Birds of prey perceive minor details at great distances, bats hear what we cannot, and dogs have a sense of smell hundreds of times more potent than ours. We see what we see but it is less than everything. Our powers of perception are small; they need to be expanded by a lifelong zeal for pondering the truth, and this involves recognition that factors inhibit or obscure our gaze.

Aurelius Cassiodorus, in the middle of the sixth century, understood this verse in terms of the removal of a veil from our eyes: "While our inner sight is darkened by a covering of ignorance, we cannot understand the holy Scriptures by the light of the heart; this veil must be removed by mercy. [The psalmist] asks that blindness and incapacity be removed so that, enlightened by divine grace, he may seek to see the Lord's wonders."[27]

It is important that we persevere in opening ourselves to God's self-revelation. As we continue on our journey through life, different aspects of it will become apparent; we view the unchanging revelation of God from different angles and, so, the message received is nuanced according to where we are. That is why our eyes need to remain open.

The Divine Liturgy of Saint John Chrysostom contains a similar prayer that begins: "Loving Master, let the pure light of your divine knowledge shine brightly in our hearts and open the eyes of our mind that we may understand the proclamation of your gospel."[28]

19   I am a sojourner in the land,
       do not hide your commandments from me.

TENTATIVENESS

In today's world, we are probably conscious of the precarious status afforded to refugees and immigrants. Such people find themselves located within a foreign country yet not accepted as citizens. It is not only their legal standing that is at risk, but socially they may find themselves unwelcome because they are different; they do not share the culture of the majority around them. This means that it is not easy or safe for them to relax because, suddenly, a situation may arise for which they are incapable of giving an automatic response. They have to be careful that, in an unguarded moment, they do not reveal themselves as unacceptable.

Even if they are only passing through a place on their way to somewhere else, they have to be careful. We may regard travel as relatively carefree, and even as a normal luxury for the leisured classes. In the ancient world travel was fraught with danger. On land, it meant passing through different spheres of influence, each with its own rules and regulations. And who knows what bandits lurk behind every bend in the road? At sea, the ships were relatively fragile, navigation was not always certain, and the possibility of unforeseen storms was always present. Safe travel involved being prepared to deal with all kinds of threatening eventualities.

When the psalmist compares our situation to that of a traveler or temporary resident we are being admonished to be careful during our life on earth. We cannot always take for granted that we possess the insight and skills to survive the dangers that may confront us. We have only one lifetime and we cannot be certain that we are really well equipped to deal with the future as it unfolds before us. We have to learn as we progress, and the lessons we draw from our past may not necessarily apply to what we are about to meet. We need to look beyond ourselves for a source of sure guidance; otherwise we will not survive.

God's self-revelation is set before us as a source of guidance for our mind and of encouragement and support for our heart. Both benefits are important. We do not to know what actions are needed to ensure that we are traveling in the right direction. Maps are useful, but often enough we find it difficult to relate what is indicated by them to what we see around us. We need a more dynamic source of direction, one that corresponds to the actual situation in which we find ourselves. We also need to have our resolve strengthened if we are habitually to make decisions based on the knowledge that has been communicated to us. Decisiveness and courage and even boldness are needed if we are to complete the course.

Above all, God's self-revelation sets a goal before us to keep in our sight as we move through the different zones with their different challenges. Conscious of our status as mere sojourners, we are encouraged to look beyond the here-and-now and to set our hearts on the ultimate goal. It is what awaits us at the end of the journey that keeps our hearts hopeful and our feet moving. By your word, Lord, reveal our goal, show us the way that leads toward it, and confirm our will to pursue the path that leads to abundant life.

20   My soul is consumed with desire
       for your judgments, at all times.

DESIRE

One of the indicators of the dynamic quality of the human condition is the universality of desire. No matter what we become or how much we possess there seems to be an unquenchable yearning for more. Dissatisfaction with the present is what drives us toward a different and, it is to be hoped, better future. If we were perfectly content with the present we would cease acting and lapse into a state of permanent dormancy. We would achieve nothing.

Desire is what we experience when we consider what we do not have at present. When I become aware of the absence of some benefit, I feel a strong affective movement to acquire that which is missing, whether it be a material and tangible product or something more interior. Sometimes I want food or money or shelter; at other times, I want peace, affirmation, or love. It seems that perfect happiness is impossible so long as so many different benefits are lacking.

In the spiritual order also desire is a prime driver of our efforts. Few of us are moved by flashy desires for high mystical states. Most of us, however, are aware that our efforts to live in accordance with the plan God has revealed for humanity are often stymied by inherent weakness, lack of insight and, sometimes, by spiteful outbursts of adolescent rebellion. We fail to make much headway in overcoming our natural inertia because we are not sufficiently motivated, either to take the first step, or to persevere with the thousands of steps that must follow.

Our dissatisfaction with our present state is a good thing because it feeds our desire to move beyond what presently obstructs our growth. Since self-motivation is unlikely to last long, we need to take our cue from beyond our habitual purview and open ourselves to some form of external direction. This is where our desire to be better can meet up with God's word and find in it a source of guidance and encouragement.

There needs to be a marriage between our inner desire and what we hear the Scriptures saying to us. It is not enough to acquire a comprehensive knowledge of biblical criticism, we must invite the text that we are reading to speak to us as we are, to address us in our current situation. Every authentic reading of the Bible is a dialogue in which what we are calls out to God, and then listens for a response. The traffic is in both directions. By a wonderful humility God's word accommodates itself to our limited receptivity and, if we are willing, points out the next step on the way to a more abundant life.

Oddly enough, self-knowledge is the first step toward the knowledge of God. The Scriptures will speak to us only to the extent that we see our limitations and consciously feel the need for direction. Only then will we earnestly desire that God will open before us the path of goodness and joy.

21   You rebuke the proud, the accursed,
     who have strayed from your commandments.

REBUKE

Alexandr Solzhenitsyn, seeking to understand the vast inhumanities of the twentieth century, recalled a Russian folk saying: "People have forgotten God; that's why all this has happened." We may well ask ourselves whether our increasingly secularized world has become more human, kinder and more tolerant. It often seems that those who become godless rarely become better. Leaving aside what had become the routine observance of religious practices may offer a temporary reprieve from boredom, but it scarcely represents a foray into a more creative and other-centered life. We can judge a tree by the quality of the fruit it produces.

Those who allow themselves to live their lives in total isolation from God's word are prone to judge matters without any reference to transcendent reality. They allow themselves to become strangers to the spiritual world. They may seek to disguise this loss by speaking flowery generalities, or to compensate for it by the public performance of good works, but there is something hollow about such manoeuvers. Religion flowers in the inner self and when it flourishes, it stamps the quality of the inner self on everything that is done. Authentic religion adds to objectively good works the seasoning of sincerity and love.

In Hebrew, the word used here for "rebuke" sounds harsh and guttural. It seems to imply that the divine response to human aberration is more vindictive than remedial. But that can also be to our advantage. Opening our lives to God's revelation is not optional; it is an integral component in the process of our becoming fully human. Those who choose to live apart from God will not enjoy the benefits that accrue to faithful service, and they will leave themselves open to errors arising from their own limitations. As the psalmist says later: "You make light of all who wander from your statutes; their deceitfulness yields no result. You treat all the wicked of the earth like dross; therefore, I love your testimonies" (Ps 119:118-119). These are hard sayings. Mostly we do not appreciate stark binary choices; we much prefer some woolly middle path. Yet every day we are confronted with decisions that, in the terms used by Deuteronomy, put before us life and death. The choices we make today will, inevitably, have a bearing on what life has to offer us in the future. Much to our chagrin, we will often have no one else to blame for life's misfortunes, but only ourselves.

Arrogance is a vice that we love to hate in others, but we are often unable to perceive its tentacles binding up our inner life. We are likely to be locked within our own presuppositions and prejudices unless we have some measure by which we can gauge the value of our unreflective judgments. The commandments of God give us the opportunity to set those immediate reactions against an objective standard so that we may be more assured that the choices we make are truly life-giving and not mere phantasms generated in the dark recesses of our unconscious self. That is why following God's commandments is a protection against those secretive delusions that constantly lie in wait for the unreflective.

22   Take away from me scorn and contempt,
          for I have carefully kept your testimonies.

REJECTION

It is usual that authentic prophets meet with resistance and opposition. This is not to say that everyone who fails to gain acceptance is automatically to be considered a prophet. But when true prophets bear witness, they speak and act from a space outside the zone of common agreement. Prophets are not demagogues. Usually they are reluctant to stand out from the common herd, yet when they do express a dissenting view, or act in a way that stands out from common practice, they often meet with vilification.

Being more diligent about the divine guidelines is unlikely to win approval from those who permit themselves a more relaxed observance. We can understand why reformers usually meet with opposition, but it is unclear why those who quietly go about their own business, doing the best they can for God and for neighbor, are often the targets of scorn and contempt. Unworthy motivations are projected on to them and every effort is made to prevent their having any influence on others. In some groups the lowest common denominator is the supreme law. In many cases, those involved lack the insight to understand that what they regard as moderation is, in fact, no more than mediocrity.

To keep the divine testimonies carefully has the effect of unseating other claims to unquestioned authority. No wonder such people are regarded as dangerous. Yet, in reality, their everyday practice is not undertaken with a view to impressing casual bystanders or making a point to those who think differently. It is not a performance for the sake of others. They are acting under the gaze of God; what they do they do for God. That others may take offence is not part of their agenda.

The inner strength to endure such outward rejection comes only from a firm confidence in the truth of divine revelation, buttressed by the certainty that it points out the truest path to human fulfilment and ultimate social harmony. But there is more. The most potent source of endurance in the face of even the most severe hardships is an awareness of the supportive presence of God. To the extent that we open our lives to God we are never alone. Because of this we can face most challenges and endure most hardships. "In God we will act valiantly; and [God] will trample on our enemies" (Ps 60:14).

The psalms of lament frequently call upon us to speak out our troubles to God in the expectation that even in the direst of circumstances God may still be found, and that help will be given us. No matter how brazen we may pretend to be, scorn and contempt always wound. Even though we may pretend to be unaffected they diminish our vitality and cripple our creativity. All we can do is to turn to God, to remind ourselves of God's utter faithfulness, and to find some bulwark against oppression in the hope that God's self-revelation provides. "O my Strength, it is you to whom I turn, for God is my stronghold, a God of kindness" (Ps 59:18).

23   Though the powerful sit to conspire against me,
         your servant muses on your statutes.

PROPHETS

Most cultures seek to maintain the good order of society by elevating those who govern it. They are given honorific titles, sometimes adorned with baubles of office and, usually, propped up by the presumption that somehow they know better than those in the ranks. This illusion is maintained by the fact that often they seek to control the flow of information, so that only what supports their opinions and preferences is given a public hearing. But all this added-on glory does not change the fact, as Ecclesiastes notes, that "Fools are elevated into many high positions" (Eccl 10:6).

Independent thought threatens those whose hold on power is precarious. To avoid alternative viewpoints gaining any traction, tyrants will often launch calculated personal attacks against those likely to submit matters to a more objective judgment. We see this clearly in the case of Jeremiah and many other prophets. The danger, for prophets and pseudo-prophets both, is that they develop a taste for persecution and decline to take any steps that might reduce unnecessary friction.

Prophets will be judged according to their adherence to the word of God. It is part of their task to make the message they transmit as palatable as possible, without diluting its content. This is why the prophets often mingled words of consolation with their pronouncements of woe. The word of God is both comfort and challenge; those who claim to speak for God must take steps to ensure that they are not delivering only part of the message.

This is why those who bear God's word must, at first, transcend earthly politics and devote their primary efforts at being hearers and doers of the word they claim to represent. This means a personal program of pondering God's law, day and night, allowing its different dimensions to cast light on the evolving contexts through which their lives move. The visible feature of the prophets is their public proclamation of a message from God, but this is preceded by something more important: their receiving a word from God in the privacy of their own pondering, allowing themselves to be fired up by its vigor, to the extent that they become unmindful of everything else. Nothing else matters but the message they have been compelled to deliver—even though obedience to this injunction will mean rejection and hardship. It is the message that matters most. "The Lord protects those whose hope is in [God], who speak with [God], who adhere to [God] with all their heart."[29]

There are two temptations that beset prophets. The first is to run away, to avoid the problems that delivering the message will cause. The second is to twist the message for their own advantage; to mingle their own personal agenda with the word of God so that God is made complicit in the realization of their own plans. If both false responses are avoided, all will be well. "It is better to take refuge in the Lord than to trust in the powerful" (Ps 118:9).

24   Indeed, your testimonies are my delight;
      they are my counsellors.

COUNSEL

Seeking counsel is an expression of human solidarity. It is an indication that I realize that the decisions I make may well have an impact on others, and even on the planet which is our common home. Prior to taking counsel is the honest admission of my own limitations: I do not know everything. There are many matters that I do not understand. The world looks different to people viewing it from a different context. I seek counsel because I do not want the good deeds that I envisaged to be blighted by defects in my appreciation of all the elements of a complex situation.

Complete human autonomy is a myth, not only because what I do always affects others, but also because I am unaware of the influence of subconscious factors when I make decisions. Seeking to complement my own resources by reference to outside sources of guidance is not a symptom of weakness but an indication of maturity and wisdom.

When, through ongoing exposure, God's word is supported by personal reflection, what I have read and absorbed begins slowly to influence my outlook on life. There may not always be a sudden or dramatic change; more often the process is more gradual. It begins with the sowing of the seeds of a wholesome self-doubt concerning the preferences and prejudices that have hitherto shaped my attitudes. A chance incident or encounter seems to echo a text that I have welcomed and alerts me to the possibility of seeing things in a different life and encouraging me to make changes in the way I respond to life's surprises.

There is nothing heavy about this process because it is driven by delight. The Hebrew verb used in this verse probably edges toward the notion of intense delight. Becoming acquainted with the self-revelation of God and moving on to some degree of familiarity involves a recurrent stream of inner pleasure. This joy outweighs any effort involved in fixing one's life to the word of God; it generates a sense that this is the right and proper way to live a truly human life.

The fact that God's word has the capacity to spark joy in the human heart is an indication of an innate compatibility between human and divine. In a certain sense, to find God is like coming home. Each new discovery somehow seems familiar. Unlike more tangible sources of gratification, however, our contact with spiritual reality does not diminish as exposure increases. The more God's word colonizes the various zones that make up our humanity, the more human we become; happier in ourselves and the source of joy to others.

An exaggerated sense of autonomy not only blocks the inflow of information and wisdom coming from outside, it also deprives us of the support and comfort that is beyond our capacity to generate on our own. We need other people. We need to be part of the universe. And we need to be in communication with the spiritual world. Otherwise our humanity fails.

25   My soul clings to the dust;
           by your word, give me life.

RE-CREATION

When God's word mingles with dust, the creation of a living being results—as we learn from the book of Genesis. The word of God is both active and life-giving; it has the power to make of the most worthless and insubstantial element, a new creature that is the most precious part of all creation: the human spirit. Our origins were in the dust on the ground; we did not make ourselves into the noble creature to whom the care of the planet was entrusted; we were made so by the action of God.

God's word is not only creative; it also has the power to re-create, repair and renew those members of the human race who yield to the gravitational pull and return to dust. These are they who, instead of lifting their eyes and their hearts to the sun and the stars dancing over their heads, habitually turn their gaze longingly toward the dust of the ground.

When I find that my soul is clinging to the dust it is because I have made choices that have led to this outcome. I have renounced loftier possibilities in order to pursue more immediate and earthier benefits. Even though acquiring them brings me no deep satisfaction. "When you get what you want, you don't want it." I simply transfer my craving to a different target, until I exhaust the possibilities and nothing else has the power to move me. I wonder why my yearning for complete satisfaction is always left unfulfilled. And, soon, even my desires lose vigor, and I am left stranded in the dust, without either hope or enthusiasm.

Dust is mere deadness. Sometimes my choices lead me into situations that are more aggressively hostile. "My soul lies down in the midst of man-eating lions" (Ps 57:5). There is a mysterious tendency to self-destruction among humans that begins with the refusal of what is truly life-giving, and slowly proceeds toward the embrace of what is positively harmful. Yet, if disaster happens to generate a spasm of sincere prayer, then God is able to intervene and reverse the effects of this death-wish. "When the poor cry out the Lord hears them and rescues them from all their distress" (Ps 33:7). Part of humanity's burden is their capability to manufacture unpleasant situations from which they cannot extricate themselves. Perhaps, then, they begin to understand their dependence on God—which previously had been only a theoretical truth. Perhaps, then, they learn to raise their hearts from the ground.

God's word is life-giving because it offers us guidance on our journey and encourages us to keep moving. It is also life-restoring because, God remembers that we are made of dust (Ps 103:14), and when we return to sit in the dust of which we are made, the word calls us to wake up to ourselves and come forth. Even though we are like dry bones scattered over a field of defeat, God's breath hovers over the wreckage, summoning us to stand up and set out from the valley of death and to take up our journey, once again, renewed in hope and vigor.

26   I narrated my ways and you responded;
        teach me your statutes.

NARRATION

"The heavens narrate God's glory" (Ps 19:2) and all over the earth the works of God are manifest. The Scriptures often teach us about mysteries of the spiritual world by narrating the wonderful deeds that God has done. We learn something about the being of God through seeing the effect of the divine energies in our own sphere of existence. Thus, the dialogue between God and humanity begins. We learn something about God.

The dialogue expands when we allow ourselves to be known by God or, more correctly, when we do not hide from the gaze of God but are content to be seen as we are. Our conversation with God is not some kind of charade in which we present ourselves as somehow different from what we are, hiding behind a mask of fake righteousness, and somehow hoping that the depths of our being remain occluded from the divine sight. This plan is futile. God searches the depths of my heart, knows my inmost thoughts and is never absent from the movements of my will. There is nothing that I reveal about myself that will come as a surprise to God.

When I narrate my ways before God it is not to inform God but to remind myself of what I am. When I do this in God's presence I reach a level of truth which facilitates a more direct approach to God. The glory of God is not only manifest in the heavens and in the beauty of the created universe but also in the depths of my being. To make contact with God the most direct path is to travel to the place where God is to be found—my own inmost reality. When I withdraw from the many false imaginings which color my daily outlook on life, when I leave aside the projections which attempt to reshape those around me according to my expectations, when I free myself from my grievances about the past, when I cease to ignore the present moment in the hope of a better future, then I begin to see my life as it really is. And this realization is the only possible springboard for prayer.

When I come before God and tell my story in all truthfulness, God responds. In the first instant I experience a warm welcome that is not diminished by the narration of the errors, failures and omissions that have bedeviled my journey through life. It seems that I am more important than the mistakes I have made. In the presence of God I find a level of acceptance of my imperfect reality that is much more expansive than anything I experience from human beings.

Without any diminishment of this total acceptance there is also a gradual revelation of a pathway which will lead me beyond my present mediocrity to a more complete realization of my innate potential and my deepest desires. God's self-revelation is instructive. In the light of the divine radiance I perceive a more wholesome future for myself, a future that is both more human and more divine.

When I tell my story to God I do so in the hope that God will instruct me in the ways that lead to an even more abundant life. Experience will teach me that this hope is not unfounded.

27   Make me understand the ways of your precepts
      and I shall ponder your wonders.

UNDERSTANDING

Devotees of obedience, whether religious or civil, usually focus on the performance of the act; they have little concern for the interior disposition of the one who obeys. They do not care much whether the person understands the reason for the action; blind obedience is perfectly acceptable. When the Taliban commanded that all men grow their beards, they paid no heed to personal tastes or circumstances; they demanded only compliance. Tyrants of all shapes and sizes are not interested in what their subjects feel or think; all they demand is that they do what they are told.

By contrast the precepts of God are not merely performative. In some cases, such as the performance of certain rituals, the fruit of obedience is more symbolic than practical. Complying with commandments signals our desire to conform to God's will and, in so doing, to conform to the rest of the universe which concords with the unfolding of the divine plan. Just as our radical rejection of authority can be indicated by trivial examples of passive aggression, so our willingness to go along with apparently arbitrary norms can easily express our loyalty in major matters.

In general, however, God's precepts are not merely performative; they are formative. They are intended to nurture in us the beliefs and values that will sustain a life of fidelity in the presence of God. Some things we can learn from a book; others, like carpentry, we can learn only from doing. Living is more like a craft than a science. We learn by doing. That is why wisdom is often associated with a long life; through much practice understanding is gained. This usually means learning from our many mistakes.

Yet because human life is not endlessly repetitive we need more than rote skills to be able to make the most of it. We need understanding to enable us to interpret the past and envisage the future, so that we make the best choices for the present. The precepts of God are a school of instruction which allow us to transcend our inclinations toward immediate gratification and to view matters from a broader perspective.

In assessing the value of a life, the work of intelligence is often underestimated. Yet we are admonished "Do not act like horse and mule, without understanding" (Ps 32:9). They may be obedient, but it is not from free choice. In our case, the whole fabric of faith depends on the operation of our intellect. As Saint Augustine comments, "Without understanding something, no one is able to believe in God."[30]

Living with the self-revelation of God constantly in our memory changes our outlook on life for the better. We begin to view immediate events in a wider context and, so, our response to them is sober and reflective. We are liberated from a tendency to over-reactiveness which sparks off so many undesired outcomes. And we develop some measure of immunity from the self-interested falsehoods so widely propagated today. "From your precepts I gain understanding, therefore I shun every way of falsehood" (Ps 118:104).

28   My soul faints through anguish
        By your word sustain me.

REVIVAL

Sometimes I am conscious that "my soul lies in the dust" and that I am not sure that I have the necessary strength to continue the journey. Those of us born since the nineteenth century are often imbued with the belief that life should keep expanding, getting better all the time. As a result, we are often ill-prepared for the inevitable slumps that punctuate our onward progress. Sometimes these are due to my failure to live up to the ideals I profess. Sometimes they seem to be caused by the actions or omissions of others. At other times, they are more mysterious. I find myself without energy to pursue the things I care about, held bound by regrets for the past or fears for the future.

The first step I need to take is to accept that every human life has its ups and down; alongside moments of exhilaration there are periods of despondency. This is normal. If I am wise I will try to work out strategies to reduce their impact, though experience will often demonstrate that it is just when I need to exert myself more vigorously that my energies fail. It becomes clear to me that a solution is to be sought outside myself.

If I am constant in opening my life to the word of God then my good habit will lead me to the point where my attention to the Scriptures and to their inner resonances will become a source of guidance and animation, to lead me forth from my anguish into a better space. Probably this will not be a dramatic revelation of the way ahead, but simply the dawning realization of a possible next step. A simple action that will cause other life-giving options to manifest themselves. A tiny act of assent that will begin to change the color of my day.

Sometimes, however, the gloom is deeper and more enduring and there are no obvious short-term measures that lead to relief. In this case, we are being led toward a more fundamental truth: we cannot save ourselves. "Only in God is there rest for my soul; from [God] is my salvation" (Ps 62:2). The word of God sometimes withholds its saving energy in order to instruct us to recognize our own powerlessness—to move us to turn to God for help. In this case, our desperation serves the purpose of forcing us to turn back to God.

Hard times break the hard shell of self-sufficiency. When we are weakened by anguish our only hope is to cry out to God. "My soul longs for your salvation, I hope in your word" (Ps 119:81). "Lord, I am badly afflicted; by your word give me life" (Ps 119:107). "Sustain me by your utterance and I shall live; let my hopes not be abashed" (Ps 119:116). "My eyes long for your saving help and your righteous utterance" (Ps 119:123).

If our times of anguish bring us to rely more fully and more confidently on the goodness of God then, maybe, they are not such a bad thing.

29   Keep me from the way of falsehood,
       by your instruction show me favor.

FAVOR

What we seek from God, above all, is acceptance. We hope that we will find favor or grace in God's eyes: "Turn to me and show me favor; according to your judgment for those who love your name" (Ps 119:132). Such petitions bespeak a recognition of the graciousness of God, who was revealed to Moses as "compassionate and gracious" (Exod 34:6). Usually, showing favor follows finding something acceptable or beautiful in the one to whom favor is shown. In the case of God, however, the giving of favor creates beauty where hitherto beauty was not. God shows favor before there is anything to merit such a response.

When God looked on creation, it was found to be "very good." Its goodness flowed from the hand of the Creator. In some way creation reflected back the glory that had reached out from God to create a world of wondrous beauty. "The skies narrate God's glory" (Ps 19:2). Whatever is touched by the radiance of divine glory is transformed into something beautiful. This is our hope when we cry out in our need: "Let your face shine on your servant." When we become aware of God's gracious regard, the context of our lives is changed. And we ourselves become worthy of acceptance.

"Let your face shine on your servant and teach me your testimonies" (Ps 119:135). The sign of our acceptance by God is that we are given access to God's self-revelation. God becomes our teacher. And so, the present verse prays: "By your instruction (*torah*) show me favor."

The instruction given by God is not merely that which is written on a scroll. It is also written in the heart. When the disciple commits God's word to memory and allows it to take residence in the heart, it becomes an internal principle of action that is somewhat autonomous from the preferences of the person. God has set the law within us, writing it on our hearts. A well-known passage from Isaiah witnesses to the power of this internalized word: it is living and active.

> O people of Zion, who live in Jerusalem, you will weep no more. [God] will show favor when you cry for help. As soon as God hears, there will be an answer for you. Although the Lord has given you the bread of adversity and the water of affliction, your Teacher will be hidden no longer; with your own eyes you will see your Teacher. Whether you turn to the right or to the left, your ears will hear a voice behind you, saying: This is the way; walk in it. (Isa 30:19-21)

It is through the constant action of this indwelling *torah* that we are protected from falsehood. It establishes within us a power of discernment so that we instinctively know what is right and what is wrong; what is good and what is evil. It is a living reminder of that fundamental injunction: "Turn away from evil and do what is good" (Ps 34:14). What greater indication of favor can there be than being gifted with an inward sense of direction in the journey of life?

30   I have chosen the way of faith,
       your judgments I have upheld.

FAITH

To walk the way of faith demands a series of deliberate choices. It is not a cultural artefact inherited from the distant past, nor is it a policy once adopted and then allowed to run. Walking the way of faith means allowing faith to have an influence on every choice that we make in our journey toward a more abundant life.

The manner in which the psalmist understands faith is not so much a matter of giving assent to certain doctrines or belief. It is close to what we would term faithfulness or loyalty, an ongoing attachment that is characterized more by warmth than by its intellectual content. It is interpersonal and historical. In the context of the I-Thou relationship constantly evoked in this psalm, it is a continuing reference to God as a Thou, and to the word of God as a precious communication that enlightens and animates, both as an external source and an internal voice.

To choose the way of faith involves the displacement of self from the center of one's life and the decision to make room for the still, small voice that Elijah heard. It means silencing the many vocal opinions that crave our attention, and the wild noises that seek to entertain, and allowing ourselves to listen in silence for the word that is spoken without words and can be heard only by an attentive heart. At first this is accomplished rarely and with considerable effort. As the years pass, the voice becomes more familiar and its presence more easily detected. Our giving assent to the word seems to add to its strength. Willing listeners always hear more than those who are reluctant.

Faith needs to be fed. It is by our loyalty to making space to listen to God's word, both in the Scriptures and in conscience, that the bond between us and God is maintained and strengthened. The relationship grows. Each time we make the effort to implement faith in our daily life we experience new aspects of it. We deepen our understanding of faith by remembering it and putting it into practice. God's self-revelation shows us the way to become more fully what we were created to be. Living our faith causes it to grow.

Faith can be lost. Usually this is not a spectacular event, it happens by cumulative erosion. It is undermined by neglect and weakened by consciously acting against it. Faith needs to develop within the context of an ever-evolving life. If it remains fixed in the forms of the past, it can never quite cope with the challenges of today and so tends to crumble if it is subjected to unforeseen demands. We are complicit in this breakdown if we have not allowed our faith to grow with us, to accompany us through all the stages of our life.

The psalmist views matters with great simplicity: "I look on those who break faith with disgust, for they do not keep your utterance" (Ps 119:158). It is by living according to the self-revealing word of God that our faith is sustained and allowed to grow.

31   I cling to your testimonies, Lord,
       Let me not be put to shame.

UNASHAMED

When we feel guilt, it is usually because of what we have chosen to do. Shame, however, is experienced because of what we are or, at least, because of what we feel ourselves to be. Shame is much deeper than guilt; it ultimately leads to radical self-rejection and despair. The first man and woman shrank back in shame, not wanting to be seen as they were. Shame seeks concealment and, once the process of hiding begins, it expands, covering more and more areas with its deadening shroud. Shame causes a shrinking in the creative powers of those whom it envelops, so that their potential is left finally unrealized.

When we pray to be free of shame we are asking for the boldness that derives from a certainty that we are of great value. That we are loved. Without reference to what we might have accomplished in life or what missteps we may have taken. Persons who know themselves to be loved unconditionally feel no shame. They live in the awareness that their value is attested by their being accepted by the One who understands the dust of which we are made.

We come to an appreciation of this unconditional love through the fidelity that binds us to God's self-revelation. In coming to know something of God we begin to learn something about ourselves. It is in the ongoing interchange between us and God that an authentic self-understanding emerges. This is why it is important that our exposure to the word of God is lifelong and regular. As it becomes the main source of our identity, it imbues us with a boldness that cannot be shaken by the plots of the powerful or the scorn of those who despise us.

The idea of clinging to the divine testimonies is worth exploring. It seems to indicate that a decision has been taken to base one's entire life on God's self-revelation. This involves more than welcoming them and allowing them to influence us. It seems to contain the idea of setting aside alternative sources of guidance and gratification. To be attached to God involves our willingness to be detached from everything else or, at least, from everything that could displace God in our lives. Clinging to God means letting go of what is not God and running away from what is opposed to God. It is a program of life that is easy to enunciate but difficult to implement.

Fortunately for us who cannot even consider such a giant step, the word of God becomes more addictive as the years pass. It becomes a necessary comfort in hard times, and adds the seasoning of challenge when things are going well. It accompanies us along the way and adjusts itself to whatever we need to keep our balance. It is the element in our life that is not under our control and so it has the capacity to spring surprises on us. If God's word truly is an integral part of our daily life, there is no danger of our succumbing to spiritual sleepiness.

"Let my heart be upright in your statutes, that I may not be put to shame" (Ps 119:80).

32   I will run on the way of your commandments,
         since you have enlarged my heart.

RUNNING

In the Bible, the verb used here usually means deliberate running, with an implied urgency. It may be in an emergency or to deliver important news, as a tactic in battle or as an expression of warm hospitality. In the present case, it seems more like an expression of enthusiasm. The psalmist embraces the Lord's commandments comprehensively, without any trace of compromise or resentment.

We know from the Bible that one of the persistent temptations faced by God's people was to seek to supplement the sober worship of the true God with an investment of devotion toward rival deities. This the prophets of every generation denounced. Of its nature, service of the Lord must be single-minded or it is worthless. We must love God with our whole heart and our whole soul and we must pour the whole of our energy into so doing. There is no room for the half-hearted. "The divided I hate, but I love your instruction" (Ps 119:113).

But how are we to arrive at this level of fervor? Not by our own efforts; we have tried but have found ourselves unable to maintain the pace. To run the way of God's commandments seems to demand a level of youthful vigor that is no more than a distant memory and a capacity for endurance that we have never known. The answer is given us in the book of Second Isaiah:

> [God] gives strength to those who are weary and increases the power of the weak. Even the young grow tired and weary, and youth may stumble and fall. But those who wait for the Lord, shall renew their strength: they shall lift up their wings, like eagles: they shall run, and not be weary, and they shall walk and not become tired. (Isa 40:29-31)

Strength to do the impossible comes from God; the word of God is empowering. It allows us to soar above ordinary constraints and to transcend our customary reluctance to exert ourselves.

God's word is living and active and those who welcome and cherish it become more lively and proactive.

There is another aspect of running that is worth considering. In its most spontaneous expression it seems to be the prerogative of the very young. Happy children never walk when they can run, there is a sense of exuberance, a sheer delight in being alive. Devotion to God's word allows us progressively to become like children, to turn back the clock, as it were. To look upon life with a simplicity that encourages us to shrug off at least some of the complications that make us miserable, and to learn to value whatever is offered us. Without a sideways glance. Without regret that it is not something different.

The promise of an enlarged heart, a deeper understanding and a broader capacity for giving and receiving affection opens before us the prospect of becoming fully human, fully alive. We too will acquire the capacity to run the way of God's commandments, powered by the unimaginable sweetness of divine love.

33   LORD, teach me the way of your statutes,
and I will keep it until the end.

ARRIVAL

The image of walking along a road is eloquent, but it implies that the walking is less important than the arrival at the destination. It is in hope of getting somewhere that the journey is undertaken. In some senses the end of the journey is its beginning. By envisaging the end we are motivated to take the first steps. And it is by keeping the end in sight that we continue walking. If the end fades from our view then our determination falters and we become more and more liable to wander off the track.

It is the word of God that keeps alive our hopes of arriving at our goal and, thereby, motivates us to keep walking, even though our feet are heavy and the road is hard. To allow God's gracious self-revelation to slip from our minds is to deprive ourselves of the energy we need to make the most of the opportunities that unfold before us.

Constancy is a virtue that is not much celebrated today. Innovation we admire and we enjoy novelty. Repeatedly doing the same thing seems very dull. We admire the Olympic athlete winning a gold medal, but we forget about the boring years of preparation that have preceded the victory. We don't want to admit that the sparkling performance of the concert pianist depends on years of repetitive exercises, honing skills and growing in sensitivity. It is not the dramatic first step that guarantees the outcome, but the long sequence of small steps that follow. It is through slow progress along the way that we grow.

The fact is, however, that constancy is not merely dead repetition; it is dynamic and alive, and not without paradox. True progress is dependent on undeviating responsiveness to changing circumstances. It is the opposite of obstinate rigidity. Sometimes the best way forward is to go back. When we find ourselves off the track and lost, we need to return to the point from which we wandered and restart from there. This means recognizing our error, admitting it, and, then, taking steps to correct it. To do this we need some kind of external criterion which can serve as a counterweight to the erroneous presuppositions which led us astray. The word of God can show us where we went wrong and indicate a way of escape from the mess we have made for ourselves.

There is not much point in beginning the journey unless we intend to bring it to completion. If we are truly seeking closeness to God, then nothing else can substitute for it. We will spend a lifetime giving this goal priority over more ephemeral gratifications. Day by day we make the choice for God. Such perseverance needs to be constantly renewed and updated, and demands of us a dynamic commitment to allow God to bring to completion the good work that has been begun in us. If we are truly disciples who are willing to learn the way of the commandments, then we will keep them until the end and we will finally come to our goal of a more abundant life.

34   Give me understanding that I may hold fast to your
         instruction
      and keep it with all my heart.

HOLDING FAST

Living in lifelong fidelity to what we have glimpsed of God is a very challenging prospect. It means that we are committed to allowing nothing to deflect us from the direction we have given to our life. This could well be an unrealistic proposition since we do not know what threats to its continuance will emerge in the future. Predictable problems can be forestalled by prudence, but who can prepare for what happens outside the range of normal expectations? If, while I am taking a stroll, an asteroid strikes or a tiger attacks, I will be bereft of options. It never occurred to me that this might happen. I am never immune from the impact of the unexpected.

Holding fast to God's instruction or *torah*, is not a once-and-for-all decision. It is, rather, an habitual stance taken as I journey through life. At each hour and at every moment I keep relating what I am experiencing to the self-revelation of God, to find in it a source of guidance and energy. God's word is living and active, it responds to the changing situations through which I pass. Electronic navigation systems are superior to maps because they not only propose a route from where we begin to the point at which we want to arrive, but they keep modifying the directions according to where we actually find ourselves. Even if we wander away from the proposed route and are heading in the wrong direction, they still are able to propose to us the most direct route from where we are to where we want to be.

God's word is not just a series of codified moral regulations that we are expected to follow. It invites us to enter into a relationship, and like every relationship it is always evolving. To hold fast to the divine instruction is not to act like a miser clutching his bag of gold with closed fist and closed heart. It is more like a family on a roller-coaster holding fast to the safety bar as they whizz through the ups and downs of their exciting ride, not knowing what is next, but confident that they can cope with whatever happens.

The wholehearted attachment to God's word enables us to face life confidently. Almost certainly there will be setbacks and disappointments and, maybe, even disasters. But God's word will continue to speak to us, gently pointing out the best way forward and urging us to pursue it. We are not alone. God does not desert us when things go badly, even when this is due to our own obstinate blindness. The still, small voice continues to whisper in our ears: "This is the path; follow it and you will live."

If we allow ourselves to be guided in this way we will find ourselves lost in wonder at how God somehow helps us to walk straight even when the pathways are crooked. No surprise then that the psalmist prays: "Make me understand the ways of your precepts and I shall ponder your wonders" (Ps 119:27).

✣

35   Make a way for me on the path of your commandments,
     for I take delight in it.

UNIQUE

We make the path by walking on it. There is no common and predetermined road which everyone must follow. Each of us walks a unique journey through time and space that no other person has ever experienced. Yes, there are commonalities, but the total experience is particular to each person. In this verse, the word sometimes translated simply as "guide" means more literally "make a way for me." It may perhaps be taken to indicate that on our journey through life, although we share many experiences with others, our life in its entirety is unique to us, and our path through it is narrow.

The way to life revealed to us in the Scriptures gives us general directions about how we are to reach our goal. Following them will bring us to fulfilment. Yet it is not the merely material keeping of the commandments that is life-giving, but our sensitivity to our own particular call. What the written word does for us is to act as an agent in the formation of our conscience, and it is our conscience, formed by God's word, that is our immediate instructor in walking the ways that lead to life.

To assert the primacy of conscience is not an invitation to individualism. A conscience instructed by God's self-revelation is not autonomous, but a partner in an ongoing dialogue. Revelation is complete only when it is received, and when it is received it is shaped by the specific needs of the receiver. God's word always provides guidance for the here-and-now—not some universal, general indications, but as a commentary on the real situation unfolding before the person's eyes.

When we ask God to make a way for us, we are really asking for the wisdom and strength to open ourselves to the divine guidance and to implement it. A clearer vision and a firmer will. The ability to be faithful to one's own inner voice and, at the same time, to live in harmony with others who are on the same path, but travelling it in accordance with their own calling. And, above all, we seek the strength to continue the journey under the divine guidance.

God's self-revelation is a gift not a burden. That is why it is a source of delight to us. When we permit ourselves to follow it we undertake a process of finding our truest and deepest self. Although God's word comes to us from outside ourselves, it seems to have a better and more profound knowledge of who we really are than we have ourselves. Too often our choices are misguided because they stem from selfishness or arrogance; as a result, they cause us to deviate from the life-giving path and get lost in the miasma of inauthentic self-gratification.

On the other hand, opening ourselves to God's word is the way to self-discovery and, ultimately, to the realization of the potential inherent in us by virtue of our being created in God's image. This is why it becomes for us a source of deep and enduring delight.

36   Incline my heart to your testimonies,
        and not to wrongful gain.

ACCUMULATION

The service of God sits uneasily with the massive accumulation of worldly goods, whether these be material, social or personal. The more we accumulate, and the more satisfied we are with what life offers us, the less inclined we are to look beyond our present contentment to care for the welfare of others or to dedicate ourselves to the service of God. Take Solomon as an example. He had everything a human heart could desire, including wisdom, yet he fell away from the service of God and, because of this, the unity of his kingdom was lost forever.

It seems that we become more aware of our dependence on God when things are not going so well for us. During the First World War it was said that there were no atheists in the trenches. Imminent danger makes us aware of the precariousness of our existence—in fact, the term "precarious" has at its heart the Latin word for prayer. It is not surprising that the largest category of psalms is that of lament. We pray most readily when we are in danger, when we are deprived of what we need, and when we find ourselves sinking toward desperation.

On the other hand, when we are passing through a stage of abundance and prosperity, prayer may seem superfluous. To the extent that our desires are limited to the acquisition of material goods, the building of a good reputation and the comfort of a harmonious life, the restlessness of our heart is stilled and, as a result, the memory of God and the keeping of God's precepts slip from our minds and hearts.

There is another aspect to accumulation. Material assets and many non-material goods are limited. This means that the more I acquire the less that others have. The word that I have translated "wrongful gain" has more than a hint of acquisition at the expense of others, perhaps through some form of violence. As soon as we begin to exalt ourselves over others we also begin to move away from God. Our relationship with God is characterized by goodness and righteousness and justice. The relationship is not the result of these noble qualities; on the contrary, they are the consequence of our attachment to God and our willingness to be formed by God's precepts.

This is a never-ending endeavor. And so, we pray that God will help us to keep turning our minds to things above material gain. We pray that God will turn our hearts away from tangible benefits and gradually initiate us into following a less travelled road. Keeping our needs simple is the key to happiness. Those who are content with little are usually content. As the book of Proverbs affirms: "Keep far from me both poverty and riches, give me only a portion of bread, lest I have too much and then disown you, and say: 'Who is the LORD?'" (Prov 30:9-10). To keep turning our hearts to the divine testimonies disinclines us to be greedy and provides us with a treasure that outweighs even the wealth of Solomon.

37   Avert my eyes from seeing what is worthless,
       in your way, give me life.

VANITY

The book of Ecclesiastes begins with the well-known observation: "Vanity of vanities! All is vanity." As the book proceeds it becomes more obvious that the context of the maxim is moral rather than philosophical. It is true that everything around us is transient, insubstantial, ephemeral and prone to decay, but this is more a premise than a conclusion. Because everything within our reach lacks the solidity on which we can base our confidence, we must look elsewhere. To put our trust entirely in things that are not the source of their own being is to risk becoming as ephemeral as they are. Ecclesiastes is cautioning us to give no more weight to the everyday realities around us than they can sustain. We must look elsewhere for guidance and meaning. This is also the view of the prophet Jeremiah who wrote: "They who walk after vanity become vanity" (Jer 2:5). We become what we pursue.

The passion for things of trivial importance finds its way into our hearts through the eyes. Surrounded as we are by a world of wondrous variety, we are able to choose what occupies our minds and hearts by what we look at. It is from the lust of the eyes that the covetousness of the heart derives its energy. Concentration involves bringing our inward gaze into a central point, it involves focusing. It is only by sustained concentration on a particular project that progress is made. Little is achieved by constantly flitting from one topic to another. Multitasking is best left to fools.

Perhaps one reason why many of our contemporaries find it hard to distinguish knowledge from opinion is that in this digital age we are constantly flooded with unfounded assertions, which we have no ready means of verifying. We are expected to be uncritical in receiving new information, trusting that the sources are reliable. In this way we expose ourselves to the possibility of accepting what is worthless.

The psalmist prays that God will endow us with the strength to turn away from such nonsense. It may be said that indulging in such things is no more than entertainment, but this is not the whole truth. A taste for the superficial gradually annuls the capacity to appreciate what is profound. Spend your life reading nothing but comics and you will find that you have no inclination to open books of greater value. As Bernard of Clairvaux wrote: "An appetite for vanity is contempt for the truth, and contempt for the truth is the cause of our blindness."[31]

In praying that God will avert our eyes from what is worthless, we are asking that we may be empowered to give more weight to those possibilities that are truly life-enhancing, that we will walk the ways shown us by God's word, and that we will grow in our appreciation for what is of greater weight. By living in the context of the spiritual world we are saved from the flippancy of so many things that cry out for our attention. This makes it possible for us to set our hearts on what leads to wisdom and a fuller life.

38   Bring your utterances to completion for your servant who fears you.

REVERENCE

Of all the attitudes which the Bible recommends, "fear of the Lord" is probably the least appreciated. In part, this is due to the fact that the term "fear" can be interpreted in several different ways. It can refer to the paralyzing terror which grips a person confronted by an imminent and deadly threat. Equally it can cover an unsubstantiated concern about our general wellbeing or social harmony. There are qualitative differences in fear as well as differences of degree. What is meant by a godly fear?

A first element of fear is that it concerns that which is not within our control and yet impinges on our lives. An asteroid strike on Jupiter or an avalanche in Greenland leaves most of us unmoved. Events closer to home, however, can upset our equilibrium, to a greater or lesser degree, and with more or less rationality. Fear is triggered by the encounter with something greater and more powerful than ourselves, even when it is mingled with delight. A huge ocean wave may be invigorating to a professional surfer, but to a person caught up unawares it is life-threatening.

Our fear of God is a recognition that we have a genuine encounter with something that is totally different from everything else that we experience, something that is beyond our control, something that is unchanged by anything we might do. There is more. We recognize that with this encounter we ourselves are being changed—or rather, we are being summoned to change. Life cannot continue as it was. The security of our previous identity is undermined. Life henceforth will be different.

If we consider the experience of Moses at the burning bush we see these two complementary responses. On the one hand, there is an attraction which draws him closer, on the other there is implicit threat in that invitation. He is instructed to perform the symbolic act of removing his shoes. He can no longer remain what he was. In our own slighter experience we find the same dynamic; we find ourselves drawn into the spiritual realm, but on entering we feel that it demands of us more than we are prepared to give.

Spiritual experience is never to be trivialized; if it is genuine it retains this sense of reserve and reverence that keeps in check the boisterous impulses of our nature and bids us recognize the seriousness of the challenge. We are being invited to live in the context of unseen realities, and this means interposing a distance between ourselves and immediate, tangible influences. For the promise inherent in God's self-revelation to be brought to completion in us we have to be prepared to reorder our lives so that they become more in accordance with the divine precepts. We do not have to be fanatical in this, but simply to act in a measured and prudent manner that does not place excessive demands on our possibilities for change.

Fear of God is not being afraid of God; it is a matter of accepting the challenge to change our lives so that they can, in some way, accommodate the presence of the infinite, eternal Creator of all. To invite God into our hearts demands a serious effort at housecleaning.

39   Avert the reproach that I dread
        for your judgments are good.

REPROACH

None of us is beyond reproach, even if our failures to practice integrity are not widely known by others. "There is no one on earth that does what is good and is free from sin" (Eccl 7:20). No matter how virtuous our present life seems to us or how reputable it seems to others, there is always a hidden zone of weakness, blindness and malice that underlies our current respectability; it has broken loose in the past, and may do so again. Few of us would be happy to be under close observation at every moment, and even if we succeeded in making our outward conduct blameless, none of us can afford close scrutiny of our inner feelings and motivations. In addition, because we develop during our lifetime, our earlier stages seem less valuable in retrospect; if we are honest with ourselves we are somewhat abashed by the things we said and did when we were younger.

The Latin translation of a line in the lament of Hezekiah has been traditionally taken as an indication of this reality. "I think over my years in bitterness of heart" (Isa 38:15). As the years pass and wisdom grows, we cannot prevent ourselves from re-assessing our past. Memories of miscalculations and misdeeds mount up before our eyes; in hindsight we become aware of the extent of our omissions, so that our achievements seem overrated. What is happening here is that we are progressing more fully into the realm of self-truth. It may be uncomfortable but it is progress. Our delusions of righteousness are being stolen from us so that we can stand naked and unashamed before God.

When the dread of discovery is dissipated, then the gratuitous goodness of God becomes manifest. We no longer fear to be revealed as the sinners that we are but, instead, accept ourselves as we are, and expose ourselves fully to the mercy of God. This is not to condone the evil that we have done or to lessen the malice that left the possibility of good deeds unfulfilled, but to insist that

God's mercy is such that it can coexist with our failures and is, in no way, lessened because of them.

To allow our life to be illumined by God's self-revelation and to endeavor to live in the context of this light is to live in the truth without fear. To understand that we are known by God in all our limitations and yet remain precious in God's sight is a great advance. If we no longer fear reproach because of our human weakness, then perhaps we shall become a little more tolerant of the failures of others. We will feel less need to project our disappointment at our own shortcomings onto others, and readier to be more benign in our assessment of their virtue.

In a mysterious way, while we remain attentive to God's self-revelation, our own limitations and failures seem less important. As Saint Augustine notes: "The just one falls and rises seven times, but is not weakened by all these evils."[32] Our failings are par for the course. Who is surprised when they happen?

40   Behold, I have desired your precepts;
in your righteousness, give me life.

LIVELINESS

There is more to life than simply living. When God enters a person's life it begins to sparkle. The divine righteousness is contagious; it transforms everything it touches. A person who begins to walk along the way of the commandments, perhaps unknowingly, is moving toward greater freedom and spontaneity. This is because true righteousness begins in the heart and slowly makes its way outward; it does not consist merely in external observances.

Being exposed to the divine self-revelation has, as its first effect, to make us carefree. We are no longer lost in the miasma of contrary opinions, but can see the way ahead with some clarity.

We have to keep walking along this way before we reach the goal of abundant life, but we can relax, knowing that the path we are following is one that will carry us to our desired destination. We can take time to enjoy the journey.

This means that we can afford to be a little playful. Life lived under the guidance of God is not deadly serious. There is a time for play. Ancient philosophers gave a name to this quality and regarded it as a virtue. They called it *eutrapelia*. They thought that anyone who lacked humor was less than fully human, that those who aspired to be like the angels ended up being less than the beasts. Being silly sometimes is part of our nature; it is a normal expression of happiness. In fact the origin of the English word "silly" is shared with the German word *selig*, blessed or happy.

A person who is fully alive is also creative. The book of Genesis tells us that we were made in the image of a creating God; we are most like God when we are creative. When we draw forth from our interior resources something that is new and beneficial. We are, as it were, continuing the work of creation, doing our part in bringing the universe to that completion which was envisaged at the beginning. We are not drones contributing nothing but our labor to the process; our participation means that the final product will be all the better for carrying something of us in its fabric. Our signature will be there along with those of others who have been co-creators.

Accordingly, there is scope for exuberance in our journey, to allow energy to flow from our center and transform the world around us. If this seems an extravagant claim, it is probably because we are thinking of ourselves too much in isolation. We do not accomplish our task alone, but as members of a corporate entity. Our work is done in the context of human solidarity. Alone our contribution is slight; together we can accomplish much.

We know that our vices hurt others. Sometimes we forget that they hurt us more. Such vices as anger, sadness, envy, resentment, and laziness impact also upon us. They reduce the level of liveliness and change our sparkle into drudgery. Cut back on vice and life becomes happier.

The glory of God is God's self-manifestation; when we welcome it we become more fully alive; our lives are lit up by liveliness.

41   Lord, let your kindness come to me,
      salvation according to your utterance.

KINDNESS

The word *chesed*, here translated as "kindness" was traditionally translated as "mercy." This rendering gave to the word a strong connotation of forgiveness which, undoubtedly, is one expression of divine kindness. Forgiveness has as its trigger, the miserable situation of the recipient thus, a connection was made, in the Latin tradition, between *misericordia* and *miseria*. Mercy was understood as God's response to our misery. Translating the word as "kindness" however, makes the point that God's benign attitude toward us preexists any damage that we may have inflicted on ourselves. The kindness of God is unconditional and unremitting; it is an essential facet of the divine nature.

The first quality to be found in God's kindness towards humanity—and, especially, with regard to the chosen people—is that it is active. More than that, it is proactive. This is to say that divine kindness is not simply a fuzzy benevolence in our regard, but generates dynamic interventions with a view to our welfare. The God of Israel is a God who acts, and it is by remembering the actions of God that our faith is sustained. To remind us of these is one function of the Scriptures. The "justice" or "righteousness" of God is not a self-contained entity, but actively imparts itself to all who are touched by it; it justifies. Just as in creation, all that come to be came out of nothingness, so God's justice brings forth that same quality in those who lack it and do not deserve it. God's kindness creates where nothing was before.

The second quality of *chesed* is that it is relational. We are saved by entering into a relationship with God—or rather, by God entering into a relationship with us. Such a relationship is marked in an eminent degree by all those qualities that we expect in a good human relationship: love, affection, truthfulness, fidelity, acceptance, tolerance, loyalty. God is often described as our *goel*, our closest relative, with a duty to uphold our rights and avenge any wrongs done to us. The relationship remains incomplete, however, if it is one-sided. Love, affection and fidelity can be experienced fully only if they are reciprocated. God's kindness calls us into a relationship of mutuality. The more we are exposed to it, the more we are expected to love God in return and to be faithful.

Kindness' third quality is endurance. It is unconditional and so is not changed by any change in us. Divine benevolence survives any failure on our part and immediately sets to work to repair whatever damage we have inflicted on ourselves. Wherever we wander and distance ourselves from the way that leads to life, there is always a way back; it is out of kindness that God is always ready to point to the path we must take. God's word is always ready to show us the way home.

The goodness and graciousness and kindness of God are realities to be celebrated. No doubt that is why Psalm 136 affirms twenty-six times: "[God's] kindness is without end."

42   I have a word to respond to those who reproach me,
       for I have trusted in your word.

RESPONSE

The meaning of our actions is not always self-evident. As Blaise Pascal once noted: "The heart has its reasons of which reason knows nothing." Those who meditate on God's law by day and night will, inevitably, have a different perspective on many issues. They tend to develop a sensitivity to aspects of reality that pass unnoticed by those concerned only with their own little world. This is not arcane or gnostic knowledge, but a deeper awareness that things are not always as they seem. It may involve an unwillingness to attribute infallibility to conventional wisdom. A similar kind of awareness is often found in indigenous peoples, who have absorbed a connatural insight into the way the world works that is not afforded to those who rely on the book learning of others.

This profound wisdom is not always easy to explain in rational or scientific language. It is a heuristic sense of aspects of reality that have not yet yielded their secrets to analytic investigation. It probably has more to do with the intuitive right hemisphere of the brain than to its rational counterpart. The fact that it cannot be explained means that it is not very marketable—most people prefer to understand what it is that they accept as true.

The knowledge of the heart reaches out to inform the conscience. It is not its function merely to inform; it carries with it a sense of obligation. The way ahead is indicated on the understanding that we will feel obliged to follow it, even though we don't fully understand why this is so. And if we ourselves do not know why we feel obliged to act, others will certainly be puzzled.

This was case with the biblical prophets. Take Jeremiah, for example. He was convinced that Judah was doomed and his message was that the best way to minimize damage was to surrender and seek some sort of compromise from the king of Babylon. He was, of course, correct in his assumptions. The diehards, however, utterly rejected any suggestion of surrender, accused Jeremiah of treason, imprisoned him so that his life was under threat. Prophets are always persecuted because their message makes no sense to "reasonable" people.

If we allow our consciences to be formed by consistent contact with God's word, it may be that we will judge some situations in a way that is different from others and will lead to scorn, reproach, and rejection. Our only defense may be that what we have said and done was in obedience to a higher law. Of course, we will have to double-check and take all necessary precautions to ensure that we are not distorting the message so that we become false prophets. But to live in strict accordance with a well-formed conscience is always going to get us into trouble.

This is where we need an abundance of confidence in the inherent power of divine revelation to achieve more than we can imagine, and to trust that it has the capacity to overcome even the fiercest resistance, not only in those to whom it is addressed but also in its reluctant carriers. Think of Jonah.

43   Never take the word of truth from my mouth
       for I have hoped in your judgements.

TRUTH

When the psalmist speaks of truth he is not thinking of the abstract and rarefied sense of the word that we associate with Greek philosophy, but he has in mind something very concrete and practical. Truth is associated with faithfulness. The word of truth is a discourse that is faithful to the reality it describes; it does not disguise it or color it, but communicates reality as it is. Truth was viewed in a holistic manner; a truthful statement conveyed the whole of the matter, in all its complexity, and omitted nothing.

This often means that truth is a matter of more than words, because words are only part of the total communication. If I say "God is love" with a scowl on my face and a whip in my hand, it is likely that the verbal message will not be received. According to the old adage: "I can't hear what you are saying because what you are is shouting too loudly." Words are important but their weight is measured by their concordance with the total reality of the person who speaks them. There are situations in which silence is more vocal than speech.

Because the human species is corporate in nature pure solitude often seems threatening to us. We are overcome by separation anxiety and seek, perhaps compulsively, to build bridges to others. Our most important means of doing this is by speech, even when we have nothing to communicate. As a result, it is important that the words we utter convey accurately the reality of the person who speaks them, otherwise the relationship that develops is based on falsehood.

To the extent that we accept the governance of God's word in our daily lives we are helped to live an authentic existence, true to our nature, true to the God who made us. In turn, this means that the words we speak have the ring of truth about them; they have a power to touch the heart, to move, to motivate, to energize. To create genuine solidarity among the people around us. Our speech becomes a means of binding neighbors together, not of creating divisions among them.

For our speech to be truthful our thoughts must also be devoid of evil intent and spurious conclusions. The brooding resentment caused by our own many failures must not be allowed to project itself on to others. To speak the truth means that our thinking must accord with reality—even though this often means that we need to be prepared to admit that sometimes the whole transcends the limits of what we can see and hear. To look more closely often means to understand more profoundly. A genuinely truthful life demands this of us.

The prophet Zechariah understood the extent of truth's reach when he wrote: "These are the things that you shall do: Speak the truth to one another, render in your gates judgments that are true and make for peace, do not devise evil in your hearts against one another, and love no false oath; for all these are things that I hate, says the LORD" (Zech 8:16-17).

44   May I always keep your instruction
        for ever and ever.

ALWAYS

I regard this verse as a prayer rather than as an aspiration and certainly not as a statement of fact. My commitment to live in harmony with God's self-revelation is not much stronger than any other commitment I make; it is buffeted by the vagaries of my will and by the assault of external forces. We live in a changing world and we ourselves are constantly formed and re-formed by the changes going on around us. Our stability does not consist in being beyond change, but in constantly changing in order to remain the same.

To promise eternal fidelity to what we have learned from God's self-revelation is probably delusional, unless we understand this fidelity in dynamic rather than static terms. A realistic commitment is something that keeps us on the track when we are on the track. But when we allow ourselves to wander and become lost, our commitment switches to making those changes in our lives that will permit us to get back on course. It may be that, for some, their fidelity is expressed by staying at home and dutifully fulfilling their domestic obligations. For others, who are beset by the inclination to drift into inaction, fidelity means constantly being active, changing directions where necessary, and casting off any tendency to doing nothing. And for those who are well and truly lost, a resurgent sense of commitment will prompt them to reverse course and come back to where they should be.

If we reflect on Israel's history we will, perhaps, be struck by the fact that it is a history in which alienation and return alternate. There are elements that are lost irretrievably; successive temples are destroyed, the system of sacrificial worship is dismantled, the land is reallocated and the population dispersed. What remains is a tribal memory of a God who acts, who is ultimately faithful, who remains for the people a rock and a stronghold. In time, these memories are written down and the scrolls on which these memories are recorded become the central point of both faith and practice; furthermore, the memories are to be inscribed on doorpost and forehead as well as on the heart (Deut 6:6-9). The Scriptures were the documentation of the covenant existing between God and the people. "There was not a word of all Moses proclaimed that Joshua did not proclaim before the whole assembly of Israel" (Josh 8:35). As much later with Ezra the scribe (Neh 8:1-3), the proclamation of the memory and the written word are the safeguards of Israel's faith and the means by which it may be transmitted to new generations.

There is a lesson for us who believe ourselves to be hearers of the word. Maintaining contact with the Scriptures will be the safeguard of our faith, enabling it to grow and adapt to the reality of a changing world. This is important for us not only as individuals but also within our communities. When we hear the same text we are all equally encouraged and admonished and some degree of consensus in action may become possible. To the extent that we become communities of faith, disciples of a common revelation, we are laying the foundation for our faith to continue to exist and to grow. We are providing for a faith-filled future. In our own way we are making sure that we keep God's instruction and continue to follow it. Maybe even for ever and ever.

45   May I walk in an open space
       for I have sought your precepts.

FREEDOM

This verse presents us with a paradox. The self-revelation of God has been repeatedly presented as a road that leads to a more abundant life, yet a road is not an open space. A road works to bring us to our destination by restricting our options. Instead of wandering all over the place, we confine our steps along a direct route that quickly takes us to where we want to be. A road brings us to freedom by limiting our choices.

Spontaneity is sometimes confused with freedom. A great musical performer, one who is able to inspire strong feelings in an audience, is harvesting the fruits of many years of disciplined learning and education. Innate talents need training if genius is to emerge. To reach a point where external restriction is minimized, a person has to develop a strong internal discipline that liberates what is noblest and best, and keeps everything else in check.

The divine precepts help us to attain a high level of freedom by giving us standards against which we may measure the instinctive impulses that often play a role in the choices that we make. When we are inclined to follow the promptings of anger, for example, the internalized word of God says to us, as God said to Jonah, "Are you right to be angry?" (Jonah 4:4). For us to reach our potential as human beings, the sub-personal forces that roil within us need to be subjected to our power of choice, and our power of choice needs to be enlightened in the context of a broader perspective into which God's word brings us. To be free means it is not sufficient to shake off all external control; it involves overcoming our inherent weakness and blindness and, even more mysteriously, neutralizing the malice that sometimes seethes within us.

True freedom is nearly invisible to those who possess it. Just as we take for granted that, when we open our eyes, the world is laid bare before our gaze. We don't think much about it; we simply look and see. Freedom is not self-conscious; it simply enables and acts. Freedom is best known by its companions: empowerment, joy, creativity, exuberance. The Flemish mystic Beatrice of Nazareth (1220–68) describes this sense of interior liberation thus:

> She is like a fish that swims in the breadth of the water and rests in its depths. She is like a bird that flies in the spaciousness and height of the sky. Thus she experiences her spirit as walking unbound in the depth and height and spaciousness of love.[33]

Walking along the way indicated by the divine precepts is a pathway to greater self-realization. This is a benefit not just for ourselves, others profit from what we have to contribute. To seek to know God's word better, and to more completely put this awareness into practice does not bespeak a servile attitude, but indicates that we have finally been liberated from the delusion that we alone are masters of our own destiny and, therefore, beholden to no one else for our fulfilment.

46 I will speak of your testimonies before kings
   and not be ashamed.

KINGS

The Deuteronomic history, roughly contemporary with much of the Psalter, leaves us in no doubt that God resisted the idea of kingship for Israel, and permitted it only with considerable reluctance. Subsequent history reveals why. Israelite kings were a sorry lot. The much-lauded David became a man of violence, a polygamist, adulterer and murderer. His son Solomon, despite having a thousand wives and immense wealth and all possible opportunities for goodness, eventually apostatized. Those who followed during the next four centuries were even worse—with the possible exception of Hezekiah and Josiah. Royal governance did not promote the welfare of the people; nor did it serve to encourage the worship of the one true God. Kings were not God's representatives; they were, often enough, usurpers of the divine prerogatives.

Ecclesiastes was probably commenting on this history when he lamented: "Fools are given high office" (Eccl 10:9). Despite the fact that those who reach the pinnacles of power use their position to promote themselves as persons of outstanding wisdom and integrity, one does not need to be very perceptive to see the hollowness of this boast. On the contrary, those whose energies have been largely devoted to attaining high office are often guilty of having neglected more important areas in which to invest their energies.

Despite their lofty claims, kings have no monopoly on truth. Whereas royal prophets are usually no more than mouthpieces for their masters, the real prophets were mavericks, speaking truths that the powerful did not wish to hear, and habitually offering more challenge than comfort. It seems that God's word is more authentic working its way from the bottom up, than from the top down. It is not exactly democracy, but it is a demonstration that those in high office have no claim to be the sole sources of guidance. God often reveals what is best to the youngest and least qualified. If it is truly God who speaks then the status of the one who delivers the message is unimportant.

The genuine prophets were those who spoke truth to power, but they faced resistance. "A poor man's wisdom is despised and his words go unheeded" (Eccl 9:16). It takes courage to speak out forthrightly, especially when we realize that our message will not be welcomed. This seems to indicate that along with the gift of prophecy is given the gift of boldness. Receiving God's word does something to its recipient. It steels the heart against future opposition, whether this be scorn, contempt, violence or the subtler rejection expressed by indifference and an unwillingness to be moved.

We may not see ourselves as major league prophets but, in our own way, we are all recipients of God's word. It is our responsibility not to allow that word to be muted. We may not have the opportunity to deliver a message to the powerful, but in our everyday life there are countless ways in which we can manifest God's self-revelation—sometimes using words. So, let us speak the divine testimonies both to the powerless and to the powerful, and never be ashamed.

47   I have delighted in your commandments,
       and I have loved them.

IMPERATIVES

The longer we live the more we become aware of certain imperatives of our nature. There are things that we cannot do without, whether because their absence directly threatens our survival or simply undermines our happiness and our willingness to keep on living. We cannot survive long without oxygen, and an existence totally devoid of companionship is not worth living. To know the conditions necessary for our wellbeing gives us the possibility of taking appropriate measures to ensure that these conditions are met.

Most of us think of God's commandments as external impositions. They come from outside ourselves and demand that we change in order to conform ourselves to them. As a result, even in the most pious observers of the divine laws, there is a certain resentment, perhaps unacknowledged. We feel that by forcing us to adapt our conduct to a rigid code, inscribed on tablets of stone—as it were—we are under some kind of compulsion to be other than what we are. The law of God seems to us as the enemy of our autonomy.

Of course, this autonomy, in whose defense we are so vociferous, is a myth. It is true that we can make decisions about what we do without reference to anyone else, but this does not mean that those choices are necessarily free. Most psychologists would tell us that many of our "free" choices would be entirely predictable if we had a comprehensive knowledge of the sub-personal influences surging under the surface of consciousness. Our much-vaunted freedom is often no more than a servitude to hidden masters, who crack the whip and demand instant obedience.

Humanity was created in God's image and likeness. The self-revelation of God is also a revelation of our truest and deepest nature. The Scriptures that we believe to be the revelation of God are also the revelation of who and what we are. They are not a foreign code imposed on us but the manifestation not only of what we are now but of what we are to become. And so they have the right to point the way to the future, even though it may not always make much sense to our limited awareness. The commandments of God reveal God and, by so doing, reveal the way forward for us; they guide us in the task of becoming more human and, thereby, more divine.

That is why the psalmist makes the seemingly paradoxical statement that the commandments of God are a source of delight. We love the divine law because it shows us the path to becoming what we were meant to be. For most of us, however, this is not the first step. What must happen before we grow in appreciation of what is offered us, is that we must become detached from the second-rate substitutes that have previously shaped our lives. Sometimes we do this spontaneously, having arrived at the point of realizing how limited the fulfilment the pursuit of such trifles offers. Sometimes, in the providence of God, these lesser goods are simply plucked from us and, in their absence, we have little alternative but to turn toward the source of all true delight and happiness.

48   I lift up my hands to your commandments, which I love; and I ponder your statutes.

ENTREATY

The word here translated as "hands" is not the usual one. Although it was used in parallel with the common term and with the same meaning, it properly refers to the palms of the hands. Of the twenty-one occurrences in the Psalter, most cover the same range of meanings as the general term, but in five cases, including the present one, there is question of lifting up the hands in prayer and entreaty before God. "Thus, I bless you [all] my life; in your name I lift up my hands" (Ps 63:5). Especially in times of trouble this earnest uplifting of hand and heart bears testimony to the sincerity of the prayer. "My eyes are dimmed by affliction, I call to you, LORD, all the day: I extend my hands towards you" (Ps 88:10). The lifting of the hands is symbolic of the prayer rising before God, making a connection between earth and heaven. "May my prayer rise like incense before you, the lifting of my hands like the evening sacrifice" (Ps 141:2).

To some people the prayer of urgent entreaty seems somehow inferior, self-centered and weighed down by earthly cares. They prefer something more metaphysical and abstract. However, although entreaty expresses our earth-bound condition, it is also a movement away from that into the presence of God. This is what the lifting of the hands connotes. We are rising above our troubles, empowered by our faith in the benevolence of God.

One aspect of the mystery of the human condition is that although we were formed from the dust of the earth, yet we stand upright with the possibility of raising our eyes and our hearts to heaven. It is from our contact with the spiritual world that we receive the wisdom and the energy to live well even while our feet remain on the ground.

The means by which we are sustained in this noble endeavor is that do not allow God's self-revelation to be clouded by the mists of forgetfulness, so that we live as if there were no God. By pondering the divine statutes, we achieve some sort of counterbalance to the continual onrush of information through our senses; we can limit the degree to which we allow our appetites to be stirred and our conduct to be governed by what is merely visible.

When we say that we love God's commandments we are affirming our experience that they are dear companions on our journey through life, offering guidance when we are beginning to stray, and encouragement when we find ourselves disheartened and ready to give up. We pray that they will continue to offer us support and that we will have a firm commitment to keep exposing our lives to God's word, permitting it to speak freely to our hearts and consciences, and ready to pay attention to the direction given.

Meanwhile we recognize the precariousness of our piety and we pray that the God who inspires our good intentions may allow them to bear fruit in a life lived according to what we have perceived through God's self-revelation.

49   Remember the word to your servant,
       on it I have waited.

DELAY

We live in hope because we have no alternative. The benefits that we have expected or which have been promised to us are nowhere to be seen. There is a gap between the word and its execution; sometimes a very long one. We willingly accept the promise implicit in what we have heard, but our faith in its realization is often tested, and we find ourselves saying in the words of another psalm: "Where are your kindnesses of the past LORD, that you swore to David in your faithfulness?" (Ps 89:50).

The idea of waiting for God's word or judgment to be fulfilled occurs in five other places in this psalm (vv. 43, 74, 81, 114, 117). In the Psalter, the idea of waiting for God to act is not merely a devotional attitude, it requires grit. It means accepting a divine intervention for which there is no visible evidence. To keep believing in God's word against the odds, requires a great deal of patience, which is why the Septuagint often translated the term by words which signified endurance. This endurance is not some spurious form of stoicism; the ability to withstand rejection, scorn, alienation and persecution is grounded in a strong personal relationship with God which serves as a buttress against human malice.

We live in the gap between promise and fulfilment. If we follow the progression often signaled by the psalms of lament, the believer is empowered to pass beyond the despair and frustration occasioned by the fact that the word of salvation seems to have been without effect. Then as mindfulness of God's faithfulness in the past begins to assert itself, the beginnings of hope emerge. When hope grows strong it is transmuted into a song of victory—even before the promised benefit has been obtained. Certainty has replaced despair and the heart of the believer is uplifted in thanksgiving—even though externally nothing has changed.

Of course, we would all like to have the kind of faith in God's word that quickly kindles hope and confidence, but this does not happen without our passing through the two previous stages. We must experience the absence of God before we can celebrate the presence. We have to hold steadfast to our belief in God's faithfulness through many difficulties and reversals of fortune before it builds up sufficient momentum to overpower our doubts and hesitations.

We remind God of the promises that have been made, yet it is really ourselves that need reminding. For us who live in the sphere of space and time there is a season for everything under the sun, and it is useless for us to anticipate the right time for events to occur—we lack the global purview that would make this possible. Instead of kicking against the goad and trying to impose our wills and our whims on the universe, we need to learn the art of waiting patiently in the firm belief that God's word to us is not subject to change, and that what has been promised will come—in God's time. Meanwhile we learn to live with inevitable delay.

50   This comforts me in my affliction;
    your utterances give me life.

COMFORT

No human life is without some form of affliction, from the wailing of the newborn infant to the expiring breath of one at the point of death. This is not gloom; it is simply reality. If, in defiance of this truth, cultures implicitly proclaim that unalloyed happiness is every person's entitlement, the result is widespread discontent and continual complaint. In such a context, there is a general belief that suffering is avoidable and, as a result, when hardship occurs someone else is blamed for it. Thus, divisions arise. On the other hand, societies that take the presence of suffering for granted are generally more compassionate; they spend more energy in comforting the sufferer than in seeking to find someone to blame.

The psalmists understood that "human life on earth is like military service" (Job 7:1), a hard slog. Beyond unmet physical needs there are the difficulties and conflicts of social existence, as well as the many doubts and anxieties which are internal and strictly personal. The present moment, in certain circumstances, may well be marked by pain or a sense of deprivation, but even these conditions can be outweighed by memories of the wounded past and fears for the future which can change the complexion of our experience and add to the burden we carry.

Because God's word establishes us in the truth of our being, it prepares us to engage with the negative elements of our life—and this is so much easier when we take it for granted that suffering is the most universal human experience. It is normal. But it is not the totality of human life. A mother cannot remove the pain from an uncomprehending infant, but she can offer comfort. And this is what the psalmist finds in God's word: a source of comfort in situations of grief, apprehension, or attack.

The dialogue between God and the people that is initiated by the divine word is an ongoing source of strength, endurance and liveliness. But it is a dialogue that must be sustained by our involvement, and not allowed to lapse. Only to the extent that we keep referring our needs to God, and allowing ourselves to be guided by the response we receive, will we experience the bracing effects of a faith sturdy enough to withstand the everyday disasters that threaten to undermine its confidence.

When the psalmist says that the utterances of God are life-giving, he is not referring to life in absolute terms, since none of us is dead—yet. Rather he is referring to some of the effects of life: responsiveness to what is around us, growth, generativity, fulfilment. It is through God's word that we become sensitive to realities that otherwise we might pass by without noticing, realities in our immediate environment, but also those unseen realities that are perceived only by the wise. God's word becomes our instructor in a life that rejoices in being more fully human. We are not mere objects tossed around by the storms of life, but we are capable of making informed choices that will effect a greater level of human-ness to our world by unleashing our creative zest, by minimizing the suffering of others, and by doing all that we can to ensure that the heavens and the earth really do proclaim the glory of God.

51   The arrogant mocked me greatly;
      I did not turn from your teaching.

SELF-ASSURANCE

To place one's confidence in an unseen and seemingly absent God is a cause for mockery on the part of those who are self-satisfied, many of whom are convinced of their own intrinsic superiority to everything around them. Humility comes hard for those who believe themselves to be the center of their own universe. The only way for them to admit God into their lives is to see God as a kind of wallpaper, mildly decorative, not interfering and, above all, completely silent.

To profess oneself a disciple of a speaking God is to lay oneself bare to all kinds of derision. When the prophet Isaiah walked around naked for three years (Isa 20:2-3), it is probable that his contemporaries concluded that he was crazy, especially during the winter. No wonder the prophet Jeremiah complains of his fate. "O Lord you have seduced me and I was seduced; you have been stronger than I, and you have prevailed. All day I have become a laughingstock, mocked by all . . . For the Lord's word has become for me daylong reproach and derision" (Jer 20:7-8).

Our call to be guided by God's self-revelation may not lead to such extremes either of behavior or of response, but we will often find ourselves unappreciated, misunderstood and pushed out to the margins. In such situations, we will need to examine our conscience: to try to establish whether our convictions truly come from pondering on the word of God or whether they are the fabrications of a mind that has stopped really listening. When we depart from the "common sense" of what is right, we need to check that we are not succumbing to delusion. There were many false prophets in Israel. In a single day Elijah slew four hundred and fifty of them—more than the total number of genuine prophets (1 Kgs 18:40). Even today there are those who claim to be speaking for God, but are not.

But if, in our own little way, we try to listen to the still, small voice of a conscience formed by years of attention to the word of God, then we may find ourselves drawn to a level of virtue of which we would never have dreamed by ourselves. Nothing dramatic: a simple act of kindness, the laying of the first planks of a bridging relationship, the refusal to join in slanderous gossip. These are not earthshaking options, but they are formative of character. Such actions are like the different pieces in a jigsaw puzzle. At first they seem to bear no relationship to one another but, progressively, as clusters grow we begin to see the full picture emerging. We have not turned from God's teaching but allowed it to influence our choices and, slowly, over the course of many years, it is healing the wounds caused by the selfishness of sin, and allowing us to grow into fully formed, intelligent, and compassionate human beings. Even the most arrogant will scarcely find grounds for mockery there.

52   I remember your judgments from long ago,
      Lord, and I am consoled.

JUDGMENT

The Hebrew word *mishpat*, which is used here, is one of the key words in this long psalm, occurring twenty-three times.[34] Its meaning is scarcely differentiated from the other words used to designate divine revelation though, of course, it sometimes has a slightly distinctive flavor due to its linkage to the word for judge or ruler. Hence there is a hint of absolute authority about it; it is a judgment which cannot be appealed.

Human judgment may well be corrupt or, at least, in error. Divine judgment is different. For one thing it is always true. For another, it is not only declarative of what is right, but it has the power to create what needs to be created. It not only recognizes what is just but is able to justify, to make just, to create justice.

Human institutions which have a limited power to rule and judge do not reflect the full reality of God's justice. The goodness and truth and compassion which are inherent in the divine nature have an impact on everything God touches. When God calls, it is not simply to issue a command that must be implemented, it is to offer an invitation to enter more fully into a relationship and, thus, to be ennobled and invigorated by our contact with the source of our being. Even when God's word seems to challenge our human ways of thinking and acting, it is not a weakening or rejection of the relationship from God's side. It is simply a correction—a directive that indicates how we might get back on track.

To transpose the "ten words" or "Decalogue" said to have been given on Mount Sinai into "Ten Commandments" is to alter their meaning. It is better not to think of them as rigid prescriptions of what to do, and more especially, of what not to do. They are not primarily external constraints on our human liberty. More fundamentally, they are indications of our identity. They tell us what we are as human beings and, more particularly, what we are as human beings who are in a relationship with God. They should be viewed more as indicative or descriptive than prescriptive. A fully mature human being does not worship false gods, commit murder or adultery, steal or tell lies. We know most of this instinctively; we just need to be reminded of it. Murder is a sin against humanity, against our victim, and against ourselves; that is why it is an abomination to God. Not merely because one of the rules has been broken. Murder, like other crimes, is contrary to the divine *mishpat*, and so it is harmful to humanity.

Clearly there are serious deficiencies in the levels of *mishpat* that we see around us—and within us. Remembering God's active interventions in the past, however, gives us the hope that the holiness of God will overflow to bring justice and judgment to full flowering on earth. This is an ongoing source of encouragement and consolation. Despite woeful appearances, God is working to restore *mishpat* to earth. This comforts me in my affliction.

53   Rage seized me because of the wicked;
        they forsake your instruction.

APOSTATES

The law of gravity is irresistible; for as long as we remain on earth, there is nothing we can do to remove ourselves from its jurisdiction. What we refer to as "the law of God" is somewhat different; it is proposed to us, rather than imposed on us. It is offered by way of guidance to a more abounding life, but the choice to follow that guidance devolves upon us alone. We can obstinately refuse to depend on its reliability but, instead entrust ourselves to our own resources, limited though they are. Then, when the inevitable mishap occurs, we tend to blame God or others because things have not worked out well for us.

Our rejection of God's commandments mostly begins without drama. We lack the conviction and courage to rebel openly, at least at first, so we tend to slide away gradually, making progressively larger compromises and using linguistic contortions to disguise what we are doing. The prophet Haggai speaks about the result of a reluctance to implement the Lord's instructions: "Consider what has happened: you have sown much but harvested little, you eat but never have enough, you drink and are never full, you earn wages and then put them in a purse with holes" (Hag 1:5). As we become aware of the inconsistency between what we publicly profess and our less-than-public behavior a profound dissatisfaction sets in. We are faced with the choice that we have long tried to avoid. Either we live in accordance with God's law or we abandon any pretense of religion. It is at this point that many turn their backs on God and on the divine law.

Not all apostates choose to trumpet the fact. Even among the ranks of those who publicly profess a religious adherence, there are those who are not only practical atheists but have lost any inner sense of connection with the spiritual world. They can maintain the pantomime of religion, if required to do so, but it is all empty gibberish.

All of us need to appreciate that a lifelong adherence to keeping the Lord's instruction is no slight matter. At the best of times it requires intelligence, integrity and endurance. Perhaps we should look on those who fail to keep their initial commitments more with pity than with blame, recognizing that our own perseverance in practice is, by no means, absolutely secure. Maybe the rage that some experience against those whom they perceive to be apostates, is really rage against their own ambivalence, projected onto others.

So often in this psalm we pray that God will light up our path and steady our steps so that we may continue walking on the road that leads to life. Despite the attractive radiance of God's ongoing self-revelation, there is within each of us, a powerful force of resistance. God's way is often not part of the future we have designed for ourselves, and so we are loath to follow it. Instead let us turn back to God's word and wait in active patience until an echo begins to resound in the depth of our being.

54   Your statutes are my songs
        in the house of exile.

EXILE

The period in which the psalms were written was one in which the notion of exile was part of the tribal memory. Even though the Babylonian exile lasted only a generation or two, its aftereffects lasted for centuries. The deportees who gradually dribbled back to Palestine found the land in a completely different state from their nostalgic memories of it. The temple was gone, cities and towns were ravaged, the population condemned to live in a quandary of uncertainty and deprivation. Most importantly, the material components of their religious faith had disappeared; the Temple and its sacrifices and pilgrimages no longer occupied a central part in popular practice. In a sense, they had become strangers in their own land, mere sojourners.

Exile can become a powerful metaphor, signaling a strong sense of alienation from our immediate environment. We feel as though we have been displaced from a space in which we felt at home and in which we could relax, and forced to reside in foreign territory. We are societal animals, by nature, when we experience a dissonance with what is around us, we feel diminished and threatened. It is as though we are estranged from all that previously enlivened us, and so our appetite for interaction wanes and loneliness sets in.

In such a situation, the psalmist finds that the songs which embodied God's word, endure. In a predominantly oral culture these were inscribed more on the memory than on scrolls. As a result, what has been internalized over the years, remained accessible, even when the external support-structure had crumbled. This is probably why, in the years following the return from exile, the emphasis moved from the temple to the synagogue, from ritual to Torah. And, in the millennia that followed the Torah has continued to be the mainstay and custodian of the faith of Israel.

We who live in a time of deconstruction, both voluntary and enforced, may learn a lesson from this history. External structures and ministries are important in sustaining our faith, but when things are difficult, and we experience a strong sense of loss, it will be our devotion to the word of God that will help us to remain on our feet. This is more than regularity in our reading of Scripture. It is allowing God's word to be taken to heart. We would do well to commit some passages of the Bible to memory, especially those that offer us a means of direct communication with God. The psalms are the most obvious example. We can choose from the Psalter a few psalms, or parts of psalms, that embody and speak to the ups and downs of our everyday existence, and use them as a means of bringing the particularities of our life before God.

Devotion to Scripture can be an effective counterweight to the troubles of life, a reminder that we are on a journey and not yet at our destination. As such we are prone to the inconveniences of travelling, the possibilities of going astray and the frustrations of not being at home. To allow the word of God to accompany us is a sure means of making our steps lighter and our hearts readier to sing.

❧

55   I remember your name in the night, Lord,
       and I keep your instruction.

NIGHT

Modern civilization has largely done away with night as it has with the Sabbath. The ugly shorthand 24/7 is an indication that we do not want to envisage a time when no one can work. Every minute of every day must be available for work or play or something else that is considered useful. We try to fill every moment. There is no room for emptiness. As a result, our thoughts are clogged by a proliferation of details which have little relevance or meaning within the total context of our lives.

This is why the night can be a friend. Most of us will never have the experience of complete night, where there is no light or sound or smell or touch, but it is possible sometimes to venture out into the darkness, to flee our hyper-stimulated world and seek out a desert of relative blankness. In such an environment, as the world around us settles into silence, we may become aware of more subtle whispers coming from the depths of our being.

Such intrusions are not under our control and, so, they do not seek to reinforce our current self-image but, instead, they offer a counterpoint to it. They bring to our awareness the things of which ordinarily we are not mindful. Sometimes it is a breath of regret or shame concerning our past. Sometimes it is a nameless dread about what might happen in the future. And, on some blessed occasions, we exult in the rich layers of the present moment, gazing with wonder on what is habitually hidden from our multi-tasking everyday self.

When the night provides us with the opportunity to shut down the busy mental processes that inform our everyday activities, it also allows some bubbles of spiritual aspiration to rise unbidden to the surface. Becoming aware of these desires is the necessary complement to the life of virtue. Without their uplifting impact, good works become increasingly burdensome, especially when they seem to yield no visible or tangible results. These opportunities for emptiness are the times when we re-connect with the spiritual world and take our bearings on our homeward journey.

The power of these moments derives from the work we have done in embracing God's word, keeping it, meditating on it, and allowing it to shape our outlook on life. Our investment is solid, but for us to be able to profit from the accrued interest, we need moments of emptiness. There is no way of knowing in advance what reverberations we shall hear in a time of silence, but we can be sure that what comes to us will be for our ultimate advantage.

It is often in the nakedness of night that we experience ourselves as known and accepted by God. "Even the darkness is not dark for you, but night is as light as day, and the darkness is as light" (Ps 139:12). When there are fewer distractions our awareness is sharpened and the presence of God looms larger, even in our enfeebled consciousness, so that its emptiness is filled, its darkness rendered radiant with light, and the silence in which we are immersed becomes an echo-chamber of the divine word.

56   This has been what befell me,
         because I have observed your precepts.

OUTCOMES

Exactly what has befallen the psalmist because of his fidelity to the word is not certain. Different psalms seem to say different things. Sometimes it seems as though strict observance of norms leads to a charge of scrupulosity; at other times, it is proclaimed as a source of happiness and esteem. We will probably experience a similar ambiguity in reviewing our own life. This means that we have to learn to live with a degree of uncertainty concerning our level of rectitude. We cannot assess the value of our piety by what we perceive to be its immediate effects. The life-changing impact of serving God becomes apparent only in retrospect. Progress occurs through a sequence of tiny steps, most of which escape our notice and some of which are counter-intuitive. Oddly, it is often when we seem to be going backwards or deviating from the ideal that we are really making solid strides forward.

If we have faith in the fidelity of God, then we have to allow ourselves to accept that whatever comes from the hand of God is to our ultimate benefit. This is not merely naïve optimism. It is a settled belief that the ways of God are not our ways and so, sometimes, they will be quite incomprehensible to us. It is simply a case of recognizing the limitations of our intelligence. We do not have a cosmic overview of the universe. At best, we have occasional glimmers of insight about our own little part of the immense totality, but the universal significance of what happens around us habitually transcends our puny intelligence.

There is something else. Human experience is subject to the principle of alternation. "There is a season for everything under the sun" (Eccl 3:1). Most of us would prefer things to remain as they are or, at least, similar to what we have already experienced. We feel uncomfortable when we have to deal with a situation that is utterly unfamiliar because it will, perhaps, demonstrate our ineptitude in dealing with it. It may well be that for us to keep developing we have to learn to go with the flow. To accept what life brings us without submitting it to our myopic judgment. Every morning to say to ourselves: "This is the day the LORD has made; let us be glad and rejoice in it" (Ps 118:24).

Especially in the West, we attribute great importance to determining the relationship of cause and effect. In the process, we often miss out on the childlike experience of simply gazing in wonder at something beautiful. Because we lack a contemplative instinct we often fail in reverence for the world around us and, because of that, reduce it to the level of something to be exploited. We are so busy calculating our potential profits that we never take the time to step back and admire. We have set ourselves up as judges of everything; whatever does not conform to our plans or expectations is to be denigrated and, perhaps, destroyed. If only we acted less as masters of the universe and recognized that we are merely sojourners, we would probably enjoy life more. We would be liberated from the tyranny of our expectations and exposed to the enchanting surprises that each day can bring.

57   I have said: You are my portion, Lord,
        and so I keep your words.

PORTION

This verse begins with a statement that is evocative of the covenant formula: "I will be your God and you will be my people." Our relationship with God is not sporadic or temperamental, but is solid and enduring, at least from God's side. By God's choice we belong together. This is a bold assertion of the bond that has been created by God's gratuitous initiative. We are not aliens or strangers but, mysteriously, we have been incorporated in God's inner circle. And because of this, we are emboldened to say: "What is there for me in the heavens except you? Apart from you, I delight in nothing on earth. My flesh and my heart may fail but God is the strength of my heart, and my portion for ever" (Ps 73:25-26).

This relationship with God is part of my portion or destiny; it defines my identity—not so much as an isolated individual, but as one of the chosen people of God. To be true to God is to be true to myself; to depart from God is to be lost. The words of God are not external impositions but the means by which we are instructed about our own nature and destiny. We are not merely the product of the interplay of forces that can be sensed and known, but there is an invisible shaping hand that both fashions us in our uniqueness and brings us into harmony with those around us.

As we make progress on our journey through life, if we are wise, we begin to appreciate some of the characteristics of the portion that has been assigned to us—not in a spirit of arrogance, but humbly recognizing the call to walk the path that divine providence has assigned to us. We may not necessarily understand its dynamics, but by keeping our consciences attuned to God's word, we are enabled to take the next step in confidence. It may be that what we are called to do is different from what others do, sometimes this may be a source of scorn or rejection, but what is important is that we follow the path that our portion opens before us.

Ecclesiastes uses the term "portion" (*cheleq*) significantly (Eccl 2:10; 3:22; 5:17-18; 9:6; 9:9). He understands by this term the span allotted to human beings by divine decree. Though the span is unalterable, what happens in it is open to human intervention. We are not passive. We are invited to make the most of the opportunities given us, limited though they be. "Behold I have seen that it is good and right to eat and drink and to find pleasure in labor and toil under the sun for the few days of life God has given—for this is [our] portion" (Eccl 5:17). We are to love this earthly life and make the most of it because—with all its liabilities—it is God's gift to us and it is intended for our benefit. The psalm already quoted continues: "For me, to be near God is good; I have made my Master, the LORD, my refuge" (Ps 73:28), "because the portion marked out for me is my delight" (Ps 16:6).

58   I have sought your favor with all my heart,
be gracious to me according to your utterance.

GRACE

The psalmist is eloquent in singing the praises of a loving and caring God who understands the dust of which we are made. However, he is not immune to thoughts which remind him of how undeserving we are of such benevolent attention. "What are human beings that you remember them, the children of earth that you bring them to mind?" (Ps 8:5). It is not so easy to understand the gratuitousness of God's affection for us, because in our experience we love what we love because we perceive goodness in the object of our regard. For God to perceive goodness in us would require a gaze far more penetrating than anything we have experienced. A gaze which easily pierces through our obvious imperfections and arrives at a core which is infinitely lovable. We quickly realize that we are nothing apart from what God has given us; our personal contribution to our lovableness is zero—at best.

The Aaronic blessing prays: "May the LORD make his face to shine upon you and be gracious to you" (Num 6:25). It is by our being invited into a face-to-face relationship that God's graciousness is revealed. The divine radiance transforms us and is reflected back to its Origin. When God's glory impacts on us, it causes to arise in our hearts a hymn of praise by which we, in turn, glorify God. The realm of grace is also the realm of glory; God's self-manifestation shines on every atom of our being and invites us to a more abundant life. Divine graciousness is self-replicating.

The lament psalms frequently seek the favor of God, especially in situations of sickness, danger or distress. Perhaps it is only in times of crisis that we think to activate, as it were, the favor which habitually surrounds us. Quite often a psalm may begin with an appeal to receive favor and gradually progresses to a recognition that the prayer has been answered. We are asking for what we have received already: God's benevolent acceptance of us, in all our imperfection.

The assurance of God's grace is given to us in the Scriptures. Often this may run contrary to the way we feel about ourselves: as falling short of our ambitions, as unworthy. Despite our tendency to project blame onto others, and despite the empty bluster of our trumpeting of our achievements, underneath we often feel the gnawings of a suspicion that we are not quite as admirable as others believe. We are imposters. This is where we have to insist on the gratuitousness of grace. God loves us because it is the divine nature to love. God loved us into being out of nothingness. Because we are created by God we are, like the rest of creation, seen to be "very good" in God's eyes. It is not due to any merit that we have superadded. Perhaps we need to be reminded that the fact that it is unearned does not make it less real.

When I seek God's favor or pray that God will be gracious, I am not really expecting change, but implicitly I am hoping that—despite the contrary appearances of my present situation—I will come to the realization of the grace which surrounds me. My situation looks different from God's point of view; it will be a great gift if I also can come to see things from that angle.

❧

59   I considered my ways
        and I turned my steps back to your testimonies.

DISSATISFACTION

The humility to admit being in error and the willingness to change course are often evidence of having arrived at a certain maturity. The temperamental obstinacy of those who believe themselves both infallible and impeccable is almost comical, though it has a dire impact on relationships with others. An inflated sense of one's intellectual or moral status is often the effect of never having experienced anything or anyone greater than oneself. Such persons are like a big fish in a small pond. They need to move out into the wider world to get some notion of their own lack of relative importance.

A normal response to being impacted by the spiritual world is a curious combination of attraction and apprehension. On the one hand, we feel drawn to venture outside our comfort zone and explore the world of spiritual reality. On the other, we feel a certain dread, since we are dealing with the unknown and our best efforts are no more than tentative. The deeper we are led into the world of the spirit the more we become dissatisfied, not only at our present behavior, but also at many aspects of our past life—even those that seemed laudable at the time.

The call to conversion does not happen only at the beginning of our spiritual journey or at pre-defined junctures as we progress; it is continuous. To the extent that we have allowed a spiritual dynamism to operate within us, we are constantly being summoned to turn our attention from the external to the inner world, to find within our immediate environment elements that speak to us of the mystery of our being, and demand of us a different mode of conduct. It is this nagging sense of dissatisfaction that drives us to abandon the security of the status quo and try to discover new ways of behaving that better suit the new vision that is emerging within us.

The itch of dissatisfaction is really the first symptom of a desire which is so deep that it cannot be defined—because it has no distinguishable object. It is simply an interior drawing that calls us to go beyond the limits of our present experience and enter into a realm which is beyond words and concepts, to set our hearts on God. This necessarily calls for a re-assessment of our values and a re-alignment of the priorities of our life.

The basis for this ongoing conversion is God's self-revelation. We keep God's word in our hearts and, often, in our thoughts. We allow it to shape our outlook on life, to govern the choices we make and, as years of fidelity pass, to form our consciences. This may well give us a distinctive attitude which is reflected in our actions. Others may not understand why we are impelled to act in a certain way, and we ourselves may be a little puzzled. It is God's internalized word acting in us, guiding us, motivating us, and giving us the energy to do what otherwise may have seemed unlikely. And this all because we keep turning back to God's word, exposing our life to its radiance and drawing on its energy, while we are in the process of considering our ways and making our choices.

60   I hurried and did not dawdle
       to keep your commandments.

DAWDLE

Dawdling can signify many things, not necessarily unrelated, including a lack of interest, a lack of energy, a lack of commitment or, in some cases, passive aggression. The psalmist is saying that when it comes to keeping faith with God's word, he is sincere and fervent in his attachment. There was no question of procrastination or delay, but an enthusiastic and total responsiveness.

Many of us live in a cynical social environment in which fervor is scorned. We want to project an image of cool indifference to religion and spirituality and, sometimes, even to the requirements of human decency. Our zeal for moderation in the practice of virtue has led us into the trap of mediocrity. We don't stand for anything; we have no personal principles. We simply cruise through life on auto-pilot conforming to the expectations of those around us and to our own convenience.

Such an existence is only half a life. As persons, we are defined by the objects of our passionate concern, whether it be football or politics or our individual ambitions. In our secular culture, most of us would hate to be known as persons whose primary interest in life is anything approaching religion. As a result, we tend to cut ourselves off from association with the spiritual world and fail even to acknowledge those transcendent intimations that sometimes arise even in the most materialist heart.

We need to shake off our reluctance to be fervently religious. We are reminded of the incident where Elijah confronted the 450 false prophets of Baal: "How long will you hobble around on one leg and then on the other. If the LORD is God, follow him" (1 Kgs 18:21). We sit on the fence and like to keep our options open. We are loth forthrightly to say with Joshua: "As for me and my house, we will serve the LORD" (Josh 24:15). What this service means was already spelled out in the first chapter of this biblical book:

> Be strong and very firm. Be careful to keep all the instruction
> that my servant Moses commanded you. Do not turn from it
> to the right hand or to the left so that you may prosper wher-
> ever you go. This book of instruction shall not depart from
> your mouth; you must meditate on it day and night, so that
> you may keep it and do all that is written in it. (Josh 1:7-8)

Good zeal begins interiorly. First we acquaint ourselves with God's word—in the Scriptures as in the events of our daily life—so that our thoughts are progressively colored by it. We see the world in a different light and assess its possibilities differently. The more we succeed in conforming our activities to what we have learned from the divine instruction, the more we discover that a zeal for good works is not alienating. It does not feel as though we are under any compulsion. What we discover is a sense of liberation—we are free to act not only in accordance with the law, but in harmony with what is noblest within us. That is why we don't dawdle in doing good, but run to implement the commandments that lead to life.

61   The cords of the wicked ensnared me
       but I did not forget your instruction.

ENSNARED

We are usually uncomfortable when reality does not conform to our expectations. We feel constricted, unable to accomplish the tasks we had intended because circumstances have changed. We are obliged to analyze the situation and devise new ways of acting that suit the new conditions that we are facing. We don't like this challenge; we prefer to remain within the limits of our familiar routines. Often we interpret change as hostile; when things are not as we anticipated, we look for someone else to blame.

If this verse seems to speak to us of our being constrained by others, unable to release our full potential, then perhaps we need to ask whether it is really by the wicked that we are bound. It is much easier to blame imagined enemies for our unpreparedness, than to stretch our own limits and meet the challenge.

To follow the ways of Scripture and to implement its directives often demands of us not only boldness and perseverance but also imagination. When we seem to arrive at an impasse, when we feel paralyzed and unable to intervene, this is the time to remember the way that leads to life. We do not allow ourselves to be defined by our apparent incapacity, but step back and reflect on the fuller meaning that our difficulties might well contain. As we think over our situation in the light of God's word, we may begin to suspect that we ourselves have been complicit in engineering the unwelcome reality we are confronting. Perhaps, not intentionally. A review of our life's experience will often lead us to conclude that many of the mishaps we have experienced are not the outcome of hostility on the part of others, or even misunderstanding. They have often been the result of misguided actions on our part. When others seem negative in their attitude to us, perhaps they are merely reacting to what they perceive to be our attitude to them. All too often we are the ones responsible for our troubles.

To be in the habit of reviewing our lives in the light of God's word is a way of coming to terms with reality instead or peremptorily imposing our own interpretations on what happens. It is often a sobering experience, but it can be liberating. When I understand how my own habitual actions have contributed to the friction I experience, then I can make changes in my behavior, with a view to reducing the irritation I am causing in others. This falls within my own purview. It may mean that I may have to give priority to social harmony over my own preferences, but I will, at least, have a sense that I am determining the quality of the social ambience rather than allowing myself to be controlled by what happens.

In this case, I will feel like singing a verse from another psalm: "My soul is like a bird that has escaped from the fowler's snare; the snare is broken and we have escaped" (Ps 124:7-8).

By way of reservation, it sometimes happens that we are wholly or mostly blameless and are, in fact, the victims of another person's unreasonable hostility. If this happens to us we have to find in God's word the endurance needed to survive such an experience. Such is life. Sometimes.

62   At midnight I will rise and thank you
       for the judgments of your righteousness.

MIDNIGHT

At a time when clocks were unknown, midnight was not just the mathematically calculated transition between one day and the next, but it was the whole period between the cessation of the day's activities and their resumption the next morning. During the winter months, this may have accounted for a major portion of the day. What happens during these hours is not insignificant.

God created the darkness and brings about the advent of night (Ps 104:20). In the privacy of this darkness, emotions which are suppressed in the daylight hours rise to the surface. The fears thrust away by activity return when activity ceases, and night can be a silent carrier of terror (Ps 91:5). I can be assailed by grief so that "at night I drench my bed with tears" (Ps 6:6). "My tears have been my food by night and by day" (Ps 42:3). The night seems long when sleeplessness occurs (Job 7:4) or pain overwhelms (Job 30:17). While the body ceases its activity, thoughts and imaginations fill the mind: the visions of the night (Job 33:15, Dan 2:19). The stillness of the night invites meditation: "At night I muse within my heart" (Ps 77:6), pondering on God's word (Ps 1:2, 63:6). At night I cry out to the Lord (Ps 88:1) and tirelessly stretch out my hands in prayer (Ps 77:2). The night is also the time of the divine visitation; God comes to put me to the test (Ps 17:3) and instruct me (Ps 16:7) in a manner not possible during the daylight hours.

Whether we like it or not, whether awake or dreaming, we are often confronted by a panorama of our life, sometimes encoded, sometimes exaggerated, often puzzling in its associations or alarming by its intensity. By midnight we have vacated the rational world and have to face the disconnected fragments of past experience. Entering the twilight zone is a useful reminder that we are not in perfect control of all aspects of our own existence—despite our deluded efforts. There remains much that we do not understand.

The middle of the night can be a school in which we learn to countenance the entropy of life. If we are wise we accept the disorder and come to terms with it, slowly arriving at a point of tranquility. One method of arriving at this point is moving towards a more rugged acceptance of the role of God's creative providence in all that concerns us. It may well be that life is a mess but, in the end, all will be well.

Maybe, having found God in the turmoil, we will be graced to move beyond even this, so that we become somewhat grateful for the disorderly basket of wild experiences that makes us who we are. We are led to feel and give expression to a sense of thankfulness for the world as it is, humbly admitting our lack of understanding but entrusting everything to God.

In such a mood, it makes sense to rise in the night and to give thanks, as we recognize the rightness of God's way of doing things, even when we are unable to see their meaning, and even if they do not meet with our approval. After all, it is God's world, not ours.

63   I am a companion to all who fear you,
       to those who keep your precepts.

SOLIDARITY

In a world that often appears, at best, to be indifferent to a life lived in fidelity to God's word, it may sometimes seem that we walk the spiritual path alone, and that upon us alone falls the responsibility for discerning the correct course to travel. This is why we need occasionally to be reminded that we have companions on our journey. There are, as God admonished Elijah, "still seven thousands who have not bowed their knees to Baal" (1 Kgs 19:18). Seven thousands: a number beyond counting. God is well able to sow seeds of spiritual life in the most unwelcoming soil—seeds of a vigor sufficient to break through even unyielding layers of unresponsiveness. If we are limiting the number of the

God-fearing, it is probably due to our drawing boundaries that are not of God's making.

In insisting on the importance of keeping God's word, meditating on it by day and night, and putting it into practice, it is possible that the impression is given of a purely solitary task. But this is not so. God's word is to be shared as widely as possible, and it is in the process of sharing that we discover new levels of meaning that were previously hidden from us. We all have selective vision, and there is danger that what we see is only that which agrees with what we already know. When an entire community receives the word, they are protected from the limiting effects of individual blind spots, and they reduce the possibility that God's word becomes a vehicle for expressing merely private preferences. Truth emerges from a plurality of viewpoints, even though it may have to endure moments of conflict. The word of God continually transcends the meagre margins of my understanding.

When God speaks, it is not for the ears alone and not merely for the mind. The word of God is not integrally received until it is put into practice. Keeping the precepts is a means of understanding its hidden content. It may well be that, on a rational level, the word of God is puzzling; more often than not it seems opposed to common sense, since it breaks into the "normal" and charts a new course. We will follow this course more confidently if we are part of a community of disciples, graced with the gift of discernment, and supported and sustained when the challenge seems great.

It makes sense that I should see myself as a companion to any who respect the word of God. There may be points on which we fail to achieve absolute agreement, but if there is reverence for God's word on their part and on mine, then harmony will result. Through our common attachment we draw nearer to one another. As the obstacles to our complete discipleship are slowly demolished so too are the barriers existing between believers.

Instead of drawing up boundaries and attaching labels, we should remember God's lesson to Jonah: even in Nineveh there are true believers. And they are worth saving.

64   Your kindness, Lord, fills the earth;
      teach me your statutes.

PROVIDENCE

To accept that the kindly providence of God permeates all space and time together with all that happens within this sphere, demands a deep faith of a kind which is built up only by a lifetime of spiritual experience. We are only too aware of the tragedies and natural disasters that darken our histories—to say nothing of the effects of human weakness, blindness and malice. Even nature itself, "red in tooth and claw," is not as innocent as the poets aver. Thanks to human weakness, blindness and malice, the Garden of Eden has become a jungle where the fittest survive by exploiting and devouring whatever comes within their ambit.

If we enroll in the school of divine self-revelation we are slowly instructed about the ways of God—which are not always our ways. This teaching does not come to us through the medium of knowledge or thoughts, but more deeply. It is by being drawn into God by the dynamism of desire that we are gradually enlightened about the nature of the divinity. We begin to experience for ourselves momentary flashes in which the infinite kindness of God is manifest.

It is in the personal experience of God's kindness that we begin to accept the possibility that there is a meaning beneath all that happens. Somehow we grasp that not an autumn leaf falls in vain, even though it does so without our understanding or our permission. This is a difficult point to reach. We live in a world tyrannized by knowledge and we tend to rebel against anything that does not concur perfectly with the limited knowledge that we have. We forget that "To the Lord belongs the earth and its fullness, the world and those who live in it" (Ps 24:1). It does not belong to us; we are mere stewards, at best or, perhaps, only sojourners. Even the most travelled among us have touched down on only a few places on the planet, and our "lifespan is seventy years, or eighty for those who are strong" (Ps 90:10). What is that compared with the millennia that have gone before?

It is delusional for us to attempt to assess the ultimate meaning of the universe; we can comprehend only minor patterns in our immediate environment. We are better advised to spend our energies coming to an understanding of what is within our reach, and working to improve matters there. Better to do a little, instead of reaching out beyond our competence, only to slump back, dazzled and defeated. Human beings are very intelligent, but the most intelligent among us are usually the first to affirm that we do not understand everything; there is much that is beyond us.

This should not prevent us from being lost in admiration at God's work in our world, where "kindness and faithfulness have met, and righteousness and peace have embraced, where faithfulness has sprung up from the earth, and righteousness gazes down from heaven" (Ps 85:11-12). If we cannot see the full beauty that surrounds us then, perhaps, it is because our vision is defective. If we have allowed our outlook to be formed by our encounter with God, then the paradoxical providence of God becomes a delight, even though we remain puzzled.

65   You have done what is good for your servant, O Lord, according to your word.

GOODNESS

Wisdom could, perhaps, be defined as the readiness to find meaning in reality. Not simply to recognize that things are as they are, but to have some degree of appreciation and admiration for the existing order, in all its paradoxical complexity. The attainment of such wisdom is largely dependent on a certain humility of mind and heart, the acceptance that one is not the absolute center of the universe, and that there is much in reality that escapes our comprehension.

Meditating on God's word brings us to the point of understanding the goodness of God, manifest both in the works of creation and in the providential interventions in human affairs. It leads us to the point of recognizing that our understanding and assessment of situations is largely dependent on many accidental factors, some as trivial as the weather, others more enduring, such as the way our lives have been impacted by the actions of others. These more immediate and urgent concerns sometimes serve as a barrier between us and reality. Their immediacy assigns a greater degree of importance than reality warrants.

A person who regularly reads the Scriptures enters an alternative universe and is invited to see the events of everyday life in the context of God's self-revelation. Done with integrity, this demands a change in perspective. It means stepping back from the immediacy and urgency of current affairs and allowing one's outlook to expand in the warmth of God's presence. Just as a person who works in a challenging occupation is helped to cope with its difficulties when the home situation is healthy and loving, so we are empowered to face up to the inevitable difficulties of interacting with an imperfect world, if we have nurtured our deeper selves through the regular encounter with the word of God. Just as a person usually cannot cope well with work challenges when the home situation is unsupportive, so we will not be able to respond creatively to the ordinary and extraordinary demands of daily life if we have, somehow, lost contact with God and drifted away from the spiritual world.

We probably do not doubt the goodness of God in the abstract but, when troubles enter our lives, we easily forget the vague theological notions that have floated over our heads, so that the situation may well seem much darker than it is, and our ability to respond creatively to it is reduced. Often enough, however, we will discover the nearness of God's care especially when life is difficult.

It is as though God is best revealed when an intervention is made to reverse the lot of the downtrodden. "From the dust [God] raises the lowly and lifts up the needy from the dung heap, to make them sit with princes, the princes of the people. He gives the barren wife a home and makes her the joyful mother of children" (Ps 113:7-9). No wonder the psalmist adds: "Praise the LORD."

66   Teach me good discretion and knowledge,
        for I have faith in your commandments.

DISCRETION

Normally when we use the term "discretion" we think of it as a quality of a person's behavior. It can be applied to diplomats, whom we expect to act with tact, prudence and reserve. The domestic servants of the high and mighty are expected to be discreet in that they do not reveal the private antics of their employers. In the present context, however, discretion means something different. Based on its Latin origins it means discernment, the ability to sort through evidence and to separate that which is more worthy of credence. It is a quality of knowledge or perception rather than of performance. A person endowed with the gift of discretion, in this sense, is one who is able to step back from impressionistic judgments and, by sifting through the facts, come to a sound and judicious decision.

It sometimes seems that discernment is a natural endowment that some people have more than others. Whether this is true or not, it should be remembered that our powers of discernment can be strengthened, and this usually comes about by practice, being prepared to examine different aspects of a proposition and being willing to find a harmony where, at first, there appeared to be only discord. This is a valuable art. It is something that can be learned and, therefore, something that can be taught. But it requires attention.

The Hebrew word used in this verse has, as its primary meaning, the idea of taste. According to a common saying, "there is no accounting for tastes." This seems to indicate that taste is a subjective phenomenon. Yet it has an objective basis: taste is experienced when a food provokes a chemical reaction in the gustatory receptors inside the mouth. You cannot positively taste sweetness if only saltiness is present. But, like cats, you may fail to perceive the sweetness, if your sense of taste is defective. And a frequent effect of the aging process is that our perception of taste is less intense. Ideally there is harmony between the objective components of the food and the subjective capacity to distinguish them, so that the sensors faithfully register what the food contains.

In the same way, the gift of discernment allows me to assess the degree of moral rectitude that a proposed course of action embodies. A lot depends on whether my moral sensitivity is intact and has been educated. This education cannot be self-generated; it comes from outside. In some sense, I have to be drawn out of myself, away from my natural preferences, and taught to look at things in accordance with criteria which are not self-serving, but are more objective. I may find it convenient, and even pleasurable, to murder someone whose views differ from mine, but this does not mean that it is a good action to perform. This is why I need to be instructed in the practice of transcending my personal feelings and giving due weight to objective factors. That is how God's word helps me to distinguish good actions from bad and, in the process, motivates me, by doing good and avoiding evil, to take some steps toward increasing the level of goodness in the world, and in myself.

67   Before I was afflicted I went astray,
      but now I keep your utterance.

EXPERIENCE

Wisdom is often viewed as an adjunct to a long life. This is not because mental faculties become sharper as the hair grows whiter—quite the reverse. What older people have is the possibility of looking back over a wide variety of experiences and, now that the heat of the moment has evaporated, make a dispassionate judgment on the value of the choices made in earlier times. Wisdom is acquired retrospectively. If we enjoyed infallible foreknowledge all our choices would be sound but, since our vision is limited, we often make mistakes. It is especially from our mistakes and misjudgments that we learn to be slow in attributing absolute infallibility not only to our reasoned conclusions but more especially to our merest opinions.

More often than most of us are prepared to admit, hard times come about because of choices that we have made. We may not have been complicit in the cyclone that demolished our house, but we did make the decision to live in a region prone to cyclones and to build a house that was less than fully cyclone-proof, maybe against the advice of those who knew better. We will often find, in retrospect, that if we had acted differently we may have avoided some of the mishaps that befell us. If we are becoming wise, we will learn from our review of the past, how to make better choices. Sometimes we will conclude that we should have been more cautious; sometimes that we should have been more adventurous. The point is that we see now what was invisible to us then.

This fragility of our decision-making teaches us that things are not always what they seem at first glance; relying on appearances is not always the wisest choice. This is a truth on which most philosophical traditions insist: truth and appearance do not necessarily coincide. As we move toward wisdom we learn to step back, to look deeper, to go beyond what, at first sight, seems obvious. This is especially true when it comes to evaluating what seem to be negative experiences. Because reality fails to live up to our expectations, we are disappointed. We are uncomfortable and confused about the choices that we are now forced to make. It is only in hindsight that we discover that what seemed negative was not; maybe we were protected from an unseen hazard, maybe in formulating a new course of action we learned something, maybe in seeking help we made new friends. Bad things may sometimes be the best thing that can happen to us, though we don't appreciate this at the time.

A good teacher allows pupils to make mistakes because usually we learn more from our failures than from the most brilliant success. Thus, the goodness of God does not prohibit us from going astray but, instead, affords us the priceless opportunity of learning for ourselves how wise is God's code of conduct for human life. Our own mistakes and misfortunes teach us to look to the utterances of God for guidance and for comfort; they come from a space that offers a purview different from our limited outlook, and they point to the way ahead in a manner that transcends our limited awareness. When we reject reality because it fails to meet our expectations, more often than not we are wrong. If we don't see that now, maybe later we will. If we are wiser.

68   You are good and you do what is good;
      teach me your statutes.

DISPERSION

By doing good we become good and, by becoming good, we spread goodness around. That is a strange feature of goodness: it replicates itself. Not immediately, not necessarily in the same form, but surely. An act of kindness echoes throughout the universe. Eventually it bounces back on us.

Without reflection, we may not appreciate this. Perhaps it is easier to grasp its opposite. A person who is immersed in unkindness usually is marked by that quality. This connection is often made in seeking leniency for criminals: it is argued they had an unhappy childhood and never had the opportunity to develop the normal social virtues. We may recognize something similar from our own experience. We are less likely to extend the hand of friendliness to those who treat us with undisguised hostility. We respond in kind. Taking this a step further, we need to be aware that how we treat people shapes how they will treat others.

If God's word is our constant companion and mentor in life, then our burgeoning awareness of God's kindness toward us cannot but influence the way we interact with others. If our consciences have been formed by contact with God, then certain divine qualities will begin to become a priority for us: kindness, understanding, compassion, forbearance, forgiveness and, progressively, a love that is boundless and unconditional. It is impossible for us to draw near to God—or for God to draw near to us—without a significant upgrading in the way that we relate to others.

Sometimes we do not readily perceive God's goodness since we are too inclined to judge things by their immediate impact on us. It happens that the goodness of God sometimes takes the form of correction, hauling us back from the wilderness onto the right road. God's intervention can seem punitive, but its purpose is remedial and not vindictive. Saint Ambrose offers the comparison of medical treatment. "Consider a physician applying an effective medicine to your wounds even though it will sting the virulent sore. Or perhaps he will cut away the festering part with a scalpel. But the physician is a good man and he does what is useful to the patient and he knows that what he does is for the patient's benefit."[35]

Daily meditation on God's word will convince us of two things. The first is that we are unable always to penetrate the providential purposes of God and, sometimes we have to accept that the seemingly uncomfortable situation in which we find ourselves is somehow conferring a benefit—although this conclusion more often arrive by hindsight. The second is, as Psalm 136 reminds us twenty-six times, God's kindness is without limit, without condition, without pre-existent worthiness on our part. As we are instructed in the divine statutes we are gradually equipped to cope with the inevitable vicissitudes of human existence, and our minds and hearts are opened to the extraordinary possibility that everything that happens to us is, in reality, a manifestation of God's goodness and kindness in our regard.

69   The arrogant smear me with lies,
        with all my heart I observe your precepts.

UNREACTIVENESS

Most of us are conditioned by our immediate environment. We are societal animals and are not unaffected by what others think or say about us. It is bad enough when our real deficiencies are publicized, it is probably worse when people utter untruths about us—it is usually hard to disprove something that didn't happen. When others denigrate me by smearing me with lies, it requires a good measure of fortitude to withstand the calumny. I need to be somewhat secure in my acceptance of who I am. Even better if I have friends who unwaveringly affirm me.

Of course, I need to examine my conscience to determine whether I am complicit in the negative attitudes taken toward me. I should not be too eager to believe that every reservation that others have about me is groundless. It can happen that I am so single-minded in implementing my own plans and projects that I do not take care to ensure that what I am doing is not offensive to others—and this includes offence taken unreasonably. I need to ensure that my choices do not diminish societal harmony even when, to my mind, the choices are eminently desirable. If others have something against me, a dispassionate assessment of how my actions may have contributed to the situation is the first step in seeking—if not reconciliation—at least, some level of resolution. I cannot change what others think or feel about me but I can, at least, ensure that I do not make matters worse by acting thoughtlessly.

It can sometimes happen that—reading this verse in reverse—it is because we observe God's precepts that others are hostile towards us and begin to smear us with lies. Religious observance, even when it is practiced sincerely and without ostentation, does not appeal to everyone. In some observers it seems to generate irrational outbursts of fury. It is as though true believers become surrogates for God. Those who are hostile to God cannot express their enmity directly, but instead project it onto those more accessible humans who take their cue from the divine precepts. By hurting them they attack God.

God, however, remains untouchable. And, to some extent, so are those who are devoted to their religious observance. If it is true that virtue is its own reward, it is probably also true that genuine religion does not need supplemental benefits to be sustained. More than that, an authentic connection with the spiritual world gives us some measure of strength in bearing with the insults that come our way.

Our dedication to the service of God, through keeping God's word, can be for us a source of identity. This is what matters. It is pleasant if others value what we cherish but, if they do not, this is to their discredit not to ours. If a person is unable to appreciate fine wine or fine music, it is not because they are of a superior sensibility. Quite the opposite. Their dullness of spirit makes it impossible for them to appreciate the delicacy inherent in the finest things in life. To those who have tasted the goodness of God, neither insult nor argument can diminish the delight that this experience brings. Reality is always stronger than mere opinion.

70 Their hearts are gross like fat,
　　but I delight in your instruction.

GROSS

This is the only occurrence of the word for "gross" in the Hebrew Bible, but its meaning is clear from related languages. The Latin translation has "curdled like milk." The underlying etymology indicates sluggishness and inertness, with undertones of discourtesy and inelegance. Most of us have met people for whom this term could be considered applicable, but would hate to think that anyone would use it to describe us.

The opposite of grossness is refinement, not in the superficial sense of having good manners, but meaning purified of whatever might defile. In some sense, a refined or pure heart has the capacity of seeing God, not by some abstract vision, but by perceiving God at work in the happenings of daily life. One who delights in God's instruction becomes more sensitive to the subtle ways in which God's hand are directing events here on earth.

Meditating on the word of God is an education in spiritual sensibility; progressively it enables us to becomes so attuned to the harmony inherent in God's interventions in human affairs that a glorious sunrise speaks to us of the beauty of God, the rhythms of nature remind us that everything on earth follows an order given by God, and a simple act of human kindness may lead us to conclude that love is the meaning of life. The footprints of God are not absent from our universe, but if we are to perceive them as such, we need to be continually schooled in detecting God's signature in what may seem to be everyday realities.

For those who have not been gifted with this sensibility, whose hearts have become gross, life is without much meaning. Its variety is not a source of wonderment and delight but an obstacle to the control they wish to assert. When no room is left for God, things fall apart, and we are deprived of the delight that results from attaching ourselves to the ultimate goal of human desire.

Bernard of Clairvaux was quite taken with this verse, seeing in it an explanation for intractable resistance to anything beyond the tangible. The eventual result is that the connection to the spiritual world is lost, and the capacity for spiritual endeavor dissipates. "Hardness of heart and stubbornness of soul come from not meditating on the law of the Lord, but on one's own will."[36]

> When pride is found in me, the Lord moves away from his servant. This is the cause of my soul's barrenness and the lack of devotion that I experience. My heart dries up, it becomes curdled like milk, and it becomes like land without water. So great is the hardness of my heart that I do not seek the tears of compunction. I have no taste for psalmody, I do not want to read, there is no delight in prayer, and I am unable to engage in my customary meditations.[37]

Cut off from the sources of spiritual renewal, spiritual sensibility withers and dies, and there is no one to blame except oneself.

71   It was good for me to be afflicted,
       so that I may learn your statutes.

AFFLICTION

When affliction strikes, it is always a good idea to step back and attempt to analyze what has happened. Affliction may be triggered by a single event or sequence of events, but it is usually the result of a more complicated series of happenings within the person. My first reaction to something bad is to consider the external causes and their effects and then, usually, to allocate blame. But is this the right way to go?

Affliction is more an ongoing state than a particular event. It is the cumulative effect of many small occurrences which, of themselves, do not amount to much. When we feel ourselves moving into a state of affliction we need to ask ourselves the question that the Lord posed to Jonah, "Is it right for you to be upset?" We need to look on the inside rather than on the outside to come to some understanding in this matter. Sometimes we are distressed because we are being castigated by an internalized parental voice for not living up to self-imposed expectations. We can be very hard on ourselves because we are not perfect, as if perfection was within anyone's grasp. Sometimes distress comes from memories which demonstrate that, in the past, we did not always live up to our present standards. Sometimes there are memories of other people mistreating us, perhaps seriously, causing lifelong trauma. These are the kind of inner factors which turn a simple negative incident into an overwhelming sense of oppression. The interpretation we give to the latest event is heavily weighted by what happened in the past.

If we are able to recognize this causal chain in ourselves then perhaps we can move toward converting our reaction into a response. This to embrace a fuller truth with its consequences, rather than hiding from the multitudinous realities that have contributed to our personal history. The first step is usually to stop being so ready to identify targets for our recrimination. Human life is so very complicated that our readiness to identify our targets for blame needs to be slowed down. We rarely know the full story of why things happen or why people act in the way that they do. If we did, our interpretation of their behavior would probably be different. We need to switch our attention from them to us. Why is it that their action causes us so much grief when, done at another time, or by another person, or in a different situation, it would be simply shrugged off.

Affliction invites analysis. And in broadening the context of our self-reflection, we may find that experiencing it has been a benefit. We come to realize that there was an appropriateness about our discomfort, because it enabled us to see some of the ways in which our approach to life can be upgraded. "I know, Lord, that your judgements are right and that in faithfulness you afflicted me" (Ps 119:75). One thing that affliction does better than almost anything else is to bring us out of our habitual distractedness and to uplift our hearts to God. "I called to the Lord in my trouble and the Lord answered and released me" (Ps 118:5). If we are wise, we don't just react to affliction; we try to respond to it—creatively.

72   The instruction from your mouth is better for me
than thousands in silver and gold.

BAUBLES

Sapiential writings often assert that wisdom is more precious than all earthly possessions. Silver and gold are mere baubles compared with wisdom. In such texts, what is being spoken about is a practical ability to get things done and to do things well. It is not a question of having a higher degree in advanced sophistry, but the ability to deal creatively with whatever life delivers to our doorstep. Biblical wisdom has its sleeves rolled up; it is fundamentally practical. It is more precious than silver and gold because it is a personal quality, not the mere possession of external objects. To gain possession of the whole world while remaining crude and crass is no permanent benefit. In the words of the prophet Jeremiah: "Those who pursue vanities become vanities" (Jer 2:5). Genuine wisdom enhances persons; it does not fill purses.

This psalm tirelessly restates the notion that it is from the divine self-revelation that all true wisdom proceeds and that making the choice to live in the context of God's word sets us on the path to a richer life. Our potential is more likely to be realized if we allow ourselves to come under the influence of this instruction and set ourselves to follow it directions. We do not make the journey alone: we are constantly encouraged and comforted as we struggle with difficulties just as we are challenged not to let our talents lie dormant but to make the most of the opportunities that open up before us.

The instruction that God gives us is not so much by means of a code of laws, engraved on tablets of stone, never to be altered. It is the word that comes from the mouth of God. It is part of an interpersonal relationship that God has initiated with us; not the heartless promulgation of universal laws, but a word spoken directly to us, that draws its strength from all that has gone before, and applies itself to the situation in which we find ourselves at present. God's law seems more like a dialogue than a decree. It takes place within the context of a covenant relationship.

And what about King Solomon? Here is someone who was gifted with profound wisdom, whose possessions excelled thousands in silver and gold and who enjoyed a high reputation among his contemporaries. Was Solomon one of whom it could be said: "Blessed is the man whose way is innocent, who walks according to the LORD's instruction. Blessed is he who observes [God's] testimonies, and seeks [God] wholeheartedly, who does not do what is evil, but walks in the LORD's ways" (Ps 119:1-3)? It seems not. It seems that wisdom cannot coexist for long with great material wealth. Most of us can never have enough of this world's benefits; there is always a hankering for more. And no matter how wise we once were, our unbridled acquisitiveness will lead us into compromises until eventually we are forced into making a life-changing choice. Our dilemma may not be as dramatic as that of Solomon and our apostasy may not be as complete, but we will soon learn for ourselves that we cannot serve more than one master. To allow ourselves to be ruled by acquisitiveness or ambition or sexual desire or self-will or other such baubles, will weaken wisdom's hold on us and eventually we too will slide into folly.

73   Your hands made me and established me;
     give me understanding so that I may learn your
     commandments.

FORMATION

When religion is subordinated to a cult of absolute obedience to external authorities, the role of understanding is diminished, as is the capacity to adapt the law or its observance to changing circumstances. The picture given us by the book of Genesis is different. It reveals that humankind was created and formed by God and that, therefore, we each have certain God-given qualities that constitute the fundamental determinant of our existence and our primary moral imperative. We are to become what we were made to be. Genesis speaks of God's Spirit breathing life into the dust of the earth and creating a new kind of being, with a natural endowment different from all other creatures.

We are formed and set in place by God's hands, with the breath of God's Spirit within us. Instead of dust, we might think of the material element in us as being constituted by the genetic and epigenetic elements we have received from our ancestors. In some way, in a manner we are currently unable to survey, our ancestors, by their lives and by their choices, have contributed to what we are today. If they had made different choices, we would never have come into existence. We were formed by the hands of God's providence to be exactly as we are; our responsibility is to become what we were made to be. And this will not happen unless we have some understanding of our destiny. And learn about who we are meant to be by gazing into the mirror of God's self-revelation.

There is a danger if we set ourselves the task of creating a human-conceived mold by which to shape our own existence or that of others. This is to ignore the God-given nature and, thereby, to usurp the role of the Creator. A first principle in self-governance and in our dealings with others is to recognize, appreciate, and respect what has been given by nature, and then to operate within its parameters. We are obliged to operate within the boundaries of reality. To seek to bypass reality in favor of our own fantasies is not only delusional but deadly.

So we gaze into God's instruction in order to come to an understanding of who we are in God's sight, what we are meant to become, and what are the choices we need to make in order to make our way toward that goal. It is not the work of a single moment, but a lifetime endeavor. "Learning the commandments" means achieving a certain interpenetration of the objective word with our own being. Understanding it in our bones. It is not enough to grasp the meaning of the words or to expound on their technicalities. We need to take possession of the text, to claim it as our own, to appreciate the fact that the story being narrated is also our story, and that understanding it is a way to a higher level of self-awareness. The word of God is not something out there; it is deep within us. To find it fully, we have also to be prepared to voyage to our own center. We were formed by God's word at the beginning and the process continues even now. Blessed are we if we grasp something of this mystery.

74   Those who fear you will see me and rejoice,
        because I hope for your word.

HOPE

This verse seems to proclaim that those who have confidence in God's word, who trust in its power to deliver, and are hopeful about the future, serve as a beacon of encouragement for all who make a place for God in their lives. This is far from the notion of privatized religion, whereby our living according to God's word is simply a matter between us and God. True religion has a contagious effect. We might call it "ontological evangelism." We proclaim the good news that we have drawn from our contact with the spiritual world by what we are, more than by anything we say or do.

Hope is a beautiful word and the reality it signifies is even more splendid. Because human life on earth is like enforced labor (Job 7:1), there are many moments in which our experience is of misery and unhappiness. Most of us pass through periods like this but, fortunately, they are passing. For a few they are habitual, and they are drawn into spasms of desperation and, perhaps, into the depths of despair. For all alike hope is a precious remedy that makes endurance of present affliction possible.

Hope's best friend is patience. It could, perhaps, be said that patience is the best guarantee of the genuineness of our faith. If we live in the context of God's self-revelation, a normal consequence will be that we are ultimately optimistic about the future. We are not naïve. We do not believe that there will be no more difficulties or reversals or failures. But there is a strong hope that, in the end, all will be well. This gives us a certain toughness even when the road on which we are traveling resists progress. It is not a delusional confidence in our own capacity to overcome obstacles, but an appreciativeness of God's utter fidelity. We will not be left to struggle alone. This seems to be the lesson that the book of Job is teaching us.

Those who have made a place for God in their lives and who have a reverence for God's word are also more finely attuned to the reality of faith in other people. There is an intuitive understanding of the forces that energize their virtues, and a strange feeling of kinship with them. Not everything that happens in the spiritual life can be explained rationally. Where there is a living faith in one person, it tends to reach out and contact those who are in a similar disposition, regardless of external differences. And this sense that we are not alone in our service of God is a source of great joy.

Hope is more a gift than a virtue. It is something that follows our attachment to God rather than a set of skills we develop through repeated efforts. As something coming from outside ourselves, it can never be overwhelmed by the troubles that bestrew our pathway through life. On the contrary it will assist us in navigating a course through the many difficulties and reversals that we may experience. Hope will bring us home. As an added benefit, it will also serve as a homing beacon to those around us.

75   I know, Lord, that your judgements are righteous,
      and that it was in faithfulness that you afflicted me.

RELIABILITY

What we cherish most in our friends is reliability, loyalty, faithfulness. We do not demand that they be glamorous or talented or rich, but we do hope to be able to rely on their friendship as the circumstances of our life change. We do not want fair-weather friends, who will desert us when storms loom on the horizon. We appreciate most those who continue to stand by us through thick and thin. And we remember with the most affection those who stood most stalwartly at our side in troubled times.

To affirm the faithfulness of God is not so much a matter of doctrine as a matter of experience. Through the years of our association we have learned to trust God, to believe that God's word is solid and true, and to hope for God's intervention when things seem to go against us. We cannot always explain why we accept God's reliability, but deep within us there is a conviction that, though God's ways are not necessarily our ways, Providence has a way of arranging things in such a way that they paradoxically lead to a good outcome for us.

Clement of Alexandria wrote of God's "pedagogical anger," which is not really anger but a tactic designed to help us learn a lesson that we have been resisting. We do not begin our lives overflowing with wisdom but, if we ever become a little wise, it is only by small increments. And the privileged occasions for such spurts of growth is when we make mistakes. But, only when we realize that we have gone astray. The function of pedagogical anger is to help us make the transition from mistake to insight—to see where we were going wrong. If we look back on our lives and conclude that we have made many mistakes, then there is a good probability that we have attained some level of wisdom. As the saying goes: the person who never made a mistake never made anything.

When we encounter hard times our first impulse is to lay the blame outside ourselves: it is somebody else's fault, the circumstances were not right, there was some kind of unforeseen accident. So long as this continues we are unlikely to unearth what it was inside ourselves that contributed to the mishap: ignorance, impatience, obstinacy, obtuseness . . . The possibilities are endless. Blaming others or blaming God blocks our coming to grips with the reality.

To affirm the utter faithfulness of God is not to deny the occasional faithlessness of others, but to accept that there is a great deal of paradox in every human life. Things are rarely exactly as they seem, and if we have total confidence in our immediate impressions and assessments, we are probably delusional. So many puzzles are solved by hindsight that we might sometimes wonder whether we ever get things right at the time they are happening. We are so enamored of a rationalist emphasis on cause and effect that we find it difficult to accept that there might be effects of which we are unable to uncover the cause. Life is not without its mysteries. The sooner we accept this, the sooner we will come to believe that God does not desert us in adverse circumstances, but is redirecting us to face in a more wholesome direction. We often make mistakes, but the judgments of God are always right.

✣

76   Please, may your kindness console me,
     according to your utterance to your servant.

PROMISES

It is easy to affirm that God's word is solid and can be relied on, so long as these assertions remain in the realm of the abstract.

It is a greater challenge to find in divine self-revelation the kind of assurance which will bolster our confidence that, in the end, all will be well. We are only too often overwhelmed by things that seem threatening because they are outside our control, and we fail to perceive anything beyond these immediate attacks on our autonomy.

This is why it is important for us to learn to live in the context of God's words to us, to see them not merely as providing information, direction or, perhaps, encouragement. God's words are promises. Not merely to do certain things, but to continue in relationship. God has initiated a dialogue; it will be interrupted only from our side. Whether our wishes are realized or not, God remains at our side, the covenant is not abrogated: "I will be your God and you shall be my people."

We tend to think that words are cheap, once spoken they fly away into the sky and are seen no more. That is why, in our culture, we demand that commitments are written down so that they can be stored away and produced when there is any doubt. A marriage contract is signed by the parties and witnessed and stored in an official archive; undoing it requires a legal process. Words are not enough. We require documentation.

In the Semitic world, as in some oral cultures today, the spoken word is both efficient and sufficient. To give one's word is to bind oneself, to make a commitment. When the Bible refers to God speaking to us, there is a certain solemnity attached to the words. They are not to be brushed away as trivial. "God speaks and it is accomplished" (Ps 33:9). What is asked of us is an undeviating acceptance of God's utterances as worthy of belief and confidence.

To believe in the promises of God asks of us an acceptance of God's kindness toward us so that even in the direst circumstances we are willing to open ourselves to receive consolation from God. Consolation does not mean removing irritants from our life. It is, rather, the assurance that we will not have to struggle alone, that we will have company in all the challenges we face on the spiritual journey. Geoffrey Chaucer described the function of consolation as, "to have another fellow in his pain."[38] What God promises us, above all, is to remain with us.

When life is hard, for one reason or another, we will find the necessary comfort in pondering God's word, in remembering the promise they imply, and searching more earnestly to perceive the hand of God at work in even the most unlikely events. What we learn about God from our immersion in the Scriptures, is that God can be trusted and that we will never be forsaken, however ugly our situation seems.

77   Let your compassion come and I shall live
       for your instruction is my delight.

SANCTUARY

The word here translated as "compassion" is plural in the original, perhaps indicating acts of compassion or signs of compassion. We do not experience God's compassion directly, because our puny intelligence is unable to comprehend the divine nature. We postulate its presence from acts of kindness done to us. If we take the trouble to ponder over our personal history, we may be inclined to join the psalmist in saying: "Lord, you have been a place of safety for us, from generation to generation" (Ps 90:1). God is for us a sanctuary, a safe space where we "dwell in the hiding place of the Most High, and rest in the shadow of the Almighty" (Ps 91:1). God is for us a protected place of peace where we find relief from the intrusive thoughts that disturb our tranquility. And so, "I will lie down in peace and fall sleep, for you alone, Lord, make me dwell in safety" (Ps 4:9). "In God alone is my soul at rest; from God comes my help. God alone is my rock, my stronghold, my fortress; I stand firm" (Ps 62:2-3). We notice the repetition of the word "alone." We will not attain deep inner peace anywhere else.

To delight in the divine compassion and to embrace it as our guide in life, it is necessary for us to place ourselves in its ambit. For most of us this involves moving from the zones in which we spend most of our time and seeking a sacred place; an inner or outer location where we find ourselves somehow more attentive to the divine presence. Although God is not constrained in making contact with us, when we try to respond to God's outreach it is easier if we have found or have created a special space in which we are encouraged to leave aside the worthy concerns of other times and open our hearts to the divine presence.

Once in the sanctuary we encourage our thoughts to move in a different direction, to revive the memory of the many acts of divine compassion which we have experienced during our lifetime, the many moments which have revealed God's particular affection for us. We do not have to begin each attempt at meeting with God as though this were a first contact. Our relationship has a long and variegated history which feeds into our present encounter. We are not strangers. We know each other well. We don't have to begin a conversation with God. We resume a conversation that has been running all our life.

As we allow the memory of many instances of God's compassion to fill our hearts and occupy our thoughts, we find ourselves being drawn closer to God and, in the process experiencing an intense quiet that is somehow more boisterous than our most frantic activity. The relationship that is submerged while we are engaged in other activities slowly emerges. We are flooded with the experience of the divine compassion and, without any qualms, we give voice to what we are feeling: "O God, my God, it is you I seek, my soul thirsts for you . . . In the holy place I have seen you, and I beheld your power and your glory" (Ps 63:1-2).

78   Let the arrogant be shamed who afflict me with falsehood,
        I will muse on your decrees.

RETRIBUTION

A theme that occurs often enough in the psalms is the notion of divine retribution. It alarms many people to find themselves praying that God will take vengeance on those who oppose them. Satisfying at one level, perhaps, but theologically confusing. Is God's nature defined by a zeal for punishing the wicked? Sometimes it seems that this is what the Bible is saying, but what does it mean?

A first distinction must be made between what we consider to be evil and what God considers evil. Usually there are two sides to every story and the fact that we find the conduct of another person disagreeable does not necessarily mean that the act is bad and the perpetrator is wicked. To kill a cow is a crime against life. To kill a cow to feed a starving village is an act of high virtue. How can the same action be ambiguous? Experts tell us that the morality of an action is determined by the intention of the one who performs that action. A slap on the face can be an assault; it can also be an attempt to halt an hysterical outburst. It is the intention that determines its moral character. It is not so much a question of whether this is an effective remedy, but of whether the one doing the action believed so. This means that it is quite difficult to be absolutely sure that an action by another person is immoral; it may be harmful, destructive and even criminal, but we cannot read the subjective state of another person with absolute certainty.

A fair indicator of the morality of a particular action is proportion; when a response is proportionate to the triggering event. A disproportionate reaction is often an indication of some subjective disorder—whether this may be regarded as wickedness is another question. Nowadays we are much more aware that there are many unseen contributory elements in a person's wrong choices which could be seen as diminishing a person's liability for what they have done.

This is to say that there may be an alternative assessment of what we regard as wickedness based on a different interpretation of the elements of the situation. There is always the danger that when we condemn another person we are imputing to them motivations that are more typical of ourselves than of them. We are projecting onto them some of the malice that lies lurking beneath the placid surface of our pious comportment. When I condemn another person for gluttony, I am likely revealing some gluttonous tendency within myself. In such a situation calling for their punishment is fraught with danger for myself.

It is probably better to leave to God the determination of what is good and what is evil in others, and to recognize the limits of our own capacity to judge them. It is much better trying to upgrade our own behavior in the here-and-now of the present situation, than to waste our breath on judicial pronouncements of what others should or should not be doing. When we call for retribution we may be making a whip for our own backs. Who knows?

79   Let those who fear you turn to me,
       those who know your testimonies.

KINSHIP

There is a mysterious kind of kinship among those who make a place for God in their lives. This is not something pre-calculated or deliberately chosen. It just is. When God finds entrance into a person's life, a great crowd enters at the same time—in fact, if not the whole of humanity, then certainly all those who revere God. If God is present these others are also present. Even before we realize it, we are united with them all.

This means that each one of us is called to be an agent in manifesting to others what we ourselves have learned from our pondering of the divine statutes. What we absorbed, we absorbed not for ourselves alone, but also for all those with whom we will come into contact. The life-giving message we received was meant to be communicated. Surprisingly, the more we pass it on, the stronger becomes our own grasp of what we have received. In evangelizing others we also evangelize ourselves.

To accept this truth demands of us a certain boldness. We know ourselves to be fragile, with only a precarious hold even on what is dearest to us. We are subject to external vicissitudes as well as to variation in our moods and dispositions. We hope to pass muster by staying under the radar. The summons to be a guide and teacher to others, who seem to us endowed with greater resources, induces a kind of dread. A fear of making a mess and leaving things worse by our intervention.

If we find ourselves thinking such thoughts, it is not because of an excess of humility. On the contrary, it is because we are attributing too much importance to our contribution. Any power that we have to influence others comes entirely from the inherent dynamism of the word we have received. It empowers us to act as its spokesperson. We are invested, for the moment, with the authority of the word, not only permitted but obliged to speak—translating it into our own idiom and coloring it with the hues of our own imagination. Yes, we have something to contribute; it is subsidiary, but it is also essential. God's word comes to others through us and when we speak the word we have received is not absent.

This is why those who are God-fearers are instructed to look to me if they want to come to an understanding of divine revelation. A shocking proposition for those of us who are not delusional. However, it involves a considerable challenge for me. I must not only live in accordance with what I have learned from my pondering of the word, I must also embody it in what I say and in what I do, in how I respond to persons and how I react to unexpected or threatening situations. This involves a much deeper assimilation of what I have learned than mere intellectual compression. I must become the message I received. And become it in a way that can be recognized and assimilated by others.

If this thought doesn't motivate me to come before God in humble petition, I don't know what will. It is a task beyond me. I need help if I am to attempt even the first steps toward its accomplishment.

80   Let my heart be upright in your statutes,
         that I may not be put to shame.

BLAMELESS

I suppose that the aspiration to be upright and blameless in God's sight is admirable, but I don't think it is very realistic. Too often the desire for perfection comes from the superego, the internalized parental voice that is constantly nagging us to try harder, to do better, and to reach for the skies. I wonder whether we are not better off keeping our feet on the ground. We read in Ecclesiastes: "Do not be over-righteous and do not be over-wise. Why destroy yourself?" (Eccl 7:16). The point seems to be that we are more likely to attain some level of perfection if we are not consciously striving for it, but attending to things as they present themselves, doing the best we can—without constantly monitoring our progress or measuring ourselves against some private standard. To have a blameless and upright heart seems to me a matter of doing the best we can under present circumstances, recognizing that these will not always be ideal. The pilot of an airliner who lands safely after a mid-air incident is more worthy of praise than one who executes a perfect, text-book landing after an uneventful flight. Battling negativity and being wounded in the process is sometimes what life expects of us; the result may not be pretty, but we have done very well even to survive.

The multiple pointers of God's pathway to a more abundant life are sometimes far from simple; they can involve contrary and sometimes contradictory principles that somehow we have to negotiate. What God expects of us is that we muddle our way through the morass, conscious that God's manner of guiding us does not always fulfil our expectations. God's ways are not always our ways. We are not expected to be masters of our own ultimate destiny; all that is required is that we take the next step in accordance with the evidence that is available to us at the moment.

If we want to be blameless, the way toward it passes through emerging self-truth. We recognize the ambiguities inherent in our human condition and the particular challenges arising from our personal history. We acknowledge what we are, and from this awareness we allow a prayer to rise from the depths of our being, directed to the One alone who can bring us to the desired goal that is beyond our capability to reach. "To you have I lifted up my eyes; to you who dwell in heaven" (Ps 123:1). With heartfelt sincerity we pray to the One who is not subject to the constraints of worldly existence and who looks upon us with the utmost benevolence. "See my affliction and save me" (Ps 119:153).

To our way of thinking it may seem strange. The only way of arriving at perfection is embracing our imperfection. Not by way of pretense or resentfully, but with total sincerity. We affirm our absolute dependence on God's saving intervention in our lives. Surely this is the lesson we learn from pondering divine revelation: our God is a God who saves. We approach God in truth when we are honest about our need to be saved. This is no cause for shame. In fact it could be a source of rejoicing because our neediness gives us cause to draw near to God, and it offers us a prompt to open ourselves for the encounter.

81   My soul longs for your salvation,
       I hope in your word.

WELL-BEING

When we hear the word "salvation" we often give it an abstract, theological meaning. In some way or other it involves attaining the goal of all our spiritual striving. And that, surely, is something desirable. But in many languages "salvation" means more than that; it signifies health, well-being and happiness. It involves the human person at all levels. To the extent that we have received salvation we are not only alive, but also lively.

When we look to God as the source of salvation, when we pray for it, we are asking to become more alive, more ourselves, less restrained, less inhibited, less dead. To the extent that a connection with God is lacking the soul languishes. "Look towards God and be radiant; let your faces not be abashed" (Ps 34:6). We are like heliotropic flowers, we blossom most brilliantly when we turn toward the radiance of God. Conversely, alas, when we turn away from God we begin to droop.

It is by our fidelity in exposing ourselves and our lives to God's word that we are motivated to turn away from evil and do good. In the first place, we begin to be assured of the welcoming goodness of God. In the process of growing up, we absorbed all sorts of notions about God's attitude toward us, some of them unhelpful. Perhaps we cannot rid ourselves of the image of God as a fearsome judge who will examine our every thought and word and deed—to say nothing of our omissions—and find us worthy of eternal punishment. Such an attitude makes it unlikely that we feel drawn to approach God; like Adam and Eve we are more likely to hide ourselves among the bushes, hoping to escape an encounter. The Scriptures teach us about a different God. One who knows the dust of which we are made and does not expect too much from us. One who is kind and content to countenance our many misdeeds and lost opportunities out of unconditional love and acceptance. Unconditional. It means that it is not determined by anything we do; not generated by our good deeds or weakened by our misdemeanors. Our regular contact with the Scriptures introduces us to the true God and sustains our relationship.

The second benefit that follows regular exposure to God's word is that we grow in self-knowledge. We shed the delusions that used to be so important in maintaining our self-esteem and begin to be willing to admit our limitations and liability—and be unabashed by them. When we experience the reality of another's love for us we may well conclude that we are not without value. As we become more aware that we are daily swathed in God's love we are less afraid to look in the mirror and see ourselves as we are. If God loves us we must, indeed, be lovable.

Salvation begins when we embrace the reality of God and the reality of ourselves; it comes to a glorious conclusion when it is no longer assailed by doubts and reservations but boldly celebrates the gift that God's love has wrought. This is the salvation that we desire so earnestly; this is the ultimate reality to which we are called.

82   My eyes yearn for your utterances,
       saying: When will you console me?

ANTICIPATION

One of our besetting sins is impatience. We want things to happen now, and we are reluctant to endure periods of waiting. As a result, we often do things hurriedly so that we can move on to something else, instead of finding delight in whatever it is that we are doing now. We can't see the beauty of the present moment because we have decided that it is only a dispensable stage in progress to a superior future. Our life is impoverished by our failure to draw from each of its moments the sustaining joy that they contain—though maybe hidden beneath the surface.

We are all aware of the promises inherent in following the spiritual path, and most of us feel frustrated that they have not been realized already. We fret because of the distance between our first steps and our arrival at our destination and, so, seek ways to speed up the process. This may well lead us to underestimate the value of giving time and energy to the various intermediary stages. To enjoy the wide variety of flavors that a long life yields.

It is good to look to the future, but this should not lead us to underestimate the value of paying attention to the present. It may be that we feel our energies waning when the time of waiting and watching is prolonged, but the watching and waiting can themselves be profitable because they encourage us gradually to reorient ourselves, to nuance our expectations, and to get rid of some of the delusional hopes that may have inspired our efforts at an earlier time.

Watching and waiting for a desired outcome that never seems to be any closer can precipitate questions about the worthiness of our hopes. Desires are plentiful, even in children; it is only as we move toward a mellower maturity that we begin to appreciate that many of our desires, in their crudest form, need to be refined; they need to be brought into harmony with the chosen direction of our lives.

While we wait, we reflect, and the more we reflect the wiser we become. Time spent in anticipating a desired outcome can sometimes mean that we become more focused on what is, at present, away in the future, and so we are gradually molded into a form that is more capable of receiving that to which we aspire. As our desire becomes more intense, in a paradoxical way, it renders the future present. Anticipation begins to be colored by that for which we are waiting. Expectation comes closer to reality.

This is not to say that we should not give expression to our hopes. The psalms frequently bid us to cry out to God to bring to fulfilment the work that has been begun. It is a good prayer so long as we do not allow it to be dominated by exasperation. It is a good prayer because it encourages us to move closer to viewing the passage of time in God's terms rather than in our own. To accept that a thousand years is as nothing in God's sight and, so, if our waiting for God's intervention has lasted less than that we have nothing to complain about. All we have to do is to slow down and enjoy the scenery, confident that we will arrive when the time is right.

83   Though I am like a wineskin shriveled by smoke,
         I did not forget your statutes.

WINESKIN

In a world in which everything seems to be made of plastic we have forgotten the way people in biblical times were obliged to create what they needed out of what was to hand, even though the result was, by our standards, somewhat inferior. The use of animal skins for the storage and transportation of water and wine was common, but they were vulnerable to many contingencies. This obscure reference seems to evoke the image of a skin dried out and hardened through exposure to smoke as a way of describing the way we sometimes feel when we seem to be making no progress and are, in addition, beset by many external contrarieties.

Those who follow the spiritual path do not always do so with a lively step and a blithe spirit. Sometimes, through no fault of their own, the going is hard. There may have been some seasonal variation in their inner life, perhaps compounded by a lack of support or affirmation. Their spirits and their self-esteem can be shriveled by having to exist in an environment that does not nourish their deepest aspirations, but constantly abrades the principles by which they strive to shape their lives.

As societal animals, we depend greatly on the support of those around us and, when this is lacking, fidelity to our deepest beliefs becomes more difficult. It may not be overt persecution that we face, but simply an active indifference that refuses to take seriously matters that are central to our approach to life. Living in a situation which constantly erodes any religious convictions means that we often have to struggle to maintain our grip even on the most fundamental tenets of our faith. There is a danger that, like the wineskin exposed to too much smoke, our faith loses its vibrancy and begins to shrivel.

To the extent that we live in such a situation, we need to strengthen our faith by a consistent remembrance of God's word, reviewing and renewing our faith as it interacts with an ever-changing world. Obviously, more than a merely mechanical recitation of Scripture is required. We need to keep imploring the text to speak to our present situation and cause the light of God's benevolent countenance to shine upon it, so that we begin to discern the path that leads to life. But there is more. We need not only knowledge, but our wills need fortifying and sustaining to offset the effects of the unbelief that surrounds us. In such a situation, our encounter with God's word becomes more intense.

And if it happens that we have been so dried out that God's word seems reluctant to address our needs—though it is really our shriveled state that is the cause of our insensibility—then we have to learn the art of patiently waiting for God to intervene, to create out of our inner confusion a moment of enlightenment that will show us the way out of the morass. Enduring such a situation tests our commitment but, without our knowing it, almost certainly strengthens our faith. We will, one day, recognize this; but not yet.

84   How many are the days of your servant?
       When will you do justice to those who persecute me?

TRANSCENDENCE

The complaints which the psalmist addresses to God about the apparent failure of divine justice to rectify what is wrong with the world are, no doubt, sincere. However, they tend to overlook one point: God's time is not our time. "In your eyes, a thousand years is like one day, it passes like yesterday, or like a watch in the night" (Ps 90:4). We become so used to addressing God in human terms that we sometimes forget that a great gulf exists between our finite world of time and space and the boundlessness of the spiritual world where God dwells. It is fine to give expression to our frustration because of the apparent delay in the arrival of relief, but we need to realize that our prayer says more about us than it does about God. Our impatience is the result of our not being able to see the big picture; we are locked in the narrow world of our own finitude and we may not be able to perceive the absolute significance of the things that are happening around us.

Divine transcendence does not, at first glance, seem like a comforting doctrine. In locating God above the ebb and flow of human affairs, it seems to make God indifferent to the plight of those who are persecuted and oppressed. This is not so. The term that is used here for the "justice" of God is not abstract and remote. The justice of God is dynamic and proactive; it is not only a quality, it is an ongoing activity. It is of the nature of God to create justice, where hitherto there was none. Just as the earth in all its splendor is the result of God's creative act, so God is—even now—in the process of creating on the earth a realm of justice.

But God's time-scale is not the same as ours. We cannot ever see the whole picture, and so our reading of situations may be off-kilter. Our experience is mostly limited to our immediate environment and what we can learn second or third hand. It is easy for us to make misjudgments because of an insufficiency of data. Our conclusions may be premature, but this does not mean that we do not feel passionately about the issues that confront us. But sometimes we need to take a step back. To do what we can to rectify things that are not right in our own environment, even if the results seem puny, and to have a sincere concern for wider issues, but also to recognize and accept that we cannot take over the running of the universe.

Meanwhile, though our days are numbered, we have to learn both the art of waiting patiently, and the skill of interacting positively with the world around us. Spending time with God's word can help us in both of these. The first benefit is teaching us to develop a strong confidence in divine providence and the willingness to step back and allow it to unfold. The second is to provide us with the guidance and the energy to whatever good becomes possible for us, boldly to step through every door that opens, and to radiate confidence that in the end all will be well.

85   The arrogant dig pitfalls for me;
      this is not according to your instruction.

REBELLION

To live in a community which takes seriously the instruction of God's Torah, is the foundation for a harmonious and fruitful existence. The fundamental requirements for living in accordance with God's self-revelation are simple and all-embracing. They exclude violence, exploitation, infidelity, envy and the other vices that undermine the solidarity of the human community. They foster a spirit of concord and cooperation in the human family with an appropriate respect for everything under the sun. Such an ambience would be like the Garden of Eden, a paradise on earth.

The disruptions we experience in life come from sin, they result from attitudes and actions which are in accordance neither with the nature God has given us nor with the pathway sketched out for us by God's word. Consciously or not, they are a rebellion against the Creator, and their effects cannot but be baneful. Whenever we try to superimpose our own self-centered will on our immediate environment or wider, we are in danger of upsetting the balance of reality. We are attempting to twist it out of shape so that it conforms to our wishes, even though we have no guaranteed vision of what the universe really needs.

Arrogance is a vice detested in others but often invisible in ourselves. It has been defined as "the proud, lordly bearing arising from a consciousness of real or supposed superiority."[39] It is the attitude most commonly derided in politicians, but it is even more ridiculous in those whose authority is minimal. Arrogance is an attempt to usurp the prestige and authority of God and, as such, cannot abide any who give precedence to God's word over its own pretentious claims. Those who observe God's law are, therefore, to be regarded as enemies and every effort must be made to reduce their influence, by scorn and contempt on the one hand and, on the other, by violence. This means that any who commit themselves to living in accordance with God's word can expect resistance. Even in nominally religious communities, there will be those who arrogate to themselves an authority which is not theirs, and they will always seek to inhibit any who give priority to God. The example of the prophets confirms this.

The psalm repeatedly sings the praises of those who are obedient to God's law, not through submission to external constraint, but stemming from a deep, inner conviction. This is a source of delight, certain guidance in the journey of life, and comfort in times of trouble. But, alas, such people become the targets of those who can countenance no authority but their own. In this case, God's word must become for them a bulwark, a shield, a stronghold—to cite some of the metaphors used in the Bible.

We should never be surprised that those who reject God's authority express their rebellion by hostility and persecution directed at sincere believers. They cannot hurt God, but they can, and often do, inflict pain on those who are God's friends. Such is life.

❧

86   All your commandments are faithful;
   help me; they persecute me without cause.

ASSISTANCE

Asking for assistance and giving it are important components of human existence. In the first place, asking for help is a recognition that our resources are limited. Secondly, it affirms our solidarity with the one to whom the request is made. The degree of comfort which we feel in asking, requesting and receiving help is an indication of the closeness of the relationship.

The fact that we ask help from God is a sign that dependence on God has become part of our personal approach to life. When human help fails, we know that, in some mysterious way, God will come to our assistance. We do not have to prescribe channels by which this help will arrive; that is God's concern. But help will come, whether by removing or reducing the external causes of our trouble, or by bolstering our inward resources so that we are better able to cope with the situation or, maybe, even turn it to some good.

Psalm 70 begins with the petition: "God, come to my help; Lord, hurry to help me" (Ps 70:2). This is a prayer than can be allowed to surface in many of the situations we face in everyday life, as well as in the occasional emergencies that confront us. We may not have to face overt persecution on a daily basis, but there will almost certainly be many occasions when we encounter a negative reaction from someone in our immediate circle. This may sometimes grow into open hostility but, more often, it will take subtler forms: distance, indifference, non-responsiveness, rudeness, contradiction. Sometimes there may be a historical basis for the unfriendliness, but more often its effective cause is a puzzle to us—and we do well not to waste too much time trying to fathom its origins. We can simply regard the difficulty as a reminder of our existential condition and use it as a springboard to strengthen both our relationship with God and our determination not to allow everyday strains to grow into a major fracture.

When we ask God for help we are not praying for vengeance to be wreaked on those who seem opposed to us, but that our own hearts be expanded to make room for a wider acceptance of others who are different. "Let your compassion come and I shall live, for your instruction is my delight" (Ps 119:77). When we enter into the sphere of divine compassion, we begin gradually to become a little less ready to hand down harsh judgments on others. Even when their behavior seems obnoxious to us, we learn to look upon their actions more in pity than in blame. And we try to build or rebuild bridges to span the gap—though sometimes we may have to await a favorable moment to begin construction.

If, through our exposure to the Scriptures, we have been impressed with the assurance of God's faithfulness, perhaps a little of it may have rubbed off on us. Instead of despairing of repairing a broken relationship, we may be inspired to work a little harder to add a few grains of sand to the balance until, in time, it tips over and a measure of harmony is restored.

87   They almost brought me to an end on earth,
       but I did not forsake your precepts.

ALMOST

The spiritual journey is not one of unimpeded progress. The road is winding, there are steep ascents and dangerous downward passages. Attractive deviations continue to present themselves which lead nowhere and will eventually require a weary reversal of course. As a result, we are prone to becoming discouraged and disheartened, especially when every step requires a major effort. Looking back, we have to acknowledge that there were times when we almost gave up hope and abandoned our spiritual quest in pursuit of an easier life. Almost. However precariously, we stayed the course.

The delicate thread that guided us out of the labyrinth created both by our conflicting inner desires and by the vagaries of the world in which we live, was our remembrance of God's promise to accompany us on our journey. This is an indication of how important it is for us to reciprocate by turning our attention to this presence and allowing ourselves to be guided and encouraged.

Here it is important that we develop a sense of proportion. When life delivers experiences which are contrary to our preferences and expectations we easily become upset. More often than not the degree of our disturbance is much greater than the situation warrants. Sometimes we are not really reacting to the triggering event, but using it as a surrogate for more deep-seated sources of resentment. A misplaced item, a misspoken word, a momentary delay, can occasion a wrathful tirade that is out of all proportion to its supposed cause—because the complaint is really against life as a whole. Those who are burdened with an unboundaried sense of grievance are continually brought to the brink of total breakdown by a sequence of trivial misunderstandings. They have forgotten God; that is why all this is happening.

By making room in our life for encountering God and for paying attention to God's word, this spiritual search serves as a counterbalance for the many irritants than can undermine daily life. This is not to deny that bad things happen, or that sometimes other people are blameworthy, but it is to take charge of our own perspective on life and not allow it to be distorted by the normal frictions of everyday existence. If this is true regarding small matters, how much more important it is, when confronted by a major crisis that threatens to derail everything we have tried to achieve in life, that we take time to reorient ourselves. To re-assert our fundamental relationship with God and endeavor to relocate the crisis within the context of that relationship. This will probably involve not only going deeper into ourselves but, also, plunging more profoundly into God's self-revelation. We will probably experience for ourselves that it is only when we move closer to the truth that we begin to experience some sense of liberation.

Even when objectively grave afflictions strike us, we will find that remembering what we have learned from our lifelong instruction by God's word, will protect us from disaster and sow the seeds of new hope in our hearts. When we are almost ready to succumb, it is this remembrance that saves us.

88   Give me life, according to your kindness,
     and I will keep the testimony of your mouth.

LIFE-GIVING

We are all happy to be the beneficiaries of another's kindness. Usually it implies some degree of recognition, acceptance and affection. And these are responses of which we can never get enough. To be seen and loved as we are, gives us the courage to step forward boldly and be ourselves; there is no need for us to shrink back or hide because we fear rejection. The love of others is life-giving for us.

If it happens that we are faithful in observing God's law, this is not wholly due to our own meritorious choices. It is usually because we feel comfortable living in its context. It assists us in being true to ourselves and in being helpful to others. Slowly, as the self is moved away from the center of our existence, new priorities develop that allow us to live more in harmony with those around us and more fully in accordance with our own deepest aspirations. Taking God's law to heart is life-giving; it endows all that we do with a lightness and liveliness that follows the de-centering of self.

Part of the dynamic in such a process is that God's law is no longer perceived as inscribed on tablets of stone or in the even harder hearts of legalists. It is a word spoken directly to us by the mouth of God. It is not a matter of juridical obligations handed down by a third party, but a new sense of what is right which follows our encounter with God. Drinking in God's presence gives us a new set of standards by which the value of different modes of human behavior may be assessed. A change of outlook occurs. It is not the imposition of a mass of external regulations, but the dawning of a new realization about right and wrong, good and evil. We may, if we are so inclined, codify our conclusions, but we will soon discover that written injunctions are insufficiently dynamic to energize us to carry them out. They remain outside us, a burden to be endured.

When we have experienced for ourselves something of the goodness and kindness of God, then the testimonies of God begin to make sense—just as they are foolish or scandalous for those as yet untouched by the divine self-revelation. We are not only to embrace what has been revealed to us, we are also to embody it, as it were, to make the message visible and so to pass it on to those around us. Not necessarily by preaching, but preferably by the way we meet others and respond to them; offering them the recognition, acceptance and affection that we ourselves love to receive.

The liveliness that God's kindness instills in us is expressed, above all, in our kindness to others. As we read in another psalm: "Blessed are the ones who attend to the weak. In the evil day, the Lord will deliver them. The Lord will keep them, give them life, and make them blessed in the land, and not give them up to the desire of their enemies. The Lord will sustain them on their bed of sickness; and restore then to health from their bed of illness" (Ps 41:2-4).

Being kind to others ensures that we will ourselves continue to be enlivened by our experience of the kindness of God.

89   For ever, O Lord,
        your word stands firm in heaven.

FOREVER

Semper fidelis. Forever faithful. This is the unlikely motto chosen by all kinds of organizations. Needless to say, it is aspirational rather than descriptive. Our experience of time is limited to the present and to the remembered past; we can have no certainty about what the future will bring. Future fidelity will likely depend on the magnitude of threats that beset it. While these are unknown, any commitment to remain forever faithful is precarious. At least for human beings.

For God the situation is different. Because God exists in an eternal and changeless present, neither the being of God nor any divine activity is subject to fluctuation. Everything God does is an unqualified expression of what God is; it is not subject to outside influence, nor is it modified by the situations in which God intervenes. God's kindness and faithfulness are absolutely stable, even though their effects in human affairs are sensitive to the changes in the world limited to space and time.

Forever does not mean static, just as *semper fidelis* does not mean *semper idem* (always the same). Rather, it is an indication of constancy in responding to changing circumstances. In other words, fidelity raises the prospect of ongoing change. To be forever faithful means being forever fresh; it is not the stale living out of past commitments, but a lively gift of oneself to the ever-changing present. There is no nostalgia in real faithfulness, no regret about change, but always an athletic keeping pace with whatever evolves.

It is by God's ever-changing faithfulness that we are accompanied in our spiritual journey. There is nothing we can do to separate ourselves from the divine presence. We may close our consciousness to it, but it remains; all we achieve is to distance ourselves from reality. In the same way, God's self-revelation is always a word that is apt for the season through which we are passing. What we read today speaks to us of today; the words on the page mysteriously change shape to suit our present circumstances—if we are willing to attune the ears of the heart to catch its accents.

Earth is often viewed as a place of ongoing change, an ever-flowing river or a roiling sea. Apart from death, the certainties of life are few. What this present psalm keeps reminding us is that God's self-revelation, conveyed to us through the Scriptures, is a source of wisdom and guidance on which we can rely. Twenty-one times in the psalms the Lord is referred to as a rock; something unmoving in the midst of fast-flowing currents; something onto which we can hold to prevent our being swept away. God is our refuge, a source of safety.

If we frequent God's word, then something of the stability of God's faithfulness will begin to manifest itself in our lives. It will impart a steadiness which will enable us to keep moving forward without losing the balance of our steps or of our thoughts. God's steadfast faithfulness will give to our aspiration to be forever faithful a chance of becoming a reality.

90　　Your faithfulness is from generation to generation
　　　like the earth you made, it stands firm.

GENERATIONS

It is easy to underestimate our indebtedness to our ancestors; most of them are dead and cannot complain. It is from them that we have received the genetic and epigenetic elements that have determined so much of our temperament and talent. If they had lived different lives, we would never have come into being. We are the result of thousands of choices made by the persons who have gone before us. And even though we share our genes with a large portion of the human race—and indeed with the animal kingdom—the specific combination of elements is unique. The genomes of even identical (or monozygotic) twins are not perfectly identical. We are all different, and even the differences are the gift of our ancestors.

On a more visible level, we have inherited cultural elements from those who preceded us. Ways of understanding the world around us, memories and connections, skills for dealing with recurrent issues are often handed down from one generation to the next in such a way that what we receive seems self-evident. When it comes to forms of religion, these also are largely what we receive from others and at least some of them are tribal or ancestral.

Our convictions about the faithfulness of God are a conclusion that comes from reviewing the instances in which this has been manifest. Faith is enriched, as Deuteronomy admonishes, by remembering the wonderful things God has done on our behalf, not permitting our consciousness to be swamped by the urgent onrush of current concerns, but taking a step back and allowing our purview to include the remembrance of times past.

This is what the Scriptures do for us; they relate instances in which the steadfast love of God is revealed beyond the expectations of those involved. From them it becomes possible to infer that faithfulness belongs to the very nature of God. It is especially when, in our own lives, the going is rough and the outcomes doubtful, that we need to bring to mind the reality that God's faithfulness has been verified from generation to generation and will certainly see us through whatever crisis we are presently meeting.

As a metaphor for God's trustworthiness, the psalmist points to the earth beneath our feet. Although we know that it is whizzing through space and rotating on its axis, in ancient times it was thought to be as steady as a rock. All sorts of things were taking place on the face of the earth, wars, rumors of wars, the rise and fall of empires, but underneath the earth was unmoved and unchanging. It has stood firm and will stand firm forever. Such is God's faithfulness.

"Lord you have been a refuge for us from generation to generation. Before the mountains were born, or the earth or the world brought forth, from age to age you are God" (Ps 90:2). All things are changing; God never changes.

91   Until today your judgments have stood firm,
       for all things are your servants.

SERVICE

Everything that happens is at the divine disposition. Nothing occurs by chance. What is unexpected is so only because of the limitations of our knowledge. This is not to say that there is no scope for free will to determine the outcome of some events, but what seem to us spontaneous choices are often predictable enough if all the evidence can be reviewed. In asserting the absolute faithfulness of God, the psalmist invites us to search out a reality that is deeper than mere appearances. We are asked to accept that everything that happens on earth is ultimately at God's behest.

It is easy to sing that the heavens tell the story of God's glory (Ps 19:2). It is easy to see the whole of creation following the mandate God has given: sun and moon, rain, clouds, winds, seas, rivers, wild asses, cattle, trees, birds, storks, goats, rabbits, sea-monsters and the rest, just as Psalm 104 celebrates. Everything that has existence is at God's service. Yet, when it comes to events that have an immediate impact on ourselves, we are hesitant to make the same assertion. We seem to have come to the conclusion that much of what happens to us escapes God's control and is somehow outside the orbit of divine providence.

This is where we need to shake off the unthinking conclusion that God is a mere spectator in the events of human history. Surely the narratives of the Old Testament paint a different picture. God is shown to be ever-watchful over our world and ever-mindful of what takes place even in the secret depths of our hearts, as Psalm 139 attests. The fact that events are incomprehensible to us does not mean that they are outside God's foreknowledge or beyond God's power to control. We are transposing our own limitations onto God, and the result is that we are led to mistaken conclusions.

God has more than a decorative function in our universe, is more than a kind of surrogate for any gaps in our knowledge or competence. God is Master of the universe; all beings are God's servants. That includes us. For us to fit in smoothly with the rest of creation involves our relinquishing any delusions of imposing our own preferences on reality, and learning to live in accordance with the natural laws embodied in every existent being. It calls us to a vast respect for the entire creation, especially for living things. We are stewards and not masters. The earth belongs to God, and to God we are responsible for the impact of our actions.

Our sincere service of God depends, in no small part, on our willingness to accept that God's providence rules over the universe and that—whatever its immediate causality—God is Master as much of human history as of the rhythms of the visible world. This demands that we take the step of accepting that what happens in our own lives is enfolded within the context of the benignity and faithfulness of God. If we cannot perceive this, it is because our powers of perception are limited and, perhaps, perverse. God's domain belongs to God and we, like the rest of creation, are merely God's servants; the sooner we accept this truth, the happier we will be.

✦

92   If your instruction were not my delight,
       I would have perished in my affliction.

PAIN

In Latin the noun *dolor* can cover all the territory between physical pain, grief, sadness, anguish, interior suffering and even compassion. In reflecting on this dolorous continuum, we soon come to the conclusion that all these manifestations are interconnected. Pain which seems to be merely external has the capacity to upset concentration and our emotional equilibrium. Psychological distress easily translates into psychosomatic illness. Pain is not isolated; usually it is the whole person who suffers, whatever be the origin of the malaise.

When the book of Job asserts that "the life of the human on earth is hard durance" (Job 7:1), the metaphor being used mainly refers to prolonged military service, subject as it is to enforced labor and deadly danger. It may be a dark vision of human reality, but it serves as a good reminder that none of us is able to escape suffering, be we ever so richly endowed or highly esteemed. And while it is true that some individuals seem to have a charmed existence and are the object of our envy, if we penetrate more deeply into their lives, we would soon discover that this insouciant ease is more appearance than reality. There is none of us who does not have a burden to carry, even though we may attempt to conceal our troubles from those around us.

Suffering, however, is not the whole story. Human life is marked by alternation. We pass through seasons of growth and fruitfulness and we also have to endure bare and barren seasons that seem closer to death than to life. It is in these hard times that we have to discover sources of consolation and strength. If we are frequenters of God's word then we will have built up a conviction of God's loving concern for us that will help us to locate the negativity in a broader context, and perhaps offset some of the mental confusion that suffering often engenders.

The Scriptures reveal to us that the path of God's people through history has not been smooth and unopposed. Quite the contrary. It was a journey that was marked by all kinds of unspeakable sufferings: war, defeat, betrayal, exile, persecution, mockery, scorn and contempt. Nor did the people respond to their difficulties in an exemplary manner. Even the most significant figures among them like Moses and David failed in their confidence in God, and among the population as a whole there was—apart from a lowly remnant—a recurrent tendency to seek other more accessible gods. This panoramic faithlessness is, however, only one side of the story. Set against human frailty is God's undeviating fidelity to the promises made to the Patriarchs and repeatedly renewed. God's faithfulness is not dependent on anything we do or omit to do. It flows directly from the heart of God.

These sufferings that we endure must not distract us from our fundamental faith that God is leading us to a conclusion so glorious that it will make our present affliction seem slight and transitory. But not yet. For the moment, with God's help, we must endure without losing the hope that the kindness of God will, in the end, remodel our pain into something good.

93   I will not ever forget your precepts,
        because in them you give me life.

FORGETFULNESS

On the road to disaster the downward slope begins with inattention. This is not only the effect of drowsiness, whereby many of our organs of perception are progressively shut down. More often it is the result of selective attention: our attention slips away from what is necessary and wanders into other areas which are more entertaining. Ultimately this is something that we choose to do, though habit may well diminish the visibility involved in switching off and turning to something else.

In fact, it seems that many of us spend most of our time flying on auto-pilot. Our capacious brains need to be able to stem the onrush of data and, so, unless something out of the ordinary is happening, our actions are governed by what is termed the "default mode network"—a coalition of regions of the brain that operates on the principle from Ecclesiastes that "there is nothing new under the sun." It is committed to the continuance of business as usual. With the help of this network we can drive on our regular route from our home to the city with scarcely a thought about navigating or how to operate the car. If there is an unexpected detour we are mildly uncomfortable and—as it were—wake up. Suddenly, we have to pay attention. But mostly, the auto-pilot does the driving.

At least for some of us, or for some of the time, living our lives under the direction of the default mode network seems like a desirable prospect. We never have to think, to weigh options in a balance, or make compromises. We trundle through life with nary a thought. We don't want to be disturbed. And as a result, we become the plaything of external influences. We are not really living our own life responsibly, just letting it happen.

It is a bold step to decide that we want to move away from forgetfulness and live more mindfully. Mindfulness admits of degrees: sometimes our concentration is intense, sometimes it is relaxed and diffuse. It is not possible to live in unbroken mindfulness—in that case we would never sleep. Besides, we need occasional recreation, so that our poor little brains do not burst from being overfed or tire themselves out from being constantly focused. However, if we are wise, we will recognize the need to pay more attention in certain circumstances and, in addition, to undertake regular reviews of our life to ensure that our fundamental priorities are being generally implemented.

Experience will probably reveal to us that we cannot rely solely on ourselves to check whether blind spots exist. We need to measure ourselves against some kind of external agency that has the power to reveal where our noblest dreams are not receiving sufficient attention. A wise and understanding counselor can be a help, but so too can regular and diligent exposure to God's word. The habit of mindfully encountering the Scriptures can be a non-threatening means of recognizing areas of potential growth. Dealing with these adds to the level of liveliness in our lives, which is a blessing not only for ourselves, but also for those around us.

✦

94   I am yours; save me;
      for I am searching your precepts.

SEARCHING

What gives us the right to claim that we belong to God? Surely it is by living in the context of God's word. If we shape our lives around God's self-revelation, then it is obvious that we will begin to develop a certain family resemblance. Created as we were to be images of God, our fulfilment comes about when we allow the likeness to God to develop in us. To say this in another way: we were made to be icons of God to an unbelieving world.

This is not an instantaneous transformation. Change in us is effected only after many years of diligent searching and gradual finding. The complete word of God is not revealed to us in a flash. Nor does it instantly communicate to us comprehensive answers to all our questions. Its purpose is to leave us wondering and wanting more. God's word presents itself to us as an invitation to go deeper. It is like the burning bush that attracted Moses and bade him approach. There is a certain trepidation, since we do not know what demands this encounter will make of us, but there is also a desire to go deeper. So, we pluck up our courage and say with the boy Samuel, "Speak, Lord, for your servant is listening."

The problem with fundamentalism is that it seeks quick, unequivocal answers. Yet, this is not the way that revelation works. Authentic revelation leaves us with questions that invite us to continue searching. Questions about God's ways upon earth. Questions about ourselves. If you consider some of the more provocative books of the Bible, like Job and Ecclesiastes, you will probably come to the conclusion that their method of leading us to wisdom is to lead us to ask more questions. And they did not supply the answers. They wanted us to develop a certain restlessness of mind that is dissatisfied with conventional and convenient propositions, so that we might begin to search and to find solutions to the great problems of life by reflecting more deeply within the context of our own experience.

The answers that our searching yields, arrive within the context of our own life's experience. In some mysterious way, reflecting on our everyday experience in the light of revelation, gives us an insight into wider and deeper realities. Like little children, we have to keep asking questions to which there is no immediate answer. In fact, a large part of wisdom is recognizing the limitations of our knowledge and our intellectual gaucheness in dealing with matters of ultimate meaning.

This is why wisdom manifests itself through humility. When we evacuate self from the center of our being we make room for wisdom. We make room for God. Humility teaches us that we are not masters of our own destiny, nor can we control what happens around us. The most that we can ask of ourselves is that we take each day and each moment as it comes, and seek to find a life-giving path. We do not have the security of being able endlessly to recycle the solutions of yesterday, we must keep searching. If we do, then we will discover for ourselves that the joy of finding far outweighs anything we invested in searching. Being saved is a gift that keeps being given and never grows stale.

95   While the wicked hope to bring me to nothing,
        I gained insight from your testimonies.

REJECTION

Often it is not easy to know why some people consistently manifest negative feelings toward us. We scrutinize our past conduct in their regard and can locate nothing important that seems to justify their attitude. And, while it is true that usually we are not fully aware of the extent of our complicity in our rejection by others, let us suppose, for the moment, that the negativity is all on the part of others. Is it merely a matter of differences in background, culture, style, opinion? Probably not. More often it is a question of subterranean envy. Something about us plugs into an ongoing grievance in the other person, so that we seem to be in confident and unchallenged possession of something that the other lacks: education, esteem, freedom, friends, glamor, good looks, reputation. The thing about envy is that it does not draw its energy from the target who is supposed to possess these benefits in abundance. Its power comes from an inner resentment that is more connected to the way such people feel about themselves than to any supposed quality in the target. Envy is self-rejection projected onto others. There is little victims can do to shield themselves from its malice.

Like everything else in life, being the target for someone else's negativity can be used for our advantage. Instead of labelling the other as a wicked person or an enemy, and building up a mental case to support their condemnation, we can reflect more calmly and more deeply on what is happening.

In the first place, we must avoid replicating the other's behavior by attaching this present rejection to our store of hurtful memories, and then implicating the other person in our pain. It is best not to be too quick in labeling them as "wicked" or "disturbed."

Secondly, we can be reasonably sure that the rejection says more about them than about us. When someone is rejected because of their race, gender, or appearance, it is the one who rejects who deserves blame. Or, perhaps, pity, because unreasonable antipathies always have their origin deep inside. Strong emotions derive their power from bad experiences. If we were to learn about these then, perhaps, we would be kinder and more understanding, even though we are still hurt by the rejection. What we see is never the whole story. In human affairs, it is always wise to be somewhat tentative in our conclusions.

Thirdly, when others turn up their noses at us, it is time for us to consolidate our own sense of worth and identity. We can listen to their complaints and, perhaps, accept that there is truth in them. But we do not have to acquiesce in their conclusions—that we are worthless, unworthy of their consideration or care. For us to continue steadfast in the face of widespread opposition, we need to have allowed our relationship with God to grow—through serious time allocated to pondering God's word and finding in it a language of prayer that echoes in our hearts. If we have frequented the Scriptures when life was relatively easy, they will come to our assistance when times are difficult.

96   I have seen that there is a limit to every achievement,
      but your commandment is exceeding wide.

BOUNDLESS

The psalms invite us to inhabit two distinct zones: the everyday world of space and time and the spiritual realm, where God exists, beyond every limitation. Juggling these two modes of existence within our consciousness is one of the skills we need to acquire if we are to maintain our focus during the spiritual journey.

We live in a world where "here" and "there" do not coincide, where things are composed of mutually exclusive parts, where moment follows moment only to be lost forever. Our minds have evolved in such a way that we are able to survive and thrive in a world that has too many holes in it for us to make perfect sense of it. We approach life in a workmanlike way, do our best to make the most of it, and don't ask too many unanswerable questions. All of this is good, but it does not equip us to explore the very different state of existence that pervades the spiritual realm.

To say that God is the ultimate Other sounds abstract and metaphysical, and so it is. However, the fact remains that it is easier for us to know what God is not, than to know what God is. We may say that God is not in this place, or at this time; God has no color or gender, but that is only half the story. The other half is this: not being in any particular place or time is not an absence because God is permanently present at all points of the spatio-temporal continuum. God has no particular color or gender because everything that colors and genders bestow is eminently present in God. To say that God lacks our particularities is to affirm the utter boundlessness of God. It is not a limitation. We cannot know God directly because our intellects are designed to deal only with finite data. And while it is true that the wise are able to extract from that limited source some indication of what is beyond, we are still unable to perceive God directly.

What we can do, however, is to contemplate the acts of God and to infer from them something of God's nature. This is where the Scriptures come to rescue us from total ignorance. By recounting the narratives in which God's interventions in human history are revealed, they offer us an indirect way of learning about God. The sacred authors perceive a pattern in God's dealings with humanity and this has shaped what they have written. If we devote ourselves to reading not only the text, but between the lines, we begin to build up for ourselves some shadowy notion of God's nature, we begin to appreciate that God's attitude to us is full of tenderness, that God is compassionate to all that has been created.

There is a complementary channel by which we can learn about God and that is by reflecting on our own experience. To the extent that we become spiritually literate and are able to read the subtle variations in our relationship with God, not only do we develop a personal approach to the mystery of God, but we become more aware of the ways in which we can conform our own lives to what we have learned. This is how our conscience is formed.

Because our world is located within the spiritual realm and not outside it, we can never really comprehend what is happening around us unless we take its broader context into consideration.

97   How I love your instruction!
        I ponder it all day long.

SYMBOLIC

The claim to spend the whole day pondering the Torah is likely an exaggeration, but it does give us a hint about the nature of the Torah. As long as we think of the Torah as law, daylong pondering makes no sense at all. Good law is brief, clear and unambiguous. It does not ask to be pondered, but merely to be put into practice. God's instruction is not like that. It yields its full richness only when it interacts with the changing cavalcade of life; we discover more of its meaning when it is viewed from different vantage points. What was unclear to us at one stage of our life, often becomes obvious later.

There is something else about revelation that often frustrates contemporary readers. Its meaning is not always obvious. This obscurity is not only the consequence of being written thousands of years ago in languages of which most of us are ignorant; it derives from the style of communication that revelation often uses for its most significant messages. Ultimate mystery cannot be conveyed in language formed to deal with the trivialities of daily life. Therefore, it makes use of a symbolic language which attempts to communicate more than it expresses.

Especially in the writings of the prophets you will find an abundance of metaphors, not all of them compatible. They purpose is not the transmission of a straightforward message. The aim is to make people think, to puzzle things out for themselves. To fret about the meaning of a message until something clicks and it begins to make some sense. It is the process that is important. Lazy minds are set to work. The people are pushed into drawing their own conclusions.

Think of the fantastical stories of Jonah and Job. They are pedagogical narratives meant to lead readers to arrive at a moral insight, whether it be the importance of obedience to the call of God or the encouragement to remain steadfast in times of suffering. They are not stories about other people; they are about us—if we choose to listen carefully.

Symbolic language is an invitation to reflection.[40] Reflection allows us to blend what we read in the text with what we have learned through our experience, so that we are able to arrive at a unique understanding of what the text means for us in our present circumstances. It expects us to make use of the intuitive right hemisphere of the brain to arrive at a conclusion rather than to go through a process of logical deduction. The same text will often yield different meanings to different people in accordance with their circumstances: different but not incompatible.

Musing on the word of God throughout the day is profitable because it enables us to unearth different nuances in the text which relate to the situations we encounter and the thoughts that are passing through our minds. Such pondering may not be a daylong activity, but it can take place at any time without forethought or planning. It acts as an interior prompting suggesting a line of thought and, perhaps, opening new avenues of possibility.

98   Your commandment makes me wiser than my enemies,
       for it is always with me.

PRACTICALITY

One of the gifts brought by fidelity to God's word is an enhanced capacity to deal with reality, irrespective of whether it seems favorable or oppressive. The verse does not say that such devotion makes me smarter than my enemies, clearly it does not. But it gives me the capacity to make the most out of what befalls, including what happens as the result of hostile intent on the part of those perceived to be enemies.

Wisdom is often associated with old age and white hair. Young people are generally more active intellectually, open to new ideas and ready to pursue unexplored pathways. As we grow older we usually become less radically innovative, but we reap the harvest of experience; we see things from a longer perspective and in a broader context, and as a result we often perceive connections that are unnoticed by those who are, perhaps, more intellectually agile. Slowing down has its advantages: it enables us to pay more attention to the landscape through which we are passing. This, in its turn, provides the possibility of our seeing opportunities which are not visible to those who pass by at high speed.

The fact is that most situations are more complex than first impressions reveal. Dealing adeptly with a challenging situation is often just a matter of stepping back and surveying the landscape, with a view to increasing the number of available options. Speedy decisions are usually based on the most blatantly obvious possibilities. Taking time to look at issues from different angles not only reveals alternatives, it also gives us time to summon our interior resources. If the quality of our life depends on the choices we make, then it is important that we give less emphasis to speedy conclusions and pay more attention to considering options from different perspectives.

If the word of God is truly our guide, we will develop a confidence that no situation will present itself in which we will be totally confused. We will be less inclined to set aside reality in favor of a delusion if there is some a consistent effort made to embrace a broader truth. To live in the context of what God has revealed gives us a truer picture of what we are meant to be, not only as members of the human race, but also as unique embodiments that somehow image God.

This reliance on God's word will, no doubt, be baffling and frustrating to any who might plot our downfall—whether in major matters or in frivolities. Supposing, of course, that there really are enemies out there! But the thing that will enable us to withstand indifference, antipathy and active hostility is our sense of who we are and what we are called to become. This will, no doubt, be a source of irritation to those who wish to control our destiny and shape our lives to suit their preferences. As a result, this may be a source of occasional hardship for us, but our first fidelity must always be to God which embraces fidelity to ourselves—for they are almost the same thing. Following God's commandment is always wiser than allowing ourselves to conform to the intrusive expectations of those who do not really have our best interests at heart.

99   I understand better than those who would teach me,
       because I ponder your testimonies.

ALTERNATIVES

When different people are exposed to a body of evidence, they often arrive at different conclusions. Inevitably, all of those involved believe that only their own conclusions are correct. Stalemates often happen because people do not always advert to the fact that the conclusions we reach are often no more than reflections of the assumptions we have fed into the process. Another word for "assumptions" is "prejudices." When we carry private prejudgments into a discussion, any creative consensus is doomed. The likely fund of knowledge that each brings to the interpretation of common experience makes a common assessment of issues and responses unlikely unless more effort is invested in identifying and reconciling hidden differences.

This is why the opinion seemingly expressed in this verse by the psalmist seems dangerous to me. We are too easily convinced that we know better than others, including those who are our instructors. Whereas we may, as teachers, encourage students to arrive at new theories on the basis of their little knowledge, this does not mean that students have the right to claim infallibility for their quickly cobbled conclusions. Truth is invariably complex in its simplicity; it takes time to unravel its various strands to arrive at its kernel. This means that we need to develop the patience to listen to alternative and maybe conflicting interpretations of reality in order to gain some level of certainty. Usually there is something of truth in what people say. However, it is always a mistake to assume that a part is identical with the whole.

Many intelligent people with wide experience and competent judgment are ready to admit that they do not know everything, and offer their conclusions tentatively. Absolute certainty is claimed only by fools. Think how many scientific "certainties" have been overturned in the course of the centuries, and what an upheaval followed when discredited theories were ejected—even when the evidence against them was overwhelming. We may find the same thing happening with ourselves. Many of the strongly held tribal beliefs that we inherited unthinkingly need to be subjected to adult assessment and, at least some of them, need to be discarded. Not because they are necessarily harmful, but because, as long as they are unexamined, they invisibly influence the way we interpret what happens around us, and we are unaware that we are shepherded in a particular direction.

There is always a delicate balance to be maintained between our personal opinions and what is commonly accepted by others. It is really a matter of humility. If what I hold to be true is correct, then an assessment of the alternatives will be enriching. It may prove that my assumptions were justified. Or more often, it will invite me to nuance my previously held beliefs by taking note of how others perceive matters. Doggedly closing my eyes and clinging to what I have always held will be of no benefit at all. Sometimes I will be compelled to admit that my previous conclusion was simply wrong. Thank God for that!

Perhaps in this era when false certainties abound, I am reacting too strongly to what the psalmist says. Maybe he is using poetic hyperbole, exaggerating the social benefits of dedication to the word of God, merely saying that meditating quietly on God's word under "the oaks and the beeches" yields more fruit than attending high-powered lectures that sail over our heads and do not connect to daily experience. What do you think?

100   I have gained more understanding than the elders
      since I have observed your precepts.

MORE

This is the third time in as many verses that the psalmist is claiming to have a superior form of knowledge; more than that possessed by enemies, teachers, and elders. At least part of the reason for this is that this alphabetical psalm has reached the letter *mem*; and it happens that the use of *mem* is a standard way of making a comparison. Maybe the psalmist is merely saying that devotion to the word of God is such a source of illumination that it transcends every human form of knowledge or instruction.

To appreciate what is being said here, it is worth remembering that the knowledge communicated by the Scriptures is qualitatively different from that which we gather by everyday observation and scientific investigation. We do not expect the Scriptures to provide us with facts, as books may do and, sometimes, newspapers.

Reading the Bible is not entertainment or information-gathering; it is activating a relationship. We go to the Scriptures to encounter God, and whatever enrichment results from that meeting is of a different order to everyday forms of knowledge.

More than that; when we put ourselves at the behest of the word of God, the sacred text itself seems to become active. It is not just something we read, but something that works upon us, creating echoes in our conscience, indications of how we are to find the road to a more abundant life. "Whether you turn to the right or to the left you will hear these words behind you: 'This is the way; follow it'" (Isa 30:21). There is a mysterious agency at work, summoning us to conversion in much the same way as the ancient prophets called the people to repent of their ways and turn back to the Lord. It can sometimes have a dramatic impact, but more often it is subtle, nudging us away from closed habits of thought and action, and catching our attention with the glimmer of something different.

The best indication that we are hearing the voice of God and not just responding to some internal process of our own, is that we become aware of an energy for change. This may be an uncomfortable experience, but there is a hidden sweetness within it. Most of us would prefer to continue living our lives as we have arranged them; we do not particularly want to have our plans interrupted. We like things to remain as they are. Even the faintest suggestion of an alternative future arouses in us a thousand contrary reasons. We say to ourselves: "It is better to change nothing, to do nothing. At least for the time being." But, take note. When we become aware of a storm of resistance brewing within us, we can be reasonably sure that God is speaking and, like Jonah, we are running away.

If we allow it, this source of admonishment will be our constant companion. We do not have to search for it; it will find us. "The commandment that I command you today is not too difficult for you, nor is it beyond your reach. It is not up in the sky that you should say: 'Who will go up into the sky and fetch it for us so that we may hear it and implement it?' It is not across the seas that you should say: 'Who will cross the seas and fetch it for us so that we may hear it and implement it?' No. The word is very close to you. It is in your mouth and in your heart to be implemented" (Deut 30:11-14).

101   I hold back my feet from every evil path,
        because I keep your word.

AND

It has been said that the bulk of moral teaching is contained in the verse of another psalm: "Turn aside from evil and do good" (Ps 34:15). Although it does not specify what is "evil" and what is "good" it does serve as a reminder that the task of moral living is twofold. On the one hand, it involves discipline. We must learn to restrain those tendencies and passions in us that yield a negative outcome: on ourselves, on others, on the world around us. Obviously, this is very important, but the avoidance of murder, adultery and theft is not the whole of our moral task. We are also obliged to be active and do good, to avoid the hidden sin of omission. This is more difficult because the good that we do cannot be seen until it is done; yet a judgment is required before we act. Because we were formed in the image of the Creator, our natural responsibility is to be creative, to continue the work of enhancing created reality with our unique contribution. We are supposed to leave the world a better place than it was when we arrived in it. Our contribution may not be stupendous but, in our own little way, we are called to make a difference—especially in our immediate environment.

The key word in the injunction "Turn aside from evil and do good" is "and." It is the combination that counts. Some people are proficient in avoiding evil, but their lives can end up being constricted and constrained, and their level of enjoyment minimal.

They are seen to be very good people because they do not do many bad things, but they are not much fun to be around. And sometimes the resentment they feel at having to be so careful about their own actions leads them to become resentful at the apparent freedom of others and, as a consequence, they may become harsh and judgmental.

On the other hand, there are people who are very creative in some area or another. They love to express their uniqueness as fully as possible, in their manner of acting and in what they produce. Regrettably, we have come to take it for granted that the energy they expend in self-expression will probably result in a somewhat eccentric lifestyle—sometimes so extreme that their life becomes dissipated and self-destructive. The greater the brilliance, the deeper the shadow formed in its light.

This is why those who are wise admonish us to be moderate in our self-discipline *and* moderate in our self-expression. We are called to a balancing act, but the balance is not achieved in every action at every moment. We can't spend our lifetime trying to calculate the exact median point between duty and fun. Perhaps we should aim simply at ensuring a general balance in our days and weeks. Sometimes equilibrium is worked out in the long term. We may pass through seasons in which we are obliged to undertake too much work, but when the necessity passes we need to take care to recuperate, to recover our strength, to allow the suppressed bubbles of creativity to rise from the depths; to recover a sense of lightness and fun. Likewise our moments of relaxation need to be checked lest we become addicted to diversion and entertainment and never exert ourselves to do the good of which we are capable.

Holding back my feet from evil paths is most likely to be effective if I make an equal effort to fill my life with what is good, true and wholesome. A great help in arriving at this balance is found when I open myself to God's word.

102   I have not swerved from your judgments
        since you yourself have instructed me.

INTERIORITY

The interaction of inner and outer worlds plays itself out in every human life. Alongside the visible and tangible influences to which people are subject, there is always a parallel process occurring within them which contributes as much, if not more, to the choices they make. This means that we can never pass a definitive judgment on another's behavior since we do not have access to the hidden forces that motivated the actions. We are limited to what we see and hear. Like an iceberg, much more is underneath the surface.

If this is true of others, it is also true of ourselves. We usually believe that we are in full control of our actions and that the choices we make are sober and responsible. However, it is only rarely that we submit our innate preferences to scrutiny, to ask ourselves why it is that we presume that one course of action is better than another. This is not to suggest that all our spontaneous responses are vitiated. It is simply to make the point that the personal content of what we do can be increased by consciously trying to ascertain why we are inclined to do it.

This leads us to ponder the basic principles by which—consciously or unconsciously—we give shape to our lives. Many of these are communicated to us in the process of growing up: we are strongly formed by our family and by those who accompany us through our early years, especially teachers and friends. Behind all these is the influence of society and its culture which imprints itself so deftly that we do not realize it has happened—until we travel and discover that in other cultures, different value-systems operate.

It is also worthwhile to consider the origin of our religious or spiritual principles. Some of them may have been imprinted on our hearts from outside: they derive from the people who impressed us, the teachers and counselors who have enriched our lives. But, if we search deeply enough, we will probably discover that our strongest spiritual formation has come from deep inside us, some kind of intense experience that may have become submerged through our involvement in other things but which resurfaces at odd moments. It is worthwhile trying to recover our awareness of this inaugural experience. What was it that started us off on our particular journey, inviting us to pursue an attraction, whose source and direction we did not, at first, fully comprehend?

The prophet Jeremiah foretold a future in which God would plant his instruction deep within the hearts of his people, so that there would be no further need of external instruction (Jer 31:33-34). Perhaps this is an exaggeration; we can always profit from what comes to us from the outside, because it often provides shape and context for what we experience inwardly. It can serve as a trigger which activates something inside us. But the fundamental source of our energy for the spiritual pursuit is interior. In a certain sense, as we become more spiritually literate, we can all say to God with the psalmist: "You yourself have instructed me."

Paying attention to this interior instruction is a great help to staying on the track.

103   How sweet to my tongue is your utterance,
       more than honey in the mouth.

STRENGTH

There is a certain truth to be found in the opposite of Samson's riddle (Judg 14:14): Out of sweetness comes strength. In an age that sometimes seems to be saturated with sugar, we sometimes underestimate the importance of the concept of sweetness. It seems like a soft and easy quality without much strength or persistence. To describe someone as being of a sweet disposition seems to suggest that they will be an easy prey for any who choose to impose their will upon them. No politician would want to be described as "sweet."

It is very strange. Nobody would like to be seen by others as "sour" or "bitter." These are the opposites of "sweet." We reserve these adjectives for people whose best qualities have gone rotten, and for those who have allowed toxic attitudes to grow. Most people cannot bear their company. But, strangely, we are reluctant to see sweetness as an attitude to be cultivated. If we think of its component parts: gentleness, pleasantness, courtesy, thoughtfulness, kindness, reasonableness, respectfulness, they are all highly desirable qualities. And they take a strong character and years of determined effort to develop. Harshness is a sign of immaturity and self-centeredness; sweetness bespeaks a mellow altruism that makes room for others.

Social sweetness, if it is genuine, stems from deep inside the person. Those who have tasted for themselves and discovered how good the Lord is (Ps 34:9) develop a different approach to life. In being drawn to the attractiveness of the divine mystery, they are themselves modified by what attracts them. Admiration leads to imitation. The self-revelation of God, in all its manifold forms, lights up the way to a more complete style of humanity than the crude examples offered by many of the rich and famous of our world. Not only are we drawn to follow a different path, but the relative intensity of the experience gives us the fortitude to continue pursuing that path even in the face of mockery, rejection and opposition. Out of sweetness come strength.

It is easy to dismiss interior devotion as mere sentimentality. It does have elements of softness about it, especially at the beginning, but it has a spine of steel. In a way, sweetness could be described as "maternal." Sweetly loving and affectionate and caring, but also determined and strong, willing to deal forcefully with any obstacles that present themselves. It proves itself far more enduring and resilient than abstract or rationalistic forms of religious response. Softness is not always weakness; it is an important component of the flexibility that makes people strong in dealing with a variety of challenges.

If we consumed more honey maybe there would be fewer people who go through life bearing the burden of bitterness. Of course, all of us have to confront negativity, but it is important that we do not allow these bad experiences to determine our dominant attitude. When life gets rough we need to step back and feed on something sweet, remembering the goodness of the Lord and strengthening our faith in God's benign providence. It is from the sweetness we experience in devouring the word of God that we slowly build up our reserves of endurance and our ability to be content even when the situation is less than ideal. Out of sweetness comes strength.

104   From your precepts I gain understanding,
        therefore I shun every way of falsehood.

FALSEHOOD

Truthfulness does not seem to be a high priority in contemporary society. We have come to expect that government announcements will be closer to political propaganda than to objective statements of fact, that media organizations will be both blatantly biased and tainted by commercial interests, and that product descriptions will be no more than self-promoting advertisements. On a more local level, there are probably people in our circle of acquaintances who seem to have developed the knack of seeing only what confirms their long-lasting prejudices, so that with every passing day their unfounded opinions become more entrenched.

Falsehood is more than telling outright lies. It can be expressed by our selection of facts. What we say may be correct as far as it goes, but the total meaning can de distorted by subtraction as well as by addition. If I criticize someone for arriving late to a meeting and fail to mention that the reason for the late-coming was that the person was giving first aid to the victim of a road accident, then the obvious conclusion is unfair. An unbalanced coverage of events through selective reporting is a safe way of communicating falsehood without actually verbalizing it. We lie by omission. And we are aware of instances of where a commercial interest that is threatened by scientific findings will quickly employ other scientists to muddy the waters by contrary assertions.

Scholarly journals regularly submit contributions to a process of peer review. Prestigious periodicals, such as *The New Yorker*, employ teams of fact-checkers to make sure that nothing untrue is printed and perpetuated. Our everyday media undergo no such scrutiny beyond that required to ensure that they cannot be sued for defamation. And in our ordinary conversations there is no defense of truthfulness except the occasional raised eyebrow. And so, more sensible people tend to receive much of what they hear with a grain of salt.

A personal commitment to speaking the truth and a willingness to suspend judgment until all the facts are known, are important components of integrity. This takes courage. The truth is not always comfortable, and it is not always popular. To be committed to the truth may demand something of us, and it may lead to a diminishment in our approval rating. We need to know the source of any certainty we have. If we say that our personal system of beliefs and values is derived from our meditation on God's word, there is one easy way to find out how sound is our confidence: if our reception of God's word challenges us and leads to action, and if it exposes us to scorn, then it is probably valid. If it makes us smugly certain that all our thoughts, words, and deeds are beyond reproach, then it is likely false.

But there is more. Genuine truth is marked by tenderness; it is not harsh or abrasive, even when it challenges. Remember what Aglaya said to Prince Myshkin in Dostoyevsky's novel *The Idiot*: "You have no tenderness: only truth and that's why you're unfair."[41] There is a certain human attractiveness about genuine truthfulness that falsehood or partial truth can never claim.

105   Your word is a lamp for my feet
       and a light for my path.

ILLUMINATION

This beautiful verse is one which is often cited. Images of light provide a feast for our eyes, whether it be a solitary beacon casting its beams over a turbulent sea or the spectacular colors of a dramatic sunrise. For those of us gifted with sight, it is hard to imagine a world without light. Movement is very difficult in total darkness, even if we are in a familiar environment. The gift of vision, along with our other senses, is the means by which we make contact with the world outside ourselves. For most of us, seeing is usually the first step we take to enter into relationships: we see, we are attracted, we approach, we encounter.

God's self-revelation is the means by which we begin to make contact with God. At different times in our lives and through various means God speaks to us. Sometimes God's voice seems to sound in the depths of our being and we are alerted to the existence of the spiritual realm by a sudden and spontaneous sensitivity beyond the borders of our ordinary experience. Sometimes it may be that the light shines out to us through other people who have received the word and embody it in themselves. Sometimes, when our life seems to break open and fall apart, we catch sight of a different reality beyond the ruins of our former existence. And sometimes the word catches us through the words in a book or the words spoken by others. They astonish us because they seem to echo deep inside us and invite us to enter into a more profound mystery. Sometimes we are called to conversion in a single moment; sometimes it builds up slowly and eventually reaches a climax. But, in whatever form it assumes, it is the word that summons us to a new and richer life. It is the word that is a lamp for my feet and a light for my path.

It is good to reflect on this inaugural vision and the power it has exercised over our choices. We should never let it slide from our memory, but invite it to keep lighting up the path before us.

This means that we need to keep returning to drink more from this fountain, not only in times of turmoil and confusion, but on a regular basis. To expose our lives to God's living word. Only rarely will we become conscious of a summons to walk in a new direction. More often what happens is a gradual process of formation which brings us into a greater sensitivity to a particular value to which we may have been inattentive. It is a slow process. Sometimes it takes years before the value rises above the surface of consciousness and begins to be a factor in the choices we make. But the progress is solid because it has been building up over a long period. Fidelity to the word of God gradually changes our lives.

Divine illumination is not without paradox. Gregory of Nyssa in his *Life of Moses* speaks about three phases in our experience. Meeting with God is first marked by illumination: we see things in a new light. From the light, we go to the cloud; we try to embody what we have seen in the choices we make; the light itself seems less brilliant because of the hurly-burly of practical activities. In the final stage we are plunged into darkness. Not the same darkness as at the beginning, but a state in which we no longer rely on external light to guide us, because we have allowed ourselves to become light. This is the state known as "faith." The light has entered into us and transformed us so we no longer seek external light, but we have become light. And others are guided by it. For most of us this stage is still in the future.

106   I have sworn an oath and will fulfil it,
      to keep your righteous judgments.

VOW

If it is true that we ought to be slow to swear an oath for fear that we may forswear ourselves, then making any promise to God is not something to be done lightly. Jepthah's vow which resulted in his having to offer his daughter as a holocaust (Judg 11:30) is one of the most shocking incidents in the Bible. The lesson it imparts is that promises made to God must be kept at all cost. The book of Ecclesiastes makes a similar point. "When you make a vow to God, do not delay paying it, for [God] has no delight in fools. Pay what you have vowed. It is better that you made no vow than that you vowed and did not pay it. Do not allow your mouth to lead your flesh to sin, nor say to the angel, that it was ignorance" (Eccl 5:3-5).

There is no room for playacting in our relationship with God. God is never fooled by any act that we put on. Others may be favorably impressed but, usually, they begin to suspect that something is wrong when the tree does not bear good fruit. The only one who is permanently misled by such antics is the one who performs them, who is led into greater delusion. If we are truly in the presence of God then, under God's penetrating gaze, we will find ourselves unable to continue our self-gratifying charade.

Accordingly, there is an obligation to ensure that our life corresponds to our religious practice. When religious people misbehave, scandal ensues in addition to whatever harm their conduct brings directly. We cannot isolate our relationship with God in a separate compartment of our life. When we enter God's presence we bring with us the residue of our whole life; we must do more than play a role. We must be ourselves. We come before God with all our compromises and failures, as well as with the good fruit that God has enabled us to bear. Our relationship with God is founded on the truth of who we are. To upgrade that relationship, we need to upgrade our life. To make a reality the pious words we utter when we pray.

The judgments of God are righteous; they are fair, unbiased, and utterly truthful. The more time I spend in the presence of God the more I will feel a certain constraint to embrace similar values in the way I live. If you are often in the presence of someone with an elevated sense of fashion, you may well feel inclined to upgrade your own clothes, lest you look bad in comparison. What previously passed muster is no longer good enough. In the same way, spending time with God and meditating on God's word, help us to become a little uncomfortable with the standards by which we live, so that we try to see the world in a different context, to change our habitual assessments and to embrace a more complete view of the reality that surrounds us. And, as the process continues we feel ourselves compelled to do things a little differently. To modify our behavior and, in effect, to be more like God in the choices that we make and in the activities in which we engage.

When our life sings in harmony with our prayers, we are no longer playacting, but we are really fulfilling the vows we have made.

107   Lord, I am badly afflicted;
        by your word give me life.

HONESTY

The more we become accustomed to truthful self-presentation, the easier it is to come before God naked and unashamed. As in the Garden of Eden. The Bible teaches us that God knows the dust of which we are made (Ps 103:18), observed our formation in the womb, and is aware of everything we have ever done (Ps 139:15-16). There is nothing we can hide from God. When we attempt to cover ourselves, it is concealment from our own eyes that we seek. Prayer to God demands a progressive self-honesty; it is hard at first but, with practice, it becomes easier.

In fact, it is a source of great consolation to pour out our troubles to the Lord, compounded as they often are of weakness, failure, disappointment, frustration and rejection by others. Mostly we do not want other people to know about our frailty and so we hide it. However, in the process of concealing our fragility from others we often lose sight of it ourselves. We begin to believe what we want others to believe and, so, begins a slide into delusion. In our assessments of events we fail to give sufficient weight to our own liabilities and, so, more often than not, we project the blame onto others.

To be badly afflicted is not only an indication of objective troubles, it can also include our subjective failure to deal with matters effectively. Every life has its negative moments; part of maturity is learning how to handle these in a way that does not worsen the situation or cause us more pain. This is standard operating procedure. However, there are times when it does not succeed in reducing the hardship we are experiencing. Maybe we are just weary of the struggle. Maybe there is an onrush of conflicting demands just at a time when we are feeling at our lowest ebb. We have all probably experienced moments in which we have felt that what is happening is too much for us.

This is a time to seize any opportunity to step back and do something different. Maybe we should go for a walk on a misty morning and, for a while, move away from the spaces that are causing so much anxiety. To declare to ourselves and before God that we are badly afflicted and not to run away from the fact that we are in serious disarray. When we have calmed down a little it will probably be helpful to take up the word of God and allow ourselves to seek out a different perspective. Probably there will be no lighting flash of inspiration. What happens more usually is a gradual shift in perspective. Often this will take the form of a gentle suggestion pointing out a systemic imbalance in our life: we are attempting to do too much, we are not relying enough on others, we are wasting time on self-indulgent activities, we are neglecting the things that support our resilience. Perhaps we will feel that Jeremiah is speaking directly to us when he writes: "They have abandoned me, the source of fresh water, only to dig cisterns for themselves, cisterns that leak and hold no water" (Jer 2:13).

When we are honest about our difficulties and bring them before the Lord and open our hearts and lives to God's word, the difficulties (plural) do not disappear, but the difficulty (singular) is often reduced.

108   Accept, I pray O Lord, the freewill offering of my mouth,
      and teach me your judgments

OFFERING

In a period when Israel's worship was moving toward emphasiz-ing the centrality of the Torah so that the role of Temple service was becoming secondary, some of the vocabulary associated with sacrificial rites was transposed into a more spiritual context. No doubt this was partly prompted by the prophetic denunciations of inauthentic worship: when interior dispositions did not match the ritualized expressions of piety (Isa 29:13; Jer 12:2; Ezek 33:31). It is as though the service once limited to a priestly caste and to a particular place was universalized. Instead of the grand ceremonial associated with the Temple, believers have only their own broken-ness to bring before the Lord. "You take no delight in sacrifice, and my burnt offering does not please you. So, my sacrifice to God is a broken spirit: O God; you will not despise a broken and humbled heart" (Ps 51:18-19). And it seems that the psalmist was convinced that such an offering was acceptable to God.

We appreciate the help that external structures and customary rituals afford to our hesitant piety and we are dismayed when these external supports crumble before us. In an alternative scenario, we become alienated from them for some reason. In the religious void that ensues we may feel lost, as many did when the Temple was vandalized and destroyed. However, instead of losing all hope of a connection with God, we have the option of creating for ourselves, a pattern of worship, making room for God's word in our life and offering to God the prayers that rise from the heart to the lips.

Structures are important, but without corresponding attitudes in the heart they are meaningless. Sometimes it is a gracious Provi-dence that allows us to pass through a stage of alienation from external practices or from the various social expressions of religion.

At times like this, perhaps after wandering in the wilderness for a while, we discover for ourselves that trying to live a life without God leads us into a deeper discontent. Then we start sending out feelers to discover whether the relationship can be resumed—perhaps in somewhat different forms and practices.

Gratitude can play a part in this recovery of piety. Things change when we begin to realize the many benefits that we experience in our life, not only through the kindness of others but, also, in more mysterious ways. This prompts in us a desire to offer thanks to the universe, to God, to reality. And, in this manner, a way of return opens for us. "How can I repay the Lord for all the benefits given? I will lift up the cup of salvation and I will call on the Lord's name. I will fulfil my vows to the Lord before all the people" (Ps 116:12-14).

Personal piety is needed to complement official worship, but when this latter fades away, personal piety can stand on its own feet to take its place. At least temporarily. A grateful heart, a listening ear, and a willingness to be instructed will help us to maintain a good level of communication with God, even when more public worship is not a possibility. It may even open up before us a way of return.

109   My soul is continually in the palm of my hand,
       but I do not forget your instruction.

SOUL

For us the word "soul" denotes something invisible and, maybe, abstract. However, the primary meaning of the Hebrew word *nephesh* is "neck"; it was simply the channel through which the life-sustaining processes of breathing and eating passed. If this channel ceased to operate, death followed immediately. It made a certain sense to affirm that the neck was—at least metaphorically—the source of all the vital activities, especially appetite and, hence, desire. When desires are met happiness results, otherwise there is disappointment and grief. The soul can signify a person's vital energy, the sum total of the passions. Thus it becomes synonymous with "life." The term *nephesh* is often used in an intensive sense as a reflexive pronoun. It deepens the emotional content of the passage as if to involve the whole person in whatever action is attributed to it. To love the Lord with one's whole *nephesh*, as in Deuteronomy 4:29, means that all one's energies are concentrated in a single tsunami of affection toward God. The human soul is not some passive mass lurking beneath the surface of consciousness, but a vibrant, pulsating engine for all the activities in which we engage.

To say that one's soul is in the palm of one's hand seems to indicate a life-threatening situation (1 Sam 19:5; 28:21). The imminent prospect of death has the effect of relativizing all other drives, so that the person concentrates only on survival. The danger is imminent. The situation is dire. As the psalms of lament often remind us, in such crises, the person of faith does not forget the faithfulness of God. A heartfelt cry for help comes from the depths of one's being. "I called to the Lord from my constraint; the Lord answered and set me free. The Lord is with me; I shall not be afraid. What can a human being do against me? The Lord is with me as my helper, I shall look down on those who hate me" (Ps 118:5-7). "Blessed be the Lord who did not allow us to be torn by their teeth. Our soul is like a bird that escaped from the fowler's snare; the snare was broken and we escaped. Our help is in the name of the Lord, who made heaven and earth" (Ps 124:6-8).

Mindfulness of God's self-revelation gives us a distinctive context in which to judge any unfavorable situation we encounter. Instead of being overwhelmed by the threat that is posed, we take a step back and allow ourselves to recover our poise. We remember the strength and goodness of God and we take heart. The hope that all is not lost is born in us and we are able to confront the challenge and respond creatively to it.

This is not to say that God's answer to our prayer is always immediate and in the form that we anticipate. Sometimes, having allowed us to be plunged into temptation, God wants us to remain in that awkward place while we learn the lessons that only negativity can impart. The situation continues to be painful, but it is not hopeless. In retrospect, we may see that it has conferred on us greater benefits than many days of sunshine. For the present, however, we are called to patient endurance, sustained by a gritty confidence that all is not lost.

Meanwhile we learn for ourselves that "The instruction of the Lord is perfect; it restores the soul" (Ps 19:8). After the storm, there is a great calm.

110   The wicked set a trap for me,
       but I have not wandered from your precepts.

TRAPS

The most effective traps are usually those that are well concealed; the unsuspecting victim falls into them unwittingly. Paths are generally kept clear of traps and are safely used by many. It is in wandering away from a recognized path that one runs the risk of falling into hidden traps. There is no sense in saying that one did not intend to fall into the trap; as soon as one chose to leave the path, it became a possibility.

In the spiritual journey there is a safe path traced out for us by God's word. By keeping close to that source of guidance we lessen the likelihood of falling into a trap. The danger begins when we start trying to live our lives autonomously, as we all do, from time to time.

The first impediments we encounter to our progress along the spiritual path come from our unwillingness to submit ourselves to the necessary self-discipline. We soon become aware of contrary inclinations within ourselves. Some of them, like gluttony and lust, directly drag us into inappropriate activities. Others like anger and sadness induce in us a negative state from which unworthy actions readily spring. And then there are others, like vanity and pride, which are mostly interior; and tend to poison whatever we do with a secret malice. And we are all beset by the most subtle temptation of all: to do nothing.

These innate tendencies are like traps because they tend to make their appearance when we least expect them; we imagine that we have made good progress and that these vicious inclinations are a thing of the past. Alas. They have merely gone into tactical remission, allowing us to come to the premature conclusion that we can relax our vigilance and be a little freer in what we allow ourselves. Once we have fallen into this trap, a further level of temptation awaits us. We lose hope. Our determination to continue the journey falters and we have to endure a period of uncertainty in which the ultimate outcome is unknown.

But these dark days do not last forever. The urgency of passion eventually yields to a renewed sense of caution as we navigate our course, keeping more or less to the path traced out for us. We achieve some success in realizing the goals we had set before us and, perhaps, we do much good. We are more assured in using our talents and confident in our ability to have a positive impact on whatever we embrace.

It is during these blithe moments of self-satisfaction that another trap awaits us. The trap of ambition. We are seduced by the notion that we could do much more good and reach a point of fuller satisfaction if we obtained a high position, one with more power, more status, and more opportunities to use our gifts. When our physical drives cease to cause much trouble, we sometimes become prey to other inclinations, in particular the prospect of exercising power. Few people are improved by gaining more power. Even if, at the beginning, it is exercised judicially, as the years pass, it is taken for granted and becomes a means not of service but of ensuring the priority of one's own preferences. Ambition is a trap that catches many and is just as crippling of goodness as the more visible vices.

However, by staying with God's word, we will manage to avoid all kinds of traps.

111   Your testimonies are my inheritance for ever;
       they are the joy of my heart.

INHERITANCE

We often experience a certain uplift in our achievements, often tinged with a certain smugness and self-satisfaction. This is quite different from the happiness that an inheritance brings. An inheritance comes to us not because of what we do or have done, it comes to us because of who we are. It is a sign that we are loved and honored. We rejoice not only in the gift, but also in the recognition that we are worthy to receive the gift. An inheritance is an affirmation of who we are.

God's self-revelation acts as a mirror in which we can view ourselves, not just as we are at this moment, but totally. We are given a key to interpret past experience with more exactness than when the events were taking place. We can see matters in a wider context and, perhaps, begin to catch a glimmer of God's working in our life for our benefit. We cannot foresee the future, but we are empowered by our openness to God to discern the most creative path to follow, and we are given the courage and the energy necessary for us to take the next step. And for the present, the fact that we are in contact with God means that for the moment our human destiny is fulfilled. We have not reached our final destination, but when the channel of communication with God is open, we are—at least temporarily—engaged in the relationship for which we were created.

It is this unique interpersonal relationship which is the source of our dignity as persons. The evolution of creation has reached a point in us that we are able to sustain a reciprocal relationship with the Creator—albeit, an asymmetrical relationship, and one that is sporadic rather than continual. This is not something that we have earned; it is a gift to us given through the emerging sophistication of created reality. It should be a source of wonderment; it is certainly not something of which we boast. We are the beneficiaries of millions of years of development. "What are human beings that you remember them; the children of Adam that you visit them? You have made them little less than gods, arrayed them with glory and splendor, given them authority over your handiwork, put everything under their feet: sheep, cattle, wild beasts, birds in the sky and fish in the sea" (Ps 8:5-9).

There is further amazement to be found in the fact that this spiritual revelation has allowed itself to be conveyed in ways that are accessible to limited human intelligence. God intervened in the history of Israel in various ways and has through various channels spoken words that reveal to us something of the divine nature, which is otherwise unknowable to us. We can know something of what God is. What is revealed to us as the central mystery of the divinity is God's care and loving kindness for what has been created: a revelation that inspires us to reach out from the dust of the earth to the heights of the heavens: in praise, in thanksgiving, in love, and in desire. And the psalms give us words to embody these affective movements: we are not left speechless.

This is our privilege. "God has not done thus for all nations, nor made the judgments known to them" (Ps 147:20).

112 I turn my heart to do your statutes,
   for ever, to the end.

TURNING

Total fidelity to what we have glimpsed in God's self-revelation is not achieved in a single movement of the will. However fervent we may feel, it is not within the realms of possibility that we can dedicate our lives to God once and for all. Our life's span is dispersed through a multitude of distinct moments, each subject to its own influences. Our onward course is subject to the choices we make, moment by moment. And while it is true that we can decide on a particular direction to pursue, yet that decision is constantly modified by unforeseen possibilities and threats that are liable to surface at any time.

Our willingness to serve God must be constantly re-affirmed, by word and by action. There needs to be ongoing commitment to re-acquainting ourselves with God's plan for us and discerning what actions concord with it most completely. This bespeaks a certain deliberateness in living, the capacity to step back from the onrush of work to consider what to do next. That many people would assert that this is a luxury that modern life does not allow is, perhaps, an indication that we are allowing ourselves too easily to be swept along by the tide of events. Have we ever thought of slowing our life down, so that we may see more clearly and think more expansively? We might find that by taking our time we may well increase our subjective enjoyment of what we do, but also its objective quality. Multitasking is a false friend. It is a form of enslavement that alienates us from our work and prevents us from giving meaning to what we are doing. Completion of the task seems to be everything and motivation is regarded as irrelevant.

We need to think more about why we are doing what we do. This is a means of reclaiming ownership of our actions. Repetitive factory work may seem to be charmless, but if it is viewed as a means of feeding a family, it becomes highly meaningful. In the same way, if we have made a general decision to follow the spiritual path and have adopted a lifestyle that seems conducive to it, there is a possibility that very little thought will be invested in our daily activities. We will keep doing what we determined we would do, but it is mostly a matter of routine which yields neither comfort nor challenge. If we conclude that we are stuck in a rut, we may be correct.

Turning to God, exposing our life to God's word, is a prime means of ensuring freshness in our efforts to follow the spiritual path. It won't eliminate the ups and downs of daily existence but will help us to navigate through them. What such a practice will probably reveal to us is how easily we slip away from the ideals we have adopted, how forgetful we become of what we think of as our fundamental priorities, and how weak and short-lived have been our resolutions to do better. However, it offers these reminders very gently and without rejection. It is as though our deepest self is knocking on the doors of consciousness, seeking admittance. We keep returning to the heart and through it returning to God, and by this means we live a richer life.

113   The divided I hate,
        but I love your instruction.

DOUBLEMINDED

There is much which is mysterious in human behavior. Our dearest-held principles are sometimes, or even often, violated by our actions. We are tenacious in recognizing the importance of particular values, but find ourselves incapable of fully implementing them in daily practice. It is too easy to say that this is a case of hypocrisy—that we do not practice what we preach. The mystery is much deeper than that. It is a question more of incapacity than unwillingness.

The reality is that, in the evolution of moral consciousness, the mental components appear much earlier than those that govern behavior. We begin to appreciate the beauty of a particular manner of acting long before we have the insight or skills to put it into practice. And so we experience an interior dividedness. Our energies are dissipated in different directions and, so, cancel each other out and we are unable to make much progress. A greater degree of singleness of heart is needed before our actions clearly embody the values we cherish.

Rabbinic teachers used to distinguish between two impulses or tendencies or inclinations to be found in the human heart: the one leading to good, the other to evil, and this may well have been an echo of Persian teaching, picked up during the post-exilic period. The drama of moral living consisted in the interplay of choices made about which tendency to follow. There was a clear acceptance of the notion that we become the kind of person that our everyday choices embody.

Few of us are ever fully good or fully bad; sometimes it seems that most of us subsist in a state of lukewarmness. We maintain our sense of self-worth by not following our worst inclinations, yet we rarely consider following the noblest possibilities that present themselves. We spend a lot of the time fence-sitting, not shaping our lives in one direction or the other, but hoping that events will intervene to make any decision by us unnecessary. This seems, at first, a harmless sort of existence, but it is worse than it seems. Omission of possible good is not less toxic that the embrace of evil. A bland and colorless life scarcely meets the expectation of the Creator who breathed into humanity a spirit of initiative and verve.

We are imbued with an innate zest for adventure which is curdled into sourness by too much risk-aversion. As Ecclesiastes wrote: "Whoever keeps watching the wind will never plant, and whoever keeps looking at the clouds will never reap" (Eccl 11:4). Agricultural success depends on good weather, but good weather is often unpredictable. Risk cannot be avoided. So it is in life. To follow our best instincts will sometimes bring us into conflict with those who think differently and with those who are opposed to any initiative. We need to be prepared to run that risk. To shrug off the mantle of inertia and to do the good of which we are capable when the time is right, accepting the risk of disapproval. In this way we have nothing but scorn for the divided heart and commit ourselves to invest our energies in putting into practice what we have learned from the fundamental divine instruction: "Be fruitful and enrich the earth."

114   You are my shelter and my shield,
in your word I have hoped.

SHIELD

The *magen* to which this verse refers was a small, round shield carried on the left arm, offering protection but leaving the right arm free to wield a weapon. In this metaphor, the divine protection does not absolve us from the obligation of engaging in battle, but supplements our offensive actions with a mobile means of defense. On the other hand, the word translated here as "shelter" seems to indicate the possibility of withdrawing from battle into a place of hiding. Two different ways of avoiding the negative consequences of warfare: concealment and active resistance.

The tribal memory of Israel was pockmarked with memories of battles by which the national identity was forged. Indeed, some have suggested that the oldest metaphor for Israel's God was that of a warrior, fighting on the side of the chosen people. The fact that this involved the discriminative slaughtering of opponents and the placing of entire populations under the ban was cause for rejoicing. When the enemy attacked, Israel called on its God to intervene. "Take up the *magen* and the *tsinnah* [the large body-sized shield], rise up and come to my help; wield spear and javelin against my pursuers" (Ps 35:2-3). Perhaps the annihilation of enemies was secondary; what was celebrated was the solid protection from attack and the ongoing welfare of God's people. "Great is the Lord, who delights in the peace of his servant" (Ps 35:27). "God has delivered us from our enemies; God's kindness is unending" (Ps 136:24).

The theme of divine defense is more fully developed in Psalm 18, which begins with a string of protective metaphors. "O Lord, my strength, I have affection for you. The Lord is my rock, my fortress, my deliverer; my God is my rock, in whom I take refuge. God is my shield and the horn of my rescue, my stronghold. I call to the Lord, who is worthy to be praised, and I am rescued from my enemies" (Ps 18:2-4). As a small nation at the crossroads of a succession of powerful empires, Israel was aware of its vulnerability, and this precariousness provided the starting point for many of its prayers. Only when it considered itself invulnerable did the temptation to run after other gods emerge.

For ourselves, although we are not in mortal peril, it does us no harm to ponder the benefit of divine protection. Firstly, it can be preventative, like immunization. By filling our minds and hearts with the word of God we are protected from all kinds of invasive philosophies that could lead us astray. If our basic beliefs and values are founded on the truth of God's self-revelation, then we have a standard with which to compare opinions which present themselves. And if we have taken the time to ponder God's word we will have formed a personal philosophy based on it, one that will not allow error an easy entrance.

Secondly, in hard times, it will be helpful if we have embraced the belief that Providence is constantly active in bringing things to a happy conclusion. Present reversals and misfortunes are given a wider context by the confidence that we have that somehow God is working for us and that finally all will be well. Our experience of God's kindness gives us the basis for a hope that helps us endure even the worst things that happen. "In God's word I have hoped." Nothing else matters much.

115   Depart from me, you doers of evil;
       I will observe the commandments of God.

SOLIDARITY

Because human beings are societal animals, much of what we consider to be intimately personal is, in reality, absorbed from the group or tribe in which we were raised. This formation is especially strong in our earliest years, but our openness to influence persists through most of our life. Because we were reliant on others for information, and lacked the intellectual skills needed to think things through for ourselves, more often than not we simply adopted the views of those with whom we mingled.

Even today our choice of company is significant, because it will probably reshape our views on many topics and ultimately influence the choices that we make. We may consider ourselves to be free agents, but others can easily observe the extent to which we unconsciously conform to those around us, even in our manner of speech and our pronunciation of certain words.

All this points to the importance of associating with those who share our fundamental beliefs and values and limiting our contacts with those who are hostile to them. Although we cannot always choose our companions, we may sometimes be led to mutter to ourselves the words of the psalm: "Depart from me, you doers of evil; I will observe the commandments of God." We are conscious that by being constantly in the presence of those who deride our faith, our own convictions are slowly submitted to a process of erosion.

We live in an era in which individualism is rife and even religion is often privatized. It may be that we cannot embrace some kind of relationship with the unseen God without becoming more fully aware that we are not alone in that relationship—we share it with all people of faith. Our own faith, interior and intimate though it is, is strengthened by association with likeminded people. This is true all the time, but it is especially important when our faith is subject to serious doubts and temptations. In such difficulties, it is often only the humility implied in the seeking and accepting of counsel from others that will help us survive the assault. We are not in possession of all the answers to the questions posed by human existence. When we reach an impasse in our own thinking, we will often find freedom by following the guidance of another. There is a paradox here: we become free by accepting direction.

Meanwhile we will continue to live in a society in which we may sometimes feel that following the way of life indicated by God's word is a minority option. Our commitment to faith may oblige us to swim against the current. This demands extra effort on our part, but we should take care that it does not lead to arrogance, obstinacy, or intransigence. Rigid religiosity is never attractive. We are more likely to win respect for our way of life if we treat everyone with respect, gentleness, and friendliness, without attempting to harangue them into accepting what we accept. We may not see immediate results of our forbearance, but we are meekly planting a seed which, in God's time, may well bear worthwhile fruit.

116　　Sustain me by your utterance and I shall live;
　　　　let my hopes not be abashed.

SUPPORT

All of us, it seems to me, sometimes have thoughts about how to live a better life, one that is more fulfilling for ourselves and of greater benefit to others. Sometimes this leads us to make resolutions about implementing these otherwise vague aspirations. And sometimes we even commit ourselves to action. The problem is that many of our good intentions have a tendency to wobble after the initial spurt of enthusiasm fades or when circumstances change.

This is where we need to recognize that external support is imperative if the good work that we have begun is to be brought to completion. It is a fact of human nature that our aspirations race ahead of our abilities; this is good because it prevents us from becoming immobile. But when progress slows we become disheartened. This is why it is important that we rely on some form of external support rather than simply taking for granted that our own resources are sufficient for the task.

The word of God offers us both guidance and encouragement, sometimes in unanticipated ways. If our situation were unchanging, it would be sufficient to keep on doing the same thing. But life never stays still; its component are constantly mutating and demanding of us—if not a radical change of direction—at least ongoing nuancing. What worked well yesterday has expired and we have to seek to respond to the challenges that today brings. This takes a bit of courage, because when we find something that works, we cling to it and are reluctant to take the risk of modifying our response to life.

God's word is a source not only of direction but also of a certain boldness that enables us to remain athletic in our commitments. It teaches us how to remain the same by constantly changing. This is not some grim form of enforcement from above, continually urging us to leave our comfort zone for the howling wilderness of uncertainty. It is more like a sweet inducement to come forth from our timidity and to trust in the powerful support of God, who never leaves us to struggle alone. It is more carrot than stick!

Attachment to God's word means that not only are we more inclined to be hopeful and positive in our outlook, but we are also more alive, less dead. Perhaps we know people who, although they are still walking around and engaging in all sorts of activities, seem to be at least half-dead. Their blood is still circulating, but the sparkle has long vanished from their eyes. They are not necessarily bad people but, somehow, all joy seems to have disappeared, and they become the easy prey for all sorts of difficulties. The solution can be simple. Re-attach ourselves to regular reading of the Scriptures. If we expose our lives to the challenges they contain, we will soon find that we are also drawing forth from God's word, strong currents of comfort, which will soften the hard edges of daily experience and kindle again the fire of spiritual desire.

God's word sustains us in our highest endeavors and leads us to the more abundant life for which our spirits yearn.

117   Uphold me so that I will be saved,
      and I shall continually gaze on your statutes.

GAZING

The earliest use of the word "gaze" seems to have been by Chaucer in 1435. It is a beautiful word, with undertones of eagerness, wonder, astonishment and a willingness to remain in the presence of the object of such attention. It has a contemplative flavor. The present text suggests that the psalmist is spending time in reflection and living in the context of God's word, that this is a source of support and a means by which his life is preserved and enhanced.

Contemplation is, however, not only a means to reach out to something beyond itself. It also actualizes the hidden powers of the whole person in such a way that nothing beyond itself is necessary or desirable. This is because contemplation is, precisely, a departure from self-centered selfhood into a zone of self-forgetfulness brought about by absorption in the Other. Like a child absorbed for some moments in the flight of a butterfly, so, for the contemplative, the "real" world temporarily ceases to exist. A person captivated by God's self-revelation briefly steps over the threshold into another world, where the priorities are different and a deep peace holds sway.

Sometimes the gaze of the heart is like a laser. A narrow band of concentrated light that eliminates every other concern. At other times, it is more like a floodlight that clothes all things in a sea of light, and embraces them all. And sometimes the two actions coincide so that light reaches out beyond itself and simultaneously includes everything in its own concentrated beam. Paradoxically, the soul is separated from everything and yet united to everything. The experience exceeds the normal constraints of time. Sometimes it passes in a second and feels like a year; at other times, it lasts longer, but there is no sense of passing time. Gazing upon the word of God's self-revelation does not follow normal rules or expectations.

And slowly the inner powers of the person are transformed. The formation of the word "contemplation" explains how this happens. The prefix *con-* indicates that it is something that continues over a long period. The heart of the word is *–temp–* from the Sanskrit, indicating a measured conformity. The suffix *–atio* points to an active process. So, we may conclude that the Latin word *contemplatio* refers to an active process taking place over time that induces a conformity to the object of our attention. A lifelong commitment to the contemplation of God makes us like God. It is not a method; it is the direct result of spending much time in the presence of God, gazing upon the word. When we are exposed to the glory of God's self-revelation we are slowly transformed into its likeness.

Mostly the person involved in this process is unaware of what is happening. Everyday life continues and although its activities are suffused with the hidden light of the godhead, this is not so apparent to the person. Others are more conscious of its radiance. Contemplation is not a method for acquiring God. It is, rather, an accepted invitation to leave other things aside, to create a vast inner space that is somehow both austere and welcoming. Keeping God's word, allowing it to form our behavior and spending time gazing upon it is the surest pathway to salvation and the fullness of life.

118   You make light of all who wander from your statutes;
      their deceitfulness yields no result.

LIGHTWEIGHTS

When the book of Ecclesiastes speaks about universal vanity, it seems to be suggesting that in this world of space and time there is no possibility of permanence. Everything is subject to change; it is unwise to rely on anything in this limited world. Within the context of the whole psalm, this verse implies a little more. Whereas we attain a degree of solidity through our adhesion to God's word, we lose that gift if we allow ourselves to drift away from what God has revealed, and live according to different standards. By our choice of vanity over reality, we become what we have chosen: ephemeral, impermanent, lightweight.

Sometimes we have a vague glimmer that our lives are not as fruitful as they could be. This faint stirring of conscience is really a summons to begin making changes in the way we do things. To modify our priorities. Most of us are reluctant to do this. Instead, we attempt to change appearances while leaving the reality untouched. We embark on a program of window dressing. Hoping that, if others are deceived by what they see, we ourselves may eventually be convinced that nothing needs to change.

"Their deceitfulness yields no result." Reality has a solidity that is unaffected no matter how many deny it or disguise it. It participates in the permanence of God. We also are called to share that benefit, but only to the extent that we allow ourselves to be conformed to reality. When we try to superimpose our dreams and delusions on reality, reality is unchanged, but we are slowly drawn into a mental fog which robs us of the capacity to distinguish between true and false, right and wrong, good and evil. Deceitfulness may deprive others of a portion of the truth, but we who are deceitful by word or deed are ourselves being led farther along a path that leads nowhere.

The psalm keeps reminding us that the way to truth and life and authentic humanity is by opening ourselves to the word of God. Because we are time-bound creatures, we cannot do this once and for all. It needs to become a regularly renewed practice. This can be a challenge for us. We have come to measure the value of activities by the degree of instant gratification that they yield. We are impressed if something dramatic occurs. We are inclined to pay less attention to changes that occur slowly over a long period of time. We are aware of the existence of massive canyons where rock has been eroded by the action of water. Yet, if we pour water over rock, nothing seems to change. What is missing is that the process has to continue for centuries. It is slow but sure. Our conversion also takes time. Maybe it appears dramatic when a tipping point is reached and a seemingly sudden change takes place, but the process has been operating underground for a long time. There is always a backstory. The fact that it went unnoticed merely indicates the limited nature of our perception. Stay close to the word of God and it will stay close to you, actively bringing about whatever needs to happen to bring you to the more abundant life for which you were created. However, it may take time.

119   You treat all the wicked of the earth like dross;
       therefore I love your testimonies.

DROSS

Technically, dross is a mass of solid impurities floating on molten metal; metaphorically it means persons or products who are considered to be of little worth and which should be thrown away. This verse describes God's judgment on all the wicked on the earth: they are of no value and should be abandoned. It is unequivocal language. Practitioners of evil will be rejected by God. Between God and evildoers there is no association.

The psalmist is looking at matters from God's side, but perhaps we might also look at it from the side of those who have become bemired in wickedness. Those who allow their relationship with God to lapse, often find it progressively harder to maintain any level of goodness in their lives. It is not so much that the relationship is lost because they are wicked but, rather, they are wicked because the relationship is lost. A Russian folk saying, quoted by Alexander Solzhenitsyn, assigned the cause of human malice simply: "Men have forgotten God; that is why all this has happened." Drifting away from God is not neutral; it exposes us to the likelihood of slowly becoming less human.

The opposite is also true. If I am aware that allowing a distance to develop between me and God, or between my community and God, will result in a decline in goodness, then I will probably conclude that it would be a good idea to make sure that the relationship is maintained. And this usually requires a positive effort because there are all kinds of alternative attractions that can seize our attention and divert our energies. When things start to go wrong in our lives and someone suggests that the cause of our troubles is that we have ceased to make room for God, we are reluctant to accept the suggestion. We consider it simplistic, and prefer to blame a tangle of social or psychological forces. Perhaps we would do well to think again.

God's testimonies are embraced out of love. It is not fear or some form of compulsion that opens our hearts and our lives to God's self-revelation, but its inherent attractiveness. We sense that spending time with the divine testimonies will slowly change us by revealing to us pathways that lead to a fuller life. We do not have to give up anything in order to be formed by God's word. We are the beneficiaries. This word reveals to us who we really are and animates us to act in accordance with our deepest nature—not to be seduced by transitory attractions, but to act in accordance with our own best interests.

The ultimate fate of the wicked is not ours to determine; we can leave that to the just judgments of God. For ourselves it can be useful to see life as a series of choices. We are constantly at a crossroads. And, as Deuteronomy reminds us, our task is simply to choose the path that leads to life, to love what is life-giving, and lovingly to embrace the means that will conduct us to our goal.

120   My flesh bristles in fear of you,
      I fear your judgments.

TERROR

In many cases where the Scriptures speak of fear of God, it seems more like a reverential awe in the presence of the divine majesty than a matter of utter terror. As such it is easily softened and explained away by commentators. Here fear seems like something more primal—an instinctive terror that immediately translates into bodily reactions, a bristling of the flesh or a shuddering. Such visceral terror is inspired by the thought of God's overwhelming power when fueled by anger, and the consequent danger of all those at whom it is directed. "Fire goes forth before

[God's] face and burns enemies all around. Lightning flashes light up the world, and the earth sees and trembles. Mountains melt like wax before the presence of the Lord, before the presence of earth's Master" (Ps 97:3-5). God is not to be trifled with. As the people of Israel discovered when they doubted the promises that had been made to them. "So, hearing this, the Lord was angry and fire was unleashed against Jacob and anger against Israel" (Ps 78:21).

The anger of God is, strictly speaking, not a theological proposition, since God is unchanged by anything that occurs in the sphere of space and time. God's wrath is not interior to God; it concerns only what happens in this world. What seems to happen is that when people are confronted by events which they judge to be negative or which are, in fact, destructive, their guilty consciences interpret these events as punishment for infidelity. If I am frightened by something or disappointed that something hoped for does not happen, it is easy enough unconsciously to blame myself. I have done something wrong or omitted to do something right and my failure has resulted in my wishes being thwarted, because God was displeased with me. When spelled out like this, it seems a very childish way of thinking, but few adults completely cast off the self-blaming reactions typical of earlier years.

The wrath of God is a human projection. It is a metaphor for something beyond our knowing. When our limited intellects are unable to find a direct cause for something, we tend to refer it to an unknown agency, that is, to "God." Instead of admitting our frustration at our ignorance, we conjure up an image of a God who acts very much like human beings and punishes those who have crossed the border between good and evil or between obedience and rebellion. The supposition is that bad things happen to bad people, if not now then later. When things go wrong, we assume that it is because God is angry at us.

The otherness of God does not permit us to make such facile assumptions. It must be averred without qualification that the nature of God is pure benevolence. How this is to be reconciled with bad things happening to good people is beyond our capacity to assess. If we abide with the word of God, then God's creative kindness must be the foundation of all that we conceive of the divinity. Instead of being afraid of God, we might allow ourselves to be a little fearful of our own weakness and blindness and malice. This is more likely to create trouble in the world than any supposed outburst on the part of God.

❧✦❧

121   I have practiced judgment and righteousness;
   do not abandon me to my enemies.

ACCEPTANCE

I suppose many of us have the idea that if we can get our own life in order, then the world around us will be a better place. It is probably true, but the improvement in the immediate environment may not be noticeable. Sometimes our good example can lead others to a minor conversion but, more often, it inspires in them feelings of resentment or envy. They chafe over the uncomfortable sense that the good deeds of others merely serve to underline their own omissions. Acts of virtue rarely attract admiration from near neighbors. We may praise the saints who lived in a distant time or place, but we are far too clever to be taken in by the antics of those whom we know only too well to be far from perfect.

If we practice judgment and righteousness in the hope of winning approval from those around us, we will likely be disappointed. Selective piety and good behavior may impress the naïve for a while, but they will soon discover evidence for the hollowness of our virtue, long before we do, and disenchantment will follow.

Genuine righteousness is its own reward. It sits easily with our conscience, even when it is confronted by external indifference or opposition. It does not measure the value of actions by the acclaim they occasion, but by their intrinsic goodness. It is not loud-mouthed in self-praise, but quietly follows the life-giving path without ulterior motivation.

At the same time, it is not so easy to live without affirmation. When our actions prompt a response of overt hostility or even of feigned indifference, it is hard not to feel the gnawings of self-doubt. We are societal animals and a moderate level of approbation from others is part of the mechanism of making moral judgments. Part of the dynamism of a healthy community is that it helps in the ever-ongoing formation of conscience through its subtle gestures of approval and disapproval. We are not as autonomous as we sometimes claim; we need the support of others if we are to persevere in turning aside from evil and doing what is good.

In the event that we are bereft of all support then we need to strengthen the quality and the quantity of the time spent in God's presence pondering the word of revelation. In the absence of human aid, this can be for us a source both of guidance and of encouragement—and it also reminds us that we are not alone. There are still seven thousand who have not bowed their knees to Baal!

God's repeated promise to accompany us on our journey means that we will never be completely abandoned into the power of those who oppress us in one way or another. Even though there may well be hard times in everyone's life, usually there are also breathing spaces, when our troubles ease and we are sustained by a glimpse of God's undeviating acceptance of us, however dire the external circumstances.

122   Promise good for your servant;
        do not let the arrogant oppress me.

PLEDGE

The verb here translated as "promise" has a background in ancient legal usage. A pledge given offers stronger assurance than a verbal promise. It guarantees the promised outcome. This verse seems to be asking God to stand surety for us, or for our goodness. In the event that we cannot achieve an appropriate level of goodness by our own efforts, we ask God to make good the deficiency. This is a very bold request and a good reminder that our relationship with God is not dependent on good works; rather it is the opposite. It is through our attachment to God that we are empowered to do good. We must not allow religion to be reduced to morality.

The idea of God accepting obligations on our behalf is, of course, an anthropomorphism. It is our human way of speaking about God's side of the covenant relationship. The idea behind both pledge and covenant is that God's promises are absolutely certain; they represent a cold-blooded commitment to our welfare that is not dependent on our worthiness, but is an expression of the abundant kindness of God. The more we allow ourselves to ponder the unqualified faithfulness of God, the more likely we are to commit ourselves to maintaining our loyalty to the covenantal obligations we have accepted.

Something to remember about lifelong fidelity is that it is more than a matter of devising a routine and sticking at it for ever and ever. Fidelity is dynamic or it is nothing. It involves responding consistently to ever-changing circumstances. If the world around us is changing, fidelity means changing with it in order to remain the same. When we acknowledge God's faithfulness to us, integrity demands that we reciprocate. Our imperfect loyalty to God and to God's word, is a reminder of God's solid commitment to us.

We live in a world of vast uncertainty which can generate within us a roiling sea of doubt and resistance that makes us reluctant to envisage anything as permanent. To base our personal philosophy of life on the steadfast and undeviating kindness of God is to provide ourselves and, perhaps, those around us, with a solid foundation on which to build the kind of life that is relatively unaffected by the madness around us. For us one thing is certain; the love of God will continue to operate in our regard even in seemingly adverse situations. We may feel confused and upset at what is happening around us, to us, and even within us, but this confusion is merely the result of the limitation of our knowledge. Our intelligence is limited and it does not have enough information to accurately assess the meaning of what is happening and where it is likely to lead. If we trust God's word and by it are inspired to leave everything in God's hands, we will be at peace. And, probably, our interaction with the world will be more effective in achieving some good. Divine providence is more than a myth.

123   My eyes long for your saving help
        and your righteous utterance.

LONGING

One of the ways by which hope is expressed is by gazing into the distance, as if willing the object of our desire to make an appearance on the horizon. What we hope for is always out of sight and so we must search for it. In fact, a synonym for "searching" is "looking for." Our eyes seek to be the first to make contact with what we cannot yet touch with our hands.

The desire for something more is the engine that drives our yearning for a reality that is beyond the confines of space and time. We have many small desires, each of which evaporates the moment it attains its object. If we are truly hungry we can think of nothing but food, but as soon as food is provided for us our hunger abates. All our small desires, even those that seem most insistent, motivate us in the pursuit of small objectives and then disappear. Their work is complete. Of course, there are larger desires which may last most of a lifetime: desire for love, friendship, achievement, recognition and the like may be the driving forces for many of the choices we make over a long period, but these too begin to wane and may eventually disappear. And sometimes they become very bitter when we discover that what we have sought with so much energy proves itself unworthy of our attention. When we get what we wanted, it may happen that we no longer want it.

Spiritual desire begins with a loss of interest in many of the goals which our contemporaries pursue. It has no clear focus. It is a strong sense of dissatisfaction, rising from the conviction that so many things fail to deliver the benefit they promise. A new car may be faultless in looks and appearance, but it cannot remedy our innate sense of inferiority. A brand of toothpaste may promise to surround us with a ring of confidence, but it cannot really cure our innate tentativeness. As we grow in wisdom—which is a positive way of describing the aging process—we begin to realize that there is yearning within us that cannot be quenched by anything that this world of space and time can offer: a yearning for eternity.

In one sense, the desire for eternal life is futile; there is nothing we can do to affect its realization. The most we can do is to hope that eternity will reach out to embrace us and take us to itself. And ultimately this is what we mean by "salvation." We yearn for God to lower the heavens and come down, to draw us into what we desire but can never achieve.

It is an amazing prospect. Created in God's image we have an inherent desire to replicate in ourselves the life of God, but yet we are unable to do that which our nature demands. Left to our own resources we are lost. Yet what we learn from the righteous utterances of God is that God is willing to make good our nature's defect. God is willing to come with saving help to pluck us out of this dilemma and bring all our deepest hopes to fulfilment. This is the lesson we learn if we are faithful frequenters of God's word. God is the One who can bring all things to a joyous conclusion, to bring to perfection the work begun by the seeds of desire and draw us into the embrace of eternal life.

124   Act for your servant according to your kindness
      that I may learn your statutes.

UNDESERVING

God's actions in our world are always a consequence of what God is, never because of what we have done or become. And the Scriptures keep informing us that the most prominent characteristic of God's actions in our regard is kindness or mercy. As for the many texts that speak of a wrathful God inflicting dire punishments on the wicked, these are, perhaps, best understood as pedagogical devices, intended to engender a wholesome fear in those who would otherwise be negligent in their pursuit of what is to their ultimate benefit. The threatened outcomes are due more to the self-inflicted injuries of the sinner than to any punitive assault by a vengeful God.

The proclamation of a benign God whose every action is stamped with the seal of kindness seems like a very soft teaching. Yet, for most of us it generates a challenge. When things go wrong in our life, for one reason or another, we find it difficult to believe in the kindly providence of an all-powerful God. A voice whispers within us: "How could God allow this to happen?" We do not understand why bad things often happen to those who deserve better. Our conclusion is like that of the psalmist: "How useless to keep my heart pure and wash my hands in innocence" (Ps 73:13). Implicit in our complaint is the sentiment voiced by Jeremiah (Jer 12:1): "Why does the way of the wicked prosper?" To our way of viewing reality, everything seems topsy-turvy. The good suffer and the wicked thrive.

All this proves is that our capacity for ascertaining the state of reality is very limited. We cannot see the whole sphere of space and time as a single unit; at best we are aware only of the small zone that is in our immediate vicinity. As God is described as pointing out to Job, we know nothing about so many things that our assessments are so parochial as to be ridiculous. What we expect of those we elect for governance is that they will have a broad experience, gained over years; we hope that this will provide a sound context in which important decisions will be made. This is precisely what we lack when we complain about events which have occurred within the providence of God; we do not have sufficient breadth of experience to judge what God has done or allowed to be done.

This is where our acceptance of the message of God's self-revelation has to enter into contest with our desire to establish causal chains. There is so much that we do not understand and never will, but what we do know is that the kindness of the Lord is everlasting and without limit. Whatever happens is the fruit of this kindness, whether we can see that clearly is irrelevant. Just as the sun and the moon go on their appointed circles without our permission, much that happens in the universe does so without reference to my convenience or to my preferences. I am a peripheral part of a very large whole; I am not its center. My happiness and my welfare will follow on my fulfilling the role that has been assigned to me, even though I may not be aware of all the ramifications of what I do. If I play my role, my vision will become unclouded and, progressively, I will begin to understand something of the mystery that cannot be reduced to rational categories. Thus will I learn God's statutes.

125   I am your servant, give me understanding
that I may know your testimonies.

SERVICE

Years ago, Georges Auzou published a volume on the book of Exodus under the title *De la servitude au service*: from servitude to service, from slavery in Egypt to the worship of the living God. It suggests a transition that all of us must make. For many of us the early stages of our religious practice are overshadowed by a sense of obligation. Because this is unfamiliar territory we must follow the lead of others, even when we are unable to sense the full significance of what we are doing. We embrace the whole package, with a certain enthusiasm, which has the effect of sidelining some of the reservations that some of its details may generate. Our service of God is sincere and responsible, but it is not yet fully adult.

As the years pass and we begin to internalize the values inherent in the practices that we have accepted, we are less constrained by external expectations and we feel more fulfilled and content in our service of God. But then things begin to change. We become conscious of a desire to stop being "good" and to start being ourselves—although we are not entirely sure what we mean by this. We feel alienated from the commitments we once freely accepted and ready to look for a new pathway. That this is a critical time is obvious, although the degree of overt crisis varies with temperaments. But a choice has to be made.

Here it is important to avoid reducing possibilities to binary options. It is better to sit quietly with conflicting values, and allow each of them to speak. Perhaps over a prolonged period. Perhaps in the company of someone who has a listening ear. More often than not, conflict simply reveals aspects of a situation that have not previously been apparent. As such, it is a blessing. In this case, we may be moving into a period in which our service of God is less a matter of conforming to external rules and expectations as of imbuing it with what is unique in our own lives and in our own journey. Potentially it is an enrichment.

The more we understand the personal dimensions of our service, the more authentic our lives become. When we are true to ourselves, created as we are in God's image, we become more capable of knowing the meaning of God's self-revelation and its implications for ourselves and our world. The best service we can render to God is to fulfil the purpose for which we were created, and what this involves becomes apparent to us only after the passage of time and many mistakes, false starts and failed endeavors. If "to err is human," then most of us are experts in humanity. We make progress through trial and error, and if we try too hard to eliminate errors, we never progress. That we do move forward—however painfully—is a miracle, but it happens all the time. If we allow it, our life unfolds in ways that we cannot control. Although we may be reluctant to admit it, there are forces at work which we do not fully comprehend. When we learn confidence in divine providence everything gets easier and our service of God is both sincere and, somehow, effective.

126   It is time for the LORD to act
        for your instruction has been contravened.

FORBEARANCE

Anyone who prays the psalms regularly will find themselves confronted with passages which call down God's wrath on sinners—on those whose behavior does not conform to our standards or expectations. When we have opened our lives to God's word and gleaned from it certain directives about how to live what we have learned, we may well experience a tendency to apply these directives to others before we begin to practice them fully ourselves. Their contravening of what we have understood to be God's instruction re-awakens in us a desire to do likewise. We are envious of their freedom to sin, while we have bound ourselves to a narrower discipline. We ignore the fact that what is for us willful disobedience to conscience and to God may be for them merely ignorance or thoughtlessness or the result of social conditioning. We condemn them and wonder why God does not do likewise.

If we take a step back and think about this situation we will encounter something of the mystery of God's forbearance. God is never in a hurry, as we are, who find it hard to grasp the truth of the principle stated in Ecclesiastes: "There is a time for everything under the sun" (Eccl 3:1). The interconnection of time and event is visible to God but, mostly, passes us by unnoticed. We know that fig trees do not ordinarily produce fruit during the winter, but we fail to appreciate the importance and sacredness of distinct moments in the lives of human beings. Not everything has to be done now. The moment has not yet come. It may be true that our neighbor lives an appalling life and needs to change direction. It may also be true that now is not the moment for conversion; things may have to get worse before the possibility of improvement dawns. Our grumbling and our urging God to intervene makes us look a bit stupid, because we don't really know what we are talking about. Our complaints say more about us than about others.

Pondering the forbearance of God can be a great consolation when we consider our own lives that are so replete with moments of weakness, blindness and malice. Our impatience with our inability to bring to perfection the good work we have begun may lead us to conclude that, somehow, God is unhappy with us. That our sins and omissions are a great disappointment. It is hard for us to believe that God created us imperfect in order to be able to take delight in watching our progress from the dust of earth to the fullness of humanity. This progression from glory to glory is spread out over an entire lifetime. Fortunately, we have no means of accelerating the progress; it is designed to reach its culmination only at the end of our journey. If we hope to live longer, then we should stop hoping to become perfect, because once we reach that point it will be all over. If you have plans for tomorrow, then you need to accept that for today, at least, you are less perfect than you hope to become. And God does not seem to be bothered by that.

127   That is why I love your commandments,
       more than finest gold.

GOLD

Gold is among the densest of metals, some nineteen times heavier than the equivalent volume of water. At the same time, it is a very soft metal; a small amount can be hammered thin until it covers a considerable area; this is how craftsmen form the gold leaf that is used for decoration. Gold has always been considered a precious metal, and to be adorned with gold was an indication of the status and esteem to which its wearers considered themselves to be entitled.

The psalmist qualifies his love of God's self-revelation as being more intense than his desire for the purest gold. This is similar to what was said earlier in this psalm: "The instruction from your mouth is better for me than thousands in silver and gold" (Ps 119:72). And in Psalm 19: "The commandments of the LORD are truth; each of them is righteous. They are more desirable than gold, than much fine gold; they are sweeter than honey dripping from the comb" (Ps 19:10-11). To express what the psalmist is saying in more metaphysical language we might say that the self-revelation of God is a good that transcends every other good that is known to human beings. This is a bold assertion and we ought not to let it pass us by without reflecting on it.

When we assert that God's word is the ultimate "good" we necessarily imply that it is also a benefit, that is to say, that it is good for us. If it is good for us, then it is life-enhancing, and its absence diminishes the quality of our life. This is a very clear statement. If we accept it as true then it means that we have to accept the proposition that the conforming of our life to God's word is not only a desirable option, but a necessary one. God's self-revelation is made in order to help us on our journey to a more abundant life; not to take advantage of its guidance is to expose ourselves to unnecessary jeopardy. We are putting our life at risk. Opening the Scriptures in a prayerful spirit is not merely a pious exercise, to be implemented when we feel so drawn. It is a necessary constant in our service of God. We need to be repeatedly reminded that God's ways are not our ways and that, unless we change our ways, we are liable to wander off into error and unhappiness.

Treasuring the word of God as we would gold, implies more than merely reading the Scriptures. It asks of us that we read them intelligently; their meaning is not always obvious and often we have to be diligent in seeking out the relevance of these texts written so long ago, in an alien tongue, and deriving from an unfamiliar culture. We have to listen not only to what the text says, but to what it does not say; we have to pay attention to the echoes generated in our own heart as the text struggles to relocate itself in our own particular culture. We have to ponder what we have understood from our reading and commit parts of it to memory and further rumination. If we do all this then it is clear that the word of God really is something that we cherish and treasure, something that we invest much effort in acquiring, preserving and making the most of. In time, we also may be able to affirm that God's word means more to us to us than worldly wealth or any other temporal advantage.

128   Thus all your precepts are for me a straight line;
       I have hated the paths of falsehood.

DEVIANCE

One of the images of sin that we find in the Scriptures is that of going astray, getting lost, deviating from the path. It is the basic meaning of the word "error." In colonial Australia, to be lost in the midst of a vast, unexplored and unfamiliar country was a nightmarish trope among the newly arrived colonists. We are so used to knowing where we are and how to arrive at our destination that finding ourselves in unknown territory inspires anxiety and, maybe, even terror.

However, the sense of being lost and unable to find our way is a later development. First we are lost and, only as a consequence, do we realize that we are lost. It takes time for us to comprehend the danger in which we find ourselves. The panic this inspires is a good thing. If we are lost and don't know it, we will continue to go deeper and deeper into the unknown, making it harder for us to find our way out.

It is also possible to be morally lost, when our conscience is enshrouded in a mental fog so that we no longer have a full capacity to distinguish between right and wrong, good and evil. Such a bedizened state is usually the result of years spent ignoring the promptings of conscience and allowing our actions to be guided by baser instincts. We get into a habit of labelling everything according to our preferences and desires, so that it is no longer a question of whether a course of action is objectively good, but of whether it corresponds to what we want to do. We become adept at giving new names that disguise the moral character of actions. We rename drunkenness as "joviality," gluttony as "self-care," fornication is just "acting according to nature," and arrogance becomes "self-esteem." And it is not only the quality of actions that is distorted, we also underestimate their seriousness and easily label as merely "inappropriate," "imperfect," or "harmless" what in others we would designate as a major failing. What this kind of moral fuzziness indicates is that we have gone astray. We are lost, enveloped by a mental and moral fog. No wonder that we are tempted to keep walking the ways of falsehood.

The remedy is that we need to have some flexible but objective standards that do not easily cave in before the demands of our instinctual tendencies. Not just an all-embracing code of conduct, but something always adapting to new circumstances. Mere rules and regulations are not enough. What we need is a living relationship with God's word that provides our conscience with sufficient light to discern the true character of the options that confront us. To penetrate the haze of falsehood and arrive at the truth.

Seeing the truth is only a preparatory phase of moral living, but it is a necessary one. Having discerned what is good, we are in a position to make a choice. We can choose the good over other desirable options, even though we are strongly drawn to act otherwise. If we want to walk in a straight line then we need the guidance of God's word on a regular basis; in this way we will avoid drifting into falsehood and finding ourselves lost.

129   Your testimonies are wondrous:
       My soul practices them.

PRAXIS

One of the puzzling elements in human behavior is that sincerity is not always a guarantee of truthfulness. I may sincerely believe that the earth is flat, but that does not mean that it is. I may sincerely promise to do some particular thing but, often enough, years will pass without the realization of what I had intended. And, although it is true that actions can be hollow and without real meaning, usually action is the most acceptable expression of sincerity. Mere words are easily uttered and easily forgotten. Weight is added to them when they lead to positive initiatives. The marriage of word and action is a large part of our credibility; if they are divorced, no one takes us seriously.

The same criterion can be applied to our relationship with God. In our devotions we profess ourselves as standing before God in reverence and humility, hoping for the coming of God's kingdom and praying that God's will be done. Very good! It would probably be regarded as churlish to ask whether these priorities are markedly present in our everyday behavior. Yes, the testimonies of God are wondrous, and we embrace them sincerely. The question that may be raised concerns the degree to which the divine testimonies have any influence on the choices that we make in the course of an ordinary working day.

At some point in our life we may come to the uneasy conclusion that, in much of what we do, we pretty well do whatever we want. We have great faith in our own preferences and they seem to allow us to live a good life without too much effort. We are too busy to commit many sins, as they are listed in the books. However, there is a kind of subliminal emptiness in our lives that seems to push God away to the farthest frontiers of our awareness.

What is required is the grace to realize that we need to do something to reverse the drift away from God and to make some kind of new beginning in our spiritual life. This is not necessarily bad news or evidence of radical infidelity. It may simply mean that we have grown out of our former system of beliefs and values and it is to time to expand beyond them.

This means that we need to do an audit on our conscience to ensure that it really is an openness to God's self-revelation and not merely a well-disguised expression of self-will, based on a spurious sense of identity. If conscience does not challenge us, make us dissatisfied, urge us to pass beyond the limits of our comfort zone then—at best—it is asleep. At worst, it could have been hijacked by a virus and re-routed into a less life-giving track.

To reactivate our conscience, we need to step back from our usual regimen, open ourselves to broader possibilities by which our service of God may be expressed. The first step of this is to our reading of the Scriptures or, if they have been a constant in our lives, to freshen up our approach to them. One good way of doing this is to approach the text with the question: What am I to do differently today? Sometimes a good deed or a better attitude may be indicated, sometimes there will be a suggestion of not doing something we had intended. A small act of compliance today will not only cause the Scriptures to come alive but will have the effect of beginning a process of rejuvenating our whole life.

130   The opening of your word illumines
     and gives understanding to the simple.

EXPANDING

The first half of this verse is explained in different ways. It can refer to the unrolling of a scroll to reveal further truths. This may then take a secondary meaning of the growth in understanding that comes with continuing meditation on Scripture. The same point can be reached by interpreting the noun as "doorway" or "portal." Doorways serve a double purpose: they give admittance to the interior, but they also offer the alternative of making possible an exit which offers entrance into the wider world. In the world of computers, the term "portal" is used of a website that provides access or links to other sites. Whatever interpretation we choose to adopt, the verse seems to be indicating that God's word contains much more than a first glance reveals.

This is an important message for all of us, a reminder to search diligently within the written text in order to uncover its deeper meanings, whether this comes about by penetrating to the inner heart of the text or by applying the text to outward situations. Or both. God's word is not static; it keeps on interacting with the ever-changing circumstances of the faithful reader. The psalm's admonition is always valid: "If today you hear God's voice, do not harden your heart [against it]" (Ps 95:7-8). We may not reduce the Scriptures to being merely objects of rational dissection, to be put under a microscope and analyzed. They are living and active, leading us both to a deeper appreciation of the mysteries of the spiritual world and to a more profound understanding of our own inner life.

This is why God's word is described as a portal leading to light. Those of us gifted with vision cannot imagine what it would be like to live in a lifelong state of blindness. So many of the words we use to describe the world in which we live presuppose the gift of sight. We speak of light and darkness, the interplay of colors, the perception of presence and absence, the subtle movements and changes around us that do not impinge on our other senses. Without light our understanding of the world and our interaction with it would be severely limited.

Parallel to physical blindness is spiritual blindness—an insensitivity to the spiritual world. Usually this is the result of choices made by individuals. They turn aside from the gratuitous intimations of immortality that often surface in the simple lives of the young, and restrict themselves to the certainties of the material world and the limitations of ordinary consciousness. They cannot comprehend what they refuse to experience, and have no language to describe what is lacking in their lives.

If, at any stage of our life, we find ourselves confused about how to respond most creatively to what is happening around us, it is not necessarily a sign of imminent disaster. It could well be an open door, an invitation to enter more deeply in God's word in simplicity of heart and lightness of step, expecting to find there, indications that will help us to make life-giving choices. Small things at first, but often progressing to something more significant. Then we also can say in all truth: "Your word is a lamp for my feet and a light for my path" (Ps 119:105).

131   I opened my mouth, panting,
       I yearn for your commandments

YEARNING

Spiritual desire is different from those ordinary desires which punctuate everyday existence. Usually, when we desire something, we know what it is that we desire—at least in general terms. And the desire automatically switches off when we get what we wanted. Different desires take its place, each with its own more or less specific target. We desire what we have not got, and when we get it the desire ceases.

What distinguishes spiritual desire from its mundane cousins is that its object transcends definition. We are conscious of a significant absence in our life yet we lack the language to describe what is missing. It is because any religious practice that takes its shape from this inner yearning of the heart is judged as foolish by those who have not paid attention to their own inner workings—or even scandalous. It is important that we take our inner experience seriously, because it interacts with the "objective" expressions of religious faith to generate a movement toward God that is distinctly intimate and personal, much more than the dutiful performance of ritual and the punctilious observance of moral precepts. A religion based on desire is dynamic because it is always stretching itself out beyond the present; it is dissatisfied with what is present and seeks what is beyond. A life marked by desire is endlessly restless, recklessly inventive, always trying to discover new ways of making more profound contact with the unknown object of its pursuit.

At some point in the spiritual trajectory, a person comes to the realization that a deeply personal feeling for transcendent reality is not one's exclusive property. Others have similar aspirations, though adapted to their own temperament and culture. We are fellow pilgrims on the spiritual path and we can learn much about our own journey from those who are travelling with us. And the collective memory, embedded in tradition, is a storehouse of wisdom to guide us on our way. We are not alone; we are engaged in a common journey and the farther we progress along the track, the closer we come to one another. "That which ascends must converge."

We do a grave disservice to the religious pursuit by reducing it to a matter of merely knowing about the spiritual world without being engaged with it. The study of metaphysics is great fun to those who like that sort of thing, but useless if it remain within the sphere of rational speculation. Equally unhelpful is the tendency to reduce religion to moral practice; instead of interacting with a boundlessly exciting mystery we are constrained to follow an accessible code of conduct, which cannot lift its eyes above the details of human behavior.

Learning from the Scriptures and from fellow-travelers how to identify the spiritual yearnings within our own hearts is a great gift. It helps us to acquire an art of discernment, so that we more readily recognize what derives from our deepest center, and we become more adept in reinforcing its drive. And we also acquire a kind of instinct that helps us to diagnose what clashes with this fundamental movement of our being and to know how to block contrary impulses. When we live from the heart's deepest desire, all will be well.

132   Turn to me and show me favor;
      according to your judgment for those who love your name.

FAVOR

I sometimes think that many of us are a little dubious when the book of Genesis speaks of God as finding the whole work of creation "very good." Maybe that was so in the beginning, before human beings began to leave their mark on the world, to exploit it for their own immediate gratification and to use it as a pretext for their belligerence against one another. And even when God chose to reorient people by successive acts of self-revelation the situation did not improve. It was found to be as easy to dismiss the voice of the prophets as it was to ignore the outraged cry of creation.

Scripture's way of describing the dissonance introduced into the world by human weakness, blindness and malice is to speak of the anger of God. This is, of course, an anthropomorphism. God is unchanged by anything that happens in the region of space and time. The disturbance to the relationship is unilaterally human. When we struggle against the natural order, which has been imposed by God, we subject ourselves to an interior tumult that destroys our peace of soul, neutralizes any energy we might have for doing good, and sows the seeds of potential conflict with others.

We misinterpret the Scriptures if our reading of them leads us to project onto God the disappointment and anger we feel at the state of the world. God's judgment that creation was very good was an assessment made outside the sphere of time; it was an eternal valuation, permanently valid. God's enduring attitude toward the world and its human inhabitants is one of persistent benevolence. God looks with favor on the whole of creation.

This is the message reiterated throughout the Scriptures. The chosen people were guilty of innumerable acts of rebellion and prolonged periods of estrangement. They did not keep their side of the covenant agreements. But God remained faithful to what had been promised. King David was a man of violence who committed murder and adultery and abused the office he had received from the hands of God, yet the promises made to him and to his lineage were never revoked. Whatever the vicissitudes of human loyalty, God remains forever faithful. The promises God makes are cold-blooded and calculated. Nothing that we can do will cause them to be cancelled.

If we go through life with the deep conviction that we are appreciated and loved by God, then many of our attitudes will change. If God's benevolence is so obstinate that nothing we do can alter it then, perhaps, we need to imitate this global acceptance and become somewhat more open to others, recognizing that their failings are more to be pitied than blamed. There is no need for us to place restrictions on our acceptance of others, making it conditional on their meeting our expectations. We can afford to move in the direction of an openhearted generosity that is more likely to pay attention to the good qualities of others than to their liabilities. It is not a matter of being naïve, but a realistic acceptance of the reality that every life has patches of light and patches of darkness. We choose to give priority to the light in the hope that encouraging it will cause it to grow so that progressively the darkness is extinguished.

133   Confirm my steps through your utterances;
        let evil not be my master.

SERVILITY

The popular image of religious people is that they are serious, perhaps a little rigid, and mostly driven by a sense of duty, whether personally chosen or imposed on them by some higher authority.

On the other hand, sinners have a lot of fun; they do what they like and they are unbound by the obligations that come from any solid commitment. Our celebrities repeatedly claim to be "spiritual" but not "religious"—with the details of their spirituality defined by themselves. Above all, they feel entitled to be free from the constrictive norms that shape the lives of other people. Perhaps this picture is an exaggeration, but it is not without some basis, if we are familiar with the kind of content favored by the tabloid media.

Religion is often presented more as a burden than a liberation. This is because it involves a lifelong struggle to subordinate what is no more than transient gratification to what is permanently enriching. To learn to play a musical instrument or speak a foreign language involves many long hours of hard work and may often seem like drudgery when compared with the leisure enjoyed by others. But acquiring new skills is an investment in the future Spending time in this way is laying down the foundation for a freer, more fruitful and fulfilling life.

Failing to take responsibility for the flowering of one's life is not freedom; it is a manifestation of being so bound to the exigencies of the present that we do not take the steps necessary to facilitate our personal advancement. It is not rational to give priority to the gratifications that are available in the present when it is known that they will necessarily bring misery in their wake. Our passionate tendencies and inclinations often lead us along paths that we know lead us to misfortune and unhappiness. We become addicts. If we are asked why we allow this to happen, our response is usually to claim that we acted under some kind of inner compulsion. In other words, we were not free. But, paradoxically, this lack of freedom is one that we ourselves ultimately embraced. We freely chose not to be free by giving free rein to the sub-personal forces that roil within us.

Scripture often speaks of sin as a state of enslavement; evil exercises a mastery over our life so that it becomes difficult to do what is good and dangerously easy not only to do what is bad but, progressively, to slide into patterns of behavior that are more inhumane. Think of the dehumanization that beset the guards at concentration camps. Any residual humanity was quickly leached out of their hearts and they slowly lost the capacity to distinguish right from wrong. On a smaller scale, this is what happens to us. Habits of sin become entrenched little by little without our noticing that our standards are slipping. We feel blameless because we are unable to perceive any alternative way of acting. We have become slaves of sin; evil has become our master.

This is not to say that we are liable to become serial murderers or compulsive adulterers; we are far more likely to sin by omission, to pass by on the other side, without noticing one who needs our help. Perhaps we have become slaves to inaction.

134   Ransom me from human oppression,
       and I will keep your precepts.

RANSOM

The word "ransom" usually indicates the payment of a sum of money in order to liberate persons from some form of captivity. Paying the ransom is a responsibility assumed by others for the benefit of the captive. It is taken for granted that those held against their will are unable to do anything to secure their own freedom; they are powerless. In calling out to be ransomed, the psalmist recognizes that the complex of elements that inhibit our full freedom is something beyond our powers to resolve. We need help.

In this case, the psalmist sees himself as the victim of human oppression. From the very beginning of humanity's journey through history, we see the emergence of a deadly rivalry between siblings. Cain killed his brother because Abel seemed more pleasing to God. Difference gave rise to envy, envy spawned murderous intent, and brooding thoughts of violence were quickly translated into action. The pattern has repeated itself through subsequent centuries—although not always visibly and violently: difference, resentment, oppression.

We ourselves cannot claim to be untouched by this malign cycle. Sometimes we feel ourselves to be victims, but we are not always blameless. We too have been perpetrators of oppression, but in our own sweet and subtle way, not soiling our hands with blood, but managing to push others down—refusing to give them room to flourish, space to expand, or time to adapt. More often than we care to admit, the negativity we experience from others is no more than payback for the way we have treated them.

How can we escape this vicious cycle of internecine malice? More often than not our efforts to change the dynamics of our situation are self-centered and so tend to make matters worse. Before we begin to fret over the lack of a ready remedy, perhaps it is good to step back and consider what is happening. Conflict is not always a bad thing. It simply reveals differences; it is not necessary for one option to overpower all others. Sincere dialogue will often reveal means of reconciling differences without substantial compromise. Cain does not have to murder his brother; the world is big enough to accommodate both.

The most effective means of resolving insoluble difference is to have recourse to outside mediation. We can start this process by unilaterally taking the situation as we see it to God, opening ourselves to perceive it in a different light and confirming our willingness to be guided by the divine precepts. This is not usually a rapid process. It is a little like a great ocean liner trying to avoid an oncoming danger. The momentum is too strong for a quick turn; any change of direction is achieved only in small increments. This is how it is when attempting to build bridges between potentially hostile parties. Meditation on God's word often yields insight into small practical steps that can make things a bit better and inspires us to act, even though what we do does not result in any dramatic improvement. We are giving practical expression of our desire for reconciliation. We will probably find that being a proactive peacemaker, at God's behest, is the best cure for a sense of bring unjustly oppressed. By being active we begin to feel less like a victim.

135   Let your face shine on your servant,
       and teach me your testimonies.

RADIANCE

The Bible insists that it is not possible for the human being to look directly on the face of God. To do so would mean instant death, and to attempt to do so could be considered an expression of hubris. There is such a gulf between human and divine that it cannot be crossed from our side of the abyss. The gap can be bridged, however, from God's side. When God engages in acts of self-revelation, it becomes possible for humanity to catch a glimpse of something of God's reality. It is not a total encounter because human existence in space and time is necessarily divided into mutually exclusive moments. One moment ends as another begins. Yet the glimpse is a rich experience; it is more like an encounter than a merely visual event. It is a moment of profound connection, which excites and animates the human soul. After wrestling with the angel Jacob exclaimed (according to the much-quoted Vulgate translation): "I have seen God face to face and my soul has been saved" (Gen 32:30). Even a fleeting vision of God has the power to change a life.

The outshining of God's face is a source of formation for us. This instruction is primarily an interior event. It is not so much the external dictating of a moral code on tablets of stone, but it is more a matter of slowly sensitizing the heart to spiritual reality. It is like the gradual initiation of a person into appreciating art or music. It is not a matter of studying encyclopedias in order to amass a huge volume of information. It is more like developing a taste for the finer qualities of a masterpiece, perceiving them more readily and loving them more expansively. If we encounter God often, we develop a taste for God; so much so that our life seems meaningless without this enhancement.

The deepest form of prayer is often likened to a visual outreach to God—an activity of quietly looking in the hope of seeing. This is reflected in the Greek term *theoría* and in the sense acquired by the Latin word *contemplatio*. "Look toward the Lord and become radiant" (Ps 34:5). There is an ontological change that follows sustained contact with God. The more often that we gaze upon God—even though this is only a dark and indirect vision—the more we are conformed to God. When the glory of God reaches out to touch us, it does not leave us unchanged. Progressively it transforms us; we become visual echoes of the divinity, unique reflections of a reality that surpasses our capacity to comprehend. There is a dynamic quality in this progressive configuration. Over the course of a lifetime we pass from one degree of glory to another. This is less a matter of cumulative increase than one of constant adaptation to the circumstances in which we live. God's self-revelation is not without purpose; it aims at nothing less than the ultimate divinization of humanity.

Complementary to our catching an occasional glimpse of God is the sense that God is looking at us, that we are the objects of God's loving concern. This is a more passive state than the act of seeing. We sit comfortably in God's presence, allowing God's face to shine on us, warming us and renewing our sense of being accepted and loved. We don't have to do anything. We don't have to deserve it. We simply become aware that God is close and that we are greatly loved.

⁂

136   My eyes shed streams of water,
    because people did not keep your instruction.

GRIEF

Grief is not the same as grievance. We live in a world where grievance is king and long-lasting resentment is its consort. In contrast, grief is a universal human sentiment; no one has ever escaped being touched by it. In a world marked by contingency and impermanence, there are many sources of disappointment. The things dearest to us, like everything else, are subject to decay. "'Vanity of vanities,' says the Preacher, 'all is vanity'" (Eccl 1:1). Part of being human involves the restless and unfulfilled search for a happiness that is beyond all threat of diminution or extinction.

The fact that we share a vulnerability to grief with the rest of humanity does not lessen its impact, though it may help us to navigate through its storm-tossed waters. The danger is, that instead of allowing the pain of genuine grief to do its work on us—because it is not without purpose—we seek to find someone to blame for the sorrow we feel: the doctors who failed to defeat the illness of a loved one, the taxi-driver who drove so slowly that I missed my plane, the friend who planned a picnic on the day it rained. In a culture of entitlement we are sorely vexed when our preferences are not realized, and our first instinct is to make someone else suffer for the pain or disappointment we feel. If this is not possible or too prone to provoke retribution, we allow our anger to internalize and to transform itself into an abiding and universal sense of resentment. At first this is directed against particular persons who are judged to be the source of our troubles, but progressively all our petty grievances tend to merge and become global, perhaps epitomized in an individual or institution viewed as the willful cause of all that has befallen us.

Grievance is a poor substitute for genuine grief. When grief is accepted and openly expressed it has a purifying effect. Sometimes it reveals our love for someone who has died, in a manner never experienced while they were living. Sometimes it allows us to recognize an inappropriate attachment or an unrealistic expectation. Sometimes it leads us to recalibrate elements of our personal philosophy of life. There is a truthfulness about feeling grief that neutralizes all attempts to ignore particular aspects of our life. In time we begin to appreciate that this perception of truth has been the basis for creativity. Our grief becomes a means not only to cope with our sense of loss, but also gradually to find new ways to live more fully.

Grief can also be altruistic; we can suffer because of what others endure. This seems to be the sense envisaged by this verse of the psalm. The psalmist looks around and sees his fellow citizens turning their backs on God's self-revelation, thus depriving themselves of the guidance it affords. They are left to rely on their own resources and will soon discover that abandoning God does not lead to a richer life; it is an impoverishment. Life without God is ultimately glum—despite its compensatory pleasures. On such as these the psalmist looks more to pity than to blame; human solidarity means that their loss is also my pain.

❊

137　You are righteous, Lord,
　　　and your judgments are upright.

RIGHTEOUSNESS

There is a certain hesitation about the English word "righteousness" because it often seems to carry a connotation of self-righteousness and to be more concerned with the details of external observance than with inner probity and simplicity. Because the term occurs over 500 times in the Hebrew Bible, especially in the poetic books, there is a certain fluidity about its meaning. As applied to God the word sometimes serves to indicate the absoluteness of divine rectitude which then serves as a standard by which human behavior is to be judged. The righteousness of God is overwhelming, as far as human beings are concerned, and not a little fearsome. Before God all human actions are defective and liable to punishment.

There is, however, another way of interpreting divine righteousness, and we see this exemplified especially in Second Isaiah. It is so complete that it overflows and, in overflowing, renders just whatever it touches. God's righteousness is not merely an immanent quality, it extraverts itself so as to transform the unrighteous into the righteous. It is the gift of salvation or deliverance. It proactively justifies the unworthy so that they become capable of a continuing relationship with God. The qualities of God's righteousness, signaled by associated terms, include truthfulness or fidelity, kindness or mercy, and a proactive peace that promises prosperity. These are also the qualities to be found in those to whom God has communicated this gift: faithfulness, kindness and peace.

Authentic righteousness is not merely conformity to a pre-existing set of rules and expectations, but a dynamic inner force for good, that conquers everything in its path. It is not a boring respectability but an uncompromising and all-inclusive benevolence. As such it represents a threat to established mediocrity, which usually panders to the self-interest of a privileged few. Despite its inherent attractiveness, righteousness almost always encounters resistance, especially from those who may be considered to be the pillars of society. Like prophets and reformers, the eminently good are frequently rejected.

This can serve as a warning to many of us. Everything in us rebels against the suggestion that we should change, especially when it involves the likelihood of extra effort. We should take for granted that any revelation of a path that is life-giving will meet with reluctance on our part, and so it is best not to be too ready to reject the unwelcome novelty, but to step back and learn how to view the option from different standpoints; we may well discover that a possibility is not as offensive as it first seemed. What is good and wholesome and righteous may seem undesirable to our unrighteous instincts. We need to go into matters more thoroughly.

The overarching righteousness of God is not a threat of damnation but an invitation to paradise. In so far as we gird our loins and enter into it we will find that it becomes a source of blessing, not only for ourselves, but for all who cross our path.

138   Righteous you declared your testimonies,
         with great faithfulness.

TESTIMONIES

One of the synonyms for God's self-revelation used 23 times in Psalm 119 is "testimonies"—the various acts by which evidence is offered concerning the nature of God. The use of the plural (except, perhaps, in v. 88) is significant. It seems to indicate that no single intervention by which God self-reveals stands on its own. Each testimony complements and completes others. They must all be taken together. The Scriptures need to be read in their totality; a single verse read out of context can be misleading. Whenever we encounter a part of the Bible that speaks powerfully to us, it makes sense to dwell on it and to extract all its meaning. But then we need to move on because there may be another text that nuances the message we have received. We need constantly to move from the part to the whole, and from the whole to the part.

The acts of God in history and the recital of those acts in Scripture are windows through which we may come to an understanding of what God is. Truly appreciating what God is leads us to a perception of what we, as God's images, might become. Revelation has moral implications for the one who receives it. It may be expressed as a command, a direct instruction to do something (such as honoring one's parents), or a prohibition (such as forbidding adultery). It can express itself in a variety of intermediary stages: encouragement, admonishment, correction, reproach, warning, threat. The texts of Scripture, as fragments of God's self-revelation, also serve as so many mirrors in which we can discern something of the state of our own souls. Their message to us is the subtle echo that the text generates in the heart of the reader. Although it derives from a single outshining of God's glory, the word that is received is unique to each. From the deep silence of eternity, a word is spoken and takes form in a particular moment of time. It is a word for today. "If today you hear God's voice, harden not your hearts" (Ps 95:7).

What is asked of us is that we accept that the text that speaks to us is, mysteriously, a faithful rendition of God's message to us at this time. It has a divine authority. It is not merely for entertainment or information; it has a profoundly existential impact. Revelation is the continuing work of creation, constantly re-orienting creatures so that they are traveling in the direction that will bring them to the destiny God intends and has intended even before time and space began.

The faithfulness of God is expressed in never retracting the word of creation—despite the mess creatures have made of it. God's only word to us and to the world is "Yes," "Let it be." Even when what we hear sounds like a rebuke or a threat, it is always a word of salvation, a word designed to serve as a compass to bring us to a more abundant life. The righteousness inherent in God's word becomes for us a lamp for our steps and a light for our path. By communicating it to us God continues to bring forth from nothingness a world of wondrous order and beauty.

139   My passion consumes me,
    for my enemies forget your words.

SELF-DOUBT

As with verse 136, it seems that the infidelity of others sometimes summons a storm in the heart of the psalmist. Many of us will have experienced something similar. We become indignant when we observe others acting in way that is contrary to our most fondly held principles, and we become angry. In such circumstances, it is probably prudent to ask ourselves the question which God posed to Jonah: "Is it right for you to be angry?" (Jon 4:9). Here, as elsewhere, a creative self-doubt is a good friend.

There are three areas especially where self-doubt serves us well: in judging our opinions, in assessing our integrity, and in estimating our degree of personal freedom. It is all too easy to assume that we are wise and blameless and the masters of our own destiny—even though there is plenty of evidence to suggest otherwise.

I do well to question my infallibility. My direct knowledge of the universe is limited and most of what I believe to be true is based on hearsay. Even cats and dogs and creeping things seem to know more about the rhythms of nature than I do. My knowledge is based on assembling a few scattered fragments and perceiving a pattern—it does not take into account the elements I have missed or ignored, and so my synthesis is always selective and partial. The mistake that I often make is to attribute absolute validity to my contingent conclusions. And I fret and fume about those who see things differently.

Of course, we are slow to admit to anything that casts doubt on our personal integrity. We all make mistakes, since "to err is human," but we dismiss these as external imperfections that cannot impugn our basic goodness. When pressed, we might admit to limitation or weakness, but we are adamant that there is no real malice in our behavior. We believe ourselves to be fundamentally good people, misunderstood and little appreciated, but beyond criticism in all that is truly important. However, the level of affront that I feel when others disagree with my self-assessment is a reliable indicator of how much my self-knowledge needs to grow.

Even while protecting myself from charges of ignorance and malice, I continue to underestimate the extent to which so many of my choices are not my own. I did not choose my own genes, and the family and society that gave me my initial formation preexisted me. My stance before reality is often molded subliminally by these early influences. And my own past continues to shape the present through attitudes, habits and routines that quietly determine how I will respond to any new situation.

A healthy self-doubt will incline us not to take matters for granted, but to step back and examine our lives to ensure that we do not forget God's self-revelation: to seek for a more expansive knowledge that is not limited to my own narcissistic universe, to recognize that my instinctual impulses and ethical standards need to be subject to scrutiny, and to seek more consciously the path to more abundant life and not to assume that my spontaneous preferences will always lead there.

140   Your utterance is most pure
      and your servant loves it.

TESTED

The reason God's word is said to be most pure is that it has (figuratively) been refined and purged of all dross. Dross is not something inherent to a metal but it is a superadded impurity that must be leached out. God's self-revelation is perfect, but sometimes it becomes contaminated by additions that we introduce into it. This happens when we do not accept God's word as it is, but we try to contort and distort it to suit our own preferences. We may not be fully aware of what is happening and our sense of self-righteousness remains unchallenged. Think of how the curse of Ham in the ninth chapter of the book of Genesis was used to justify slavery in the United States and apartheid in South Africa. But before we rush to condemn these abuses of Scripture, we should make sure that, in our own little way, we also are not using the Bible to legitimate our inhumane treatment of others.

The text of Scripture is one thing; the interpretation we assign to it is something quite distinct. This is why, as we read the Bible and take it to heart, we need to initiate a twofold checking process.

Firstly, we need to verify that the message we are receiving is really what the text is expressing. This means going back to read the text again, this time more closely. Perhaps we may need to exercise some ingenuity in consulting commentaries and the like in understanding the language and the wider context of the text. We must never forget that the Bible was composed a long time ago in a language and a culture with which we are unfamiliar. We have probably never been tempted to amputate limbs that lead us into sin, as Jesus seems to recommend, but there may well be other texts that we embrace that need preliminary work if they are not to lead us astray.

Secondly, the Bible is not primarily addressed to individuals, but to those who collectively form God's faithful people. In more important cases, we need to verify that our interpretation concords with what God has revealed to others, through the centuries. It does not have to coincide with what others have previously received, but our reading should be in fundamental harmony with the received image of God. There will be variations and nuances, of course, but we need to remind ourselves of the corporate quality of revelation; it is a word for God's people and not a private communication.

This means that the fundamental requirement for understanding God's utterances in their original purity is humility. We recognize our own limitations and we seek to offset them. And there is something else. If we approach God's word with an anticipatory willingness to accept its practical implications, we will be much more likely to penetrate to its inner meaning. God's word is there to guide us and it will do this best if we purge our reading of false presuppositions, and be really open to hear and receive and obey what is communicated to us, even when it seems to go against our foregone conclusions.

141   I am small and despised,
      but I am not forgetful of your precepts.

SMALL

In our ordinary way of looking at things we usually regard large as better than small, more is better than less, and many better than few. More often than not our assessment criteria are quantitative rather than qualitative. Greatness is something to be celebrated whereas puniness is a target for mockery. Most living creatures are able to calculate relative size; determining quality demands a higher intelligence.

The prophet reminds us that God's ways are not our ways; God does not judge according to surface impressions but goes to the heart of things. So it was that God's choice fell on Jacob, the younger son rather than on his privileged elder. With God's support, David as a puny youth felled the giant Goliath, and the mighty armies of Egypt were outwitted by the ragtag band of Israelite escapees. It seems that what is highly esteemed by human beings is rejected by God in favor of what is lowly and insignificant. Deuteronomy states this clearly: "The Lord did not set his heart on you and choose you because you were more numerous than other nations, for you were the smallest of all nations" (Deut 7:7).

It is the poor and lowly that are the prime objects of God's beneficence. Solomon in all his glory fell short of what God expected of him. When Israel and then Judah went into exile, it was the humble people of the land who remained as a precious remnant, and the recipients of God's covenantal beneficence. The great ones of the earth were laid low and the lowly were exalted.

What message can we draw from reflecting on God's way of dealing with humanity? The most obvious lesson is not to place excessive emphasis on the accumulation of material goods. The so-called "prosperity gospel" that teaches that God rewards the pious—and especially those who donate money to its preachers—with wealth and good fortune in this life, is an abomination. It is a perversion of everything we know about God. But it is not only wealth that we might hope to receive as a collateral benefit of our religious practice. We can also aspire after a certain status in the community, a good reputation, acceptance and respect. Life is certainly sweeter when these advantages are ours, but in themselves they have little relevance to our worthiness. While it is true that the Lord gives and the Lord takes away, our change in fortune is not an indication of the quality of our relationship with God. Unless, in all circumstances, we can say with Job: "Blessed be the name of the Lord."

If we can be content in our smallness, then it will be much easier for us to be true disciples of God, never forgetting the divine precepts, but living in harmony with what God has revealed. We do well to remember that the archetypal temptation that ensnared Adam and Eve was the possibility of becoming godlike. If we are happy to be human, with all the limitations that this involves, we will probably find ourselves less liable to be tempted toward an unreal greatness and, as it happens, loved more sincerely because of that.

142   Your righteousness is forever righteous
       and your instruction is truth.

EVER-CHANGING

When a human being exuberantly qualifies a commitment as being "forever," we instantly regard it as an exaggeration. The term "forever" means very little when it applies to things done in the zone of space and time. Here nothing is forever. Circumstances change and reality changes color with them. What was appropriate yesterday, or last year, or last century is no longer appropriate. Walk through a cemetery and view the crumbling tombstones inscribed "forever remembered," long neglected and clearly past their expiry date. Here nothing is forever.

The spatio-temporal universe is composed of mutually exclusive parts. Time flits by and we cannot delay its passage. If we are here we cannot be there. We are like shipwrecked sailors desperately clinging onto some floating object in a boisterous sea. Nothing is permanent. Everything is in a constant state of change. All we can do is to allow ourselves to change, match the changes all around us and not allow rigidity to be the cause of our being overwhelmed.

There is a kind of laziness in our brains that gives rise to a preference that things remain as they are, so that we can pass through life without having to think much about it. As a result, we may feel somewhat resentful when events around us demand a changing response. The recent pandemic provided us with many examples of this attitude. We have a kind of yearning for ultimate permanence, even when it is viewed as the outcome of revolutionary change.

This is the point at which we need to realize that we have here no abiding city. Eternity is the sphere of God, and we enter it only by invitation—as it were. We become sharers in God's eternal stability by allowing ourselves to be re-formed in the likeness of God by making room for God's active self-revelation in our hearts. Of course, it is not an instant transformation, but a process that is lifelong. By receiving God's word, by keeping it, by pondering it, and allowing our choices to be determined by it, we begin to recover our own deepest identity that had hitherto been obscured and lost by being alienated from God. We shine forth as images of the timeless God. God's inherent righteousness is unchanging but it is also active in so far as through the instruction offered by revelation it leads us into the sphere of unchangeable truth.

Everything in our universe is in a state of flux and so our certainties are precarious. What is different about the true God is the total lack of capriciousness, such as was evidenced in heathen deities. God is faithful. God is steadfast. As Psalm 136 sings no less than twenty-six times: "God's kindness is forever." This is the sum total of God's self-revelation. The divine attitude toward human beings is not determined by anything that we do. It is total and unconditional acceptance. To the extent that we allow ourselves to be shaped by the realization of God's faithful love, we become empowered to deal with whatever changes life brings, with something of the divine constancy. "We will not be afraid though the earth quake or the mountains are submerged in the depths of the sea . . . The Lord Sabaoth is with us" (Ps 46:3-4). We will not be afraid.

143   Anguish and distress have found me,
         but your commandments are my delight.

ANGUISH

These words could well have been uttered by Job. During our earthly pilgrimage, none of us will escape times of great mental anguish when our faith is tested and our willingness to go forward wavers. It is almost impossible to offer a prescription about how to handle such transitions, because the components of the crisis are particular and personal. Part of the confused anguish that we feel is a sense of isolation and loneliness, compounded of disparate elements such as anger, resentment, shame, self-pity, sadness or jealousy. It is only by passing through such rough patches and coming out the other side that we begin to acquire some measure of wisdom. We have learned what is helpful in confronting the negative elements of our life, and what is not. Trouble will almost certainly find us again. If we are becoming wise, then we will prepare ourselves to struggle against the self-destructive tendencies that stand ready to unleash themselves and to invade.

The great bulwark that defends from such hostile intrusions is to locate our most cherished resources beyond their reach. This means transferring our basic affiliation away from the vicissitudes of spatio-temporal existence and placing our major investments in the untouchable spiritual world. If we take our basic identity from the word of God, and allow it to shape the daily choices we make, then there will be less upheaval when trouble strikes and everything seems to go wrong.

If we incorporate into our personal philosophy of life, the recognition that hard times are inevitable, not only will we cope more effectively with our own difficulties, but we will have a broader understanding when those around us are smitten with similar afflictions. The only way we can develop real compassion is through the experience of our own suffering. When we know what it feels like to pass through hard times, it is easier to have some feeling of fellowship with others who are being buffeted by misfortune.

This solidarity is, perhaps, more important than any external action we take to ease their pain. By it their feelings of isolation are assuaged. Chaucer defined consolation as: "to have another fellow in his pain" (*Troylus* I, 102). Instead of marginalizing those who suffer, we embrace them. If we are wise, this is what we learn during our own dark days.

The word of God, like the spiritual universe to which it alludes, establishes itself as a point of reference that adds a broader context to what happens in our world of space and time. Just as the travails of traveling are eased by turning our attention to the delights awaiting us at our destination, so we need to keep reminding ourselves that everything that happens around us has merely relative importance. Yes, we must take the present moment seriously, even though it seems trivial. Yes, we must do what we can if not to make things better, at least, to ensure that they do not get worse. Yes, this is the day the LORD has made, and there is no other. Yet beyond the visible present there is an invisible and transcendent world which God inhabits and which is revealed by God's word. Taking our cue from this will often instill in us the strength to endure the trials the come our way and, in some paradoxical way, to profit from them, and by their agency to move toward a richer life.

144   Your testimonies are forever righteous,
      grant me understanding and I shall live.

GLIMMERING

In the Genesis story of the origins of our universe, God's first action is to create light. The same priority can be observed in the slow trajectory of every human being from the immediate exigencies of material existence toward the transcendent reality from which ultimately we take our origin. The journey begins with the faint flickering of uncreated light in our created consciousness—what Wordsworth termed an intimation of immortality. The shape and content of the inaugural experience is distinctive for each person, but always has two characteristics. On the one hand, it brings together multiple particularities of a person's history so that it is both strange and yet familiar and, for all its novelty, it exudes an aura of warmth and acceptance. On the other hand, despite its inherent attractiveness, this glimmering of light can easily be ignored or dismissed. It does not force itself upon us. It is an invitation to a different future, not an invasion of our freedom. This is why many turn aside from it or drown it in a flood of procrastination. However, their subsequent lives often demonstrate at what price the invitation is declined.

It used to be thought that goldfish lived a happy and carefree life because their intelligence was so dim—though more recent research has cast doubt on this assertion. But the principle derived from it is sure enough. As we read in Ecclesiastes: "The one who adds knowledge also adds grief" (Eccl 1:18). To be guided by blind instinct and not to grasp alternatives is a recipe for a simple life. Everything is straightforward. The more knowledge we have the more we are compelled to sift and weigh evidence and, when we make a choice, we are burdened with regret for the loss of what we did not choose. This is why we often contrive to pass our days making as few decisive choices as possible. We drift. Drifting aimlessly doesn't sound like a great crime, even though it involves renouncing the possibility of personal growth. This is possible because the challenges that reach us from the spiritual world are always subtle. They don't shout their claims. They merely murmur softly. The light that shines in the darkness begins as no more than a faint dawning glow. We can ignore it, if we so decide, and it will go away. And our impoverished life will be untroubled.

The other possibility is that we move toward the light. Yes, it is feeble at first and ambiguous but, as we move toward it, it beams more strongly. Never overwhelmingly—it does not impose itself. It is never bombastic. But it is persistent, and the more we look upon it the more it impresses itself on the deepest layers of our being. It becomes for us a star of guidance pointing to the way that more directly leads to abundant life. Inviting us, cajoling us, it comes to us in meekness, submitting itself to our choice. Yet, once the choice to follow it is made, it seems to become confident and unhesitating. Pointing the way with a clarity that challenges our inertia and, at the same time, encouraging us to take the first steps.

Maybe the divine light is not so faint when it shines upon us. Maybe it is simply a case that our power of vision is so feeble that even infinite luminescence scarcely registers. However, if we pay attention to its slight glimmerings then our cataracts are progressively cured and we become able to perceive more clearly the light that beams down from heaven. When this happens we are slowly transformed.

145   I have cried out with all my heart, answer me, O Lord;
       I will observe your statutes.

WHOLEHEARTEDNESS

One of the saddest words in our language is "half-hearted." It bespeaks persons unable to give themselves completely to something that they have decided is worthwhile. And while it is true that there are always obstacles between us and our ideals, these can come from outside us. Half-heartedness indicates an interior flabbiness that lacks the vigor to implement its own proposals. A divided heart, always in two minds, with a preference for compromise over commitment. Politicians who attempt not to displease anyone come across as spineless and wishy-washy; they seem to stand for nothing. No wonder the psalmist said earlier: "The divided I hate, but I love your instruction" (Ps 119:113).

Even when we disagree with someone over a particular issue, it is hard for us not to admire their dedication if they are really wholehearted. I think that we instinctively recognize that to remain undeviating in our adherence to our principles is costly. It usually involves a degree of detachment from alternatives. To be wholehearted in our concern for the environment may well involve using more expensive alternatives to plastic, reducing our carbon footprint by traveling less, and by giving first preference to local produce. Noble sentiments are not enough. To be wholehearted means pushing the principles through to practice, and paying the price.

In fact, integrity is a rare quality—so rare that, in English, there is no adjective corresponding to it. There are so few opportunities to describe a person of integrity! Most of us have experienced the truth of what Job said: "Is not humanity's time on earth a military campaign?" (Job 7:1). There is a war going on within us between our ideals and our practice. Even sincerely held beliefs and values often fail to have much influence on the choices we make. Inner dividedness is the source of most human drama; without it we would be angels.

It is the dissatisfaction—or even disgust—with our lack of integrity and consistency that can serve as a springboard from which to raise our hearts to God. Of ourselves we will always be scattered into disparate and often hostile parts but, to the extent that we take our focus from the spiritual world, we will gradually achieve some level of interior unity. This is more likely to happen toward the end of our spiritual journey than at the beginning or halfway through. It is the culmination of a lifetime of little choices, trying to align our lives with the ideals we cherish. It is a gradual process and is subject to slowdowns and stoppages.

The best means of energizing ourselves to keep moving toward the goal is to keep experiencing how far distant we are from what we desire and, as an outcome, to keep on calling out to God for help in doing what we cannot achieve through our own limited resources. And by keeping God's instruction ever in our minds and hearts, we allow it to bring about a deeper level of inner cohesion, and a greater harmony between what is inside and what is outwardly expressed.

146   I call you: Save me
        and I will keep your testimonies.

DESPERATION

Sincere prayer to God is always tinged with desperation. Many of us are most comfortable when we feel that our life is behaving itself and everything is under control. In such a situation, delusional though it may be, we have no real need for God. We may include a nod in God's direction as a component in the culture we have absorbed, but mostly we take charge and carry on with our life, adjusting its various elements to suit our own preferences.

It is only when the universe resists our efforts to reshape it that we begin to feel distressed, and we often mistake our subjective upheaval for an objective reflection of the state of reality. In fact, the world will not end because I am upset. It is merely a matter of my realizing that the path to a more creative future begins when I conform to reality and not the other way around.

We all experience periods when it feels as though everything about us seems to be in a state of disorder, and nothing is going right. To outsiders our panic can seem almost comical, but it is real enough to us as we confront our difficulties. These will last until, eventually, we make the discovery that we are not able to reach a solution on our own resources alone. We need the help of others. This can prove to be a valuable learning process and a step in building a stronger sense of interdependence. "No man is an island" and we are most human when we actively depend on others and allow them to depend on us. And this, despite the fact that it may seem like a tragedy to depend on others, especially if we have devoted our lives to escaping the dependence of childhood and to postponing for as long as possible the dependence that will mark our final days. Being autonomous, avoiding heteronomy, is a delusion that adverse circumstances often teach us to abandon.

In addition to human interdependence, we have to learn to relish those situations that bring us to the awareness that we also need God's help and support. During World War I it used to be said: "There are no atheists in the trenches." In the same way, it is often when things go wrong, when disaster strikes, when our whole world seems to be deconstructing, that we are given the grace to look beyond the world of physical cause and effect and seek safety and security elsewhere. This is what it means when we call out for salvation; we are asking to be saved because we cannot save ourselves. Deliverance is one of the hallmarks of God's interventions in our history.

It needs to be remembered, however, that being delivered from evil is only part of what is implied in the biblical term "salvation." It includes also the notion of ultimate wellbeing, happiness, fulfilment, harmony, universal fellowship. We can strive to taste some of these blessings through our own focused virtue, but ultimately they must come to us as a gift of God. When I cry out "Save me," I am asking for more than rescue, I am opening myself to receive from God the all-encompassing gift of eternal life.

147   I anticipated the changing of the light and cried out:
       Your word is my hope.

TWILIGHT

The word usually translated as "dawn" more generally applies to the evening transition from light to darkness, and to the breeze that blows at that time. More broadly, it can refer either to pre-darkness or post-darkness: a passing period of half-light, a time of ambiguity. Twilight is a special time, which softens the sharp contours of full daylight and yet is not shrouded by the complete obscurity of night.

Twilight is an apt metaphor for human life with its interplay of light and darkness. This is discernible at the level of knowledge, where what we know about almost any topic is usually outweighed by the vastness of our ignorance. In fact, we usually regard one of the qualities of a genuine expert as being their recognition of the limitations of their expertise and the willingness to admit what they do not know.

Twilight is also evidenced in the sphere of morality. People may be scrupulously honest in their business dealings while allowing serious inconsistencies in their personal lives. We often speak of a "blind spot" such as most of us have, where we fail even to be aware of our defects in meeting our obligations. This is something on which the tabloid media thrive: the trumpeting of the private crimes of some eminent public figure—to the gleeful satisfaction of readers who resent their own lack of recognition—bringing high-achievers down to their own level. We love to hear about the shadows that are the inevitable consequence of recognized brilliance.

Despite what is commonly believed, there are relatively few situations which may be described as black-and-white, where on option is unqualifiedly good and the alternative is completely evil. Our adversarial legal system is built on this presupposition. A defense lawyer may bring forward arguments to excuse or mitigate even the most heinous crimes. There are two sides to most questions. We tend not to see this because we are locked into our own perspective. This is where conflict can be creative, if we are willing, forcing us to see aspects of questions that were hitherto unnoticed.

There are two components that will enable us to live creatively in a world in which there are few absolutes and much is open to negotiation. The first is discernment. If we have the patience to step back from the immediate fray and consider matters from different angles, we will probably end up with a more nuanced view of the issues. This includes subjecting situations to the probing of God's word, seeking beyond and beneath mundane realities the deeper, spiritual significance of the matter. When this has been done, we are called upon to make a conscious choice between alternatives, recognizing that every compromise, no matter how necessary, results in both loss and gain, in relief and regret. We live in a world of mixity; all we can do is to attempt to minimize the negative and advance what is good.

Perhaps the mildness and mixity of twilight can be seen as a call to reconciliation, learning to live with opposites, seeking harmony rather than the suppression of differences, renouncing the tendency to judge everything from a binary standpoint. Human life is often more complex than we are prepared to admit.

148   My eyes anticipated the watches of the night
       as I pondered your utterances.

ANTICIPATION

Clockwatching is one of the most obvious signs of boredom. We are impatient to have done with whatever is presently occupying us so that we can move on to something else. However, counting the moments can also be an indication of a great desire for whatever is about to happen. It looks forward with eager anticipation. In this verse, the psalmist is awake and vigilant, opening himself for whatever is to be revealed as the hours pass.

Many people regard religion as uninteresting and, as a result, devote little time to spiritual pursuits. Even if something happens in their lives that generates a flicker of spiritual arousal, they quickly turn aside to more accessible gratifications. Their attitude becomes a self-fulfilling prophecy. Having dismissed the reality of the spiritual world, they are ensconced in an existence from which its outreach is barred.

If we hope to be touched by the spiritual world, we must leave ourselves open to its embrace. This means leaving empty spaces in our day in which the message can reach us. Filling the hours with all kinds of necessary or entertaining activities will probably mean that there are no gaps in our consciousness through which something unexpected may pass. Creative living demands intervals, periods in which we are somewhat disconnected from our usual occupations so that what is submerged deep within us may rise to the surface, and what is outside us but has long been unnoticed may have an impact on us. These precious moments of revelation will not happen if we have shoehorned so much into our days that there is no space for anything else. And, as we have probably experienced for ourselves, even the most banal physical tasks demand a degree of mental and emotional energy.

If we are to grow in wisdom, there needs to be some expenditure of time in which we are busy doing nothing. Stepping back, reflecting, thinking about something else, opening ourselves to inspiration. Looking at matters from a different standpoint. This happens easily to people of a naturally reflective temperament, but for the rest of us it comes at a price. We can never find time for interior activity; we have to make time. This necessarily involves taking time from other activities and deliberately leaving it empty.

The psalmist sees the hours of darkness as providing the opportunity to ponder the word of God. In biblical times, of course, the world was mostly closed to business when the sun went down. Lamplight was limited in what it allowed and it was presumed that only rogues were abroad during the night. Thus, these hours of relative leisure could become the occasion for activities that are incompatible with the hurly-burly of the daily round. Conversation, intimacy, rest, certainly, but also meditation. When activities cease and the sensory load is reduced, the mind is free to wander into areas that have been left unvisited during the day: to process experience, to hear the echoes of the day, to listen to inner voices that demand to be heard. Undoubtedly a rich time, but one which our modern world has largely eliminated. Unless we want to be different and make the effort to restore it.

149   Hear my voice, in accordance with your kindness,
     give me life in accordance with your judgment.

CONCORDANCE

What is intimated in this verse is the certainty that the One who is revealed in the various channels of divine self-revelation corresponds to the reality, that the nature and attitude of God is truthfully conveyed by the Scriptures and by God's other revelatory actions. People who ponder the word of the LORD day and night become imbued with an image of God that is wholly dependent on divine self-revelation. They are less influenced by what others think or say about the divinity. In a certain sense, their perspective on God is the result of sustained encounter. It is direct and experiential. On the other hand, "the gods of the heathen are nothing" (Ps 96:5), mere confections of uninspired imagination, or convenient constructs designed to support a political system.

Because the picture of a loving God communicated by revelation is guaranteed, then we can allow ourselves to incorporate it in our philosophy of life. In particular, we can take as a given God's unconditional benevolence. Whatever we experience as life passes through its many changes, one thing is certain, as Psalm 136 reiterates: "God's kindness is for ever." When things do not happen as we hope, or when our plans go astray, it is easy to assume wrongly that the reason for this lies in an all-powerful indifference to our welfare. Or worse. It may seem to us during dark days that God does not care about our troubles or, maybe, we are inclined to see God as the ultimate cause of our afflictions. We may come to the conclusion that God is punishing us for something we have done or left undone.

Whatever we may feel when things go wrong, we need to keep reminding ourselves that God's actions in our regard are not determined by our conduct. God is beyond the changeable universe of space and time and acts only in accordance with the divine nature. And, revelation keeps insisting, God's nature is to be kind and life-giving, to bring forth beauty and fruitfulness out of nothingness, to repair the evil wrought by sin, and to wipe away the tears of the afflicted. These are the actions typical of God.

If it seems, in our present situation, that God is acting differently, that conclusion is necessarily a distortion of reality. Our perception is skewed. We need to step back and take a longer view. Not everything is comprehensible to us at the moment that it happens. Sometimes it takes years, or even decades, before we begin to recognize the creative function of something that we had long dismissed as merely crucifying. What we are praying for, in this verse of the psalm, is the wisdom to be somewhat detached from immediate impressions and snap judgments, and willing to wait while the deeper meaning of events is unveiled. We pray that we may begin to perceive that God's response to a cry for help is always one of benevolence and beneficence. If we cannot yet perceive this, our hesitation is due to our incapacity and not to God's. We are praying that an understanding of God's all-pervasive kindness may gradually dawn in our hearts and minds.

150 Schemers are near,
   but they are far from your instruction.

SCHEMERS

God's instruction, or *torah*, is proposed to us as a means of guidance toward a fuller life. By following it we learn to transcend the immediacy and urgency of instinctual demands and live a life of ordered goodness. This means that our actions are governed by something outside our subjective universe which is likelier to serve a more universal good. Revelation will often provide us with a useful question mark to set alongside many of the judgments we form so hastily. It serves as a second opinion, providing an alternative purview.

Schemers—sometimes including ourselves—are people who hatch plots that they hope will deliver the outcomes that they desire. It sounds devious and it usually is. To be single-minded in the pursuit of a goal, without any reference to its impact on others, bespeaks a person with a tendency to narcissism, one strongly stamped with a sense of entitlement. There is no room for negotiation, compromise, or altruism; what I want is regarded as the only criterion for judgment. The needs or preferences of others are irrelevant. Sometimes quite a lot of time and thought is devoted to maneuvering into a position which might improve the chances of achieving the desired result. Nothing else matters.

Building into our lives an openness to the word of God, helps to undermine the claims of the Ego to absolute authority. It teaches us to step back and consider the impact that our plans have on others. This is not to say that we should not make plans. Plans are a necessary part of interacting with a complex world. They are so important that they need to be subjected to intelligent and compassionate scrutiny. Those who hatch schemes often have a disproportionate confidence in the rightness of their own spontaneous proposals, but this confidence derives from excluding any evidence that derives from outside themselves. If it feels good, do it. The more people savor the desired outcome, the less likely they are to pay much attention to its collateral damage.

To live in the context of God's word means that our self-serving inclinations are subject to challenge. We are invited to consider the broader implications of what we are about to do—and of what we decide not to do. How it will impact other people, how it will affect society and the world in general, and even what will be its less visible and long-term effects on myself. The word of God is alive and dynamic; it is not a dead letter. It provides us with up-to-date directives on how to live more fully and more fruitfully. Allowing it the freedom to interact with the present moment releases us from the tyranny of unexamined initiatives and poses the possibility of a greater level of prudence.

In a sense, slowing down to consider all things carefully makes life heavier; it adds gravitas to our lives. That need not be a bad thing. Perhaps we need to remember that heavy objects are usually more stable, less moved by ambient change. We see more when we slow down, and taking the time to reflect on the larger picture will often give us greater confidence and verve in the course we eventually adopt.

✺

151   You are near, O Lord,
        and all your commandments are truth.

CLOSENESS

The closeness of God is both comfort and challenge. A distant God can be honored perfunctorily and then easily ignored or forgotten. A God who is close is one who must be taken into account in every choice and every action of every day. "Whether you turn to the right or to the left, your ears will hear a voice behind you, saying: This is the way; walk in it" (Isa 30:19-21). One indication of the genuineness of our devotion is this double character: on the one hand it is a source of consolation and encouragement but, on the other, it makes demands on us. Often enough these are not alternatives, but mysteriously simultaneous. God expresses support of us by asking us to do more. We grow through meeting the challenges that God's lovingkindness sets before us.

A distant God is a God from whom we have become alienated. There will, perhaps, be periods in our history when this is a reality. This can be caused by either strength or weakness. When we feel strong and everything is going well, we exult in our autonomy. God is banished to the sidelines. On the other hand, when we are weighed down by failure and when we feel that we are unable to cope with what life delivers, we may come to the conclusion that God has deserted us and left us to manage on our own. In both cases we have written God out of our life.

Our feelings are deceptive. God remains close to us and God's benevolence is unchanging. Opening our hearts and our lives to

God's word grounds us in the truth at a level deeper than mere appearances. Because our powers of perception are conditioned by space and time they are not always free from error. We may not publicly claim to be all-knowing, but we often act as if we were. We do not engage in self-doubt to the extent that prudence demands, but rush to put our plans into effect as though no alternative is worth considering. More frequently than we care to admit, the blunders that we make are the consequence of failing to take the time to consider matters from all angles; we often act on partial truth without a care to envisage the whole. By remaining fixedly in our own frame of reference, we drift away from the whole truth and, as a consequence, do damage to others, and to ourselves.

The word of God is close and constantly invites us to an ampler awareness: "The word is very close to you; it is in your mouth and in your heart so that you may put it into practice" (Deut 30:14). Ongoing contact with God's self-revelation serves as a mirror for our souls. It forms our consciences and binds them more completely to the truth. This is a burden for those who prefer to live thoughtlessly, but a great blessing for those who cherish authenticity and who aspire to attain an ever-greater degree of humanity. Living in response to God's life-giving commandments renews the divine image in us so that we become more like God. By responding positively to God's closeness, we become close to God at the deepest level of our being. God is always present to us and we are no longer absent from God.

152   From antiquity I have known from your testimonies
        that they are established for ever.

ANTIQUITY

In this translation, the psalmist seems to be saying that the wisdom of divine revelation transcends his own experience of it.

Beyond the written text, there exists an ever-growing tradition that receives, adapts, and hands on what has been revealed. God has spoken in many and varied ways through the centuries, and what has been communicated to humanity is embodied not only on the pages of Scripture, but also in the lives of people, in their attempts to express in words what they believe, and in the institutions which they have developed as a result of what they have learned.

This reality reminds us that God's self-revelation is corporate. It is addressed ultimately not to individuals but to the whole of humanity and it is meant to serve as a cohesive agent among different races and cultures and languages. Of course, it has to be translated from the language and idiom in which it was first received and, inevitably, there are variations in the different renderings. However, the word of God was never intended to become domesticated, subservient to particular preferences and prejudices. It retains its independence. A translation or interpretation that attempts to control the wildness of divine revelation so that it does not pose a challenge to the established order is not only inadequate, it is verging on the blasphemous.

Before we allow our minds to race to a rapid conclusion about the meaning of a particular text, it is necessary for us to recognize that Scripture comes from a different age and a different culture and addresses situations that are alien to what we are experiencing. Of course, there is the bond of a common humanity which allows us to feel some degree of empathy that spans the centuries, but we need to restrain our inclination to believe that we can immediately and effortlessly understand the full meaning of what we are reading. Just as it is hard work to enter into negotiation with a person of another culture, so drawing sustenance from the Scriptures requires a judicious degree of preparation and a high level of attention. A radically fundamentalist approach to the Bible is not only lazy, it is stupid.

Opening the Scriptures is best understood as entering a different world. Not only the world of the patriarchs and prophets, but one in which we are in a state of connection with the whole of humanity, finding within ourselves echoes of their joys and hopes, their griefs and anxieties. It is from within this maelstrom that we lift up our hearts to God, given confidence by the assurances of age-old revelation. We step out from our familiar environment not to abandon it, but to search for its deeper meaning, to understand its vicissitudes in a broader context. In some sense this means that we have to leave ourselves behind in order to find ourselves. To listen to the Scriptures with a purified heart—not to reinforce our existing preferences and prejudices, but to challenge us to see things from a different perspective. Every day to make a fresh start. God's word is eternal and ever-new. By opening ourselves to the divine testimonies we sow the seeds of eternal life in ourselves and in the world of which we are a part.

153   See my affliction and rescue me,
     for I have not forgotten your instruction.

AFFLICTION

In the course of a lifetime, all of us have the experience of affliction. Sometimes our troubles are widely known, on other occasions they are more interior and subtle. Our characters are largely formed by how we deal with these interludes of pain. Dealing with good fortune usually does not precipitate us into a crisis, but there are always feelings of inadequacy and confusion when disaster strikes, even when it involves something considerably less than a catastrophe. If we were confident in our ability to handle a negative situation, and we had the resources needed to do so, it would simply be a challenge. Nothing more. It is our sense of being unable to respond appropriately that upsets us.

Few adults are pleased to admit their helplessness, even in minor matters. Our society encourages us in the delusion that absolute autonomy is desirable. And so, we become distressed when confronted with something that demands more than we can give. The solution is relatively simple. Since interdependence is a strong bonding factor in human relationships, it makes sense that we should make an effort to overcome our reluctance to be dependent on others, to appreciate their different gifts, and to rely on their kindness. To the extent that we embark on such a course, a crisis can become an experience of human solidarity. We feel closer to those who have come to our assistance and, perhaps, to humanity in general. And the seeds are sown in us, whereby we become more likely to step forward and render aid when we encounter somebody else who needs it.

The same dynamic operates in our relationship with God. We are likely to experience God's kindness most fully when we are extricated from some difficult situation, whether by some extraordinary intervention, or by the kindly action of another person, or by the unexpected activation of hidden sources of strength and resilience in ourselves. We feel that we have been saved. Salvation is not something that we can manufacture from our own resources; it comes as a gift from outside ourselves. Even if we cooperate with what is happening, we are largely passive in the process; the credit belongs to another.

It is because we are mindful of the lessons we have learned from God's self-revelation that we cry out for help when trouble looms. Perhaps only when trouble looms. If we are gifted with a more profound self-knowledge we will begin to discover how precarious life is, and how shallow our goodness. We will begin to feel more acutely our absolute dependence on God, not only as a philosophical conclusion but as a lived experience. Conscious that, from the beginning, we were formed in the divine image and likeness, we are aware of how far short we have fallen of God's glory, and the consequent need for radical re-formation. Even without an impending crisis to trigger a cry of alarm, this sense of falling short of our possibilities motivates us to turn toward God for help. Even when affliction is not present, the prospect of it can prompt us to re-activate our relationship with God and to remain connected by maintaining regular contact with the word of God which has been given to us as a source of guidance and strength.

154   Be an advocate in my case and act as my kinsman,
      for I have not forgotten your utterances.

ADVOCACY

The psalmist asks God to take his side in the struggle with his adversaries. The legal language is quite particular. Not only does he pray to be supported in forensic proceedings, but, in the evocation of the term *goel*, the psalmist is calling on God to intervene as his kinsman and avenger and wreak punishment on those who have unjustly risen up against him.

In a world far less individualistic than our own, to be alone and surrounded by enemies was a nightmare scenario. To be secure meant having allies nearby. To be without family and friends was to be unprotected and exposed to the whims of the powerful.

In the ancient world might was right; those in positions of authority were subject to few restraints. They could do whatever they wished. To become the focus of the hostility of a king or queen meant certain death. As we see when Ahab and Jezebel decided to confiscate Naboth's vineyard. Or when David lusted after Uriah's wife. Resistance was futile. A king imposed the law; he was not subject to it. There was no legal protection for those who found themselves in conflict with the monarch. The same pattern repeated itself throughout society at the various levels where power was exercised. As it has been throughout history; absolute power is inevitably corrupt—however much specious rhetoric might seek to disguise the fact.

The only check on absolute power in biblical times was the word of God spoken through the prophets; we see this in the prophetic denunciations of royal crimes. God's word was unchained and not in servitude to any earthly ruler. It had the right to speak the truth to power. To disregard the rights of humble folk was not subject to any earthly sanction but it incurred the wrath of God. It was an affront to the social order God has established. Unjustly to cause pain to other human beings was an offense against God and deserved punishment. It is in the context of this truth that the psalmist calls on God to fight on his side.

If we have the right to appeal for God's assistance, so do others. It may be that we are the victims of injustice, but it is also possible that sometimes we are its perpetrators. When we forget God's utterances and become estranged from the divine vision for humanity, we may find ourselves believing that the only criterion for action is our personal advantage. I will do it if it feels good, if it brings me a profit, if it advances my cause. When I am the sole arbiter of what is right and wrong, it is almost inevitable either that I will drift into a state of relative lawlessness or I will be confronted by a sudden challenge that leaves me powerless to do what is right and good.

Being mindful of God's word protects me from reaching the point where I give consent to evil and turn my back on what is good. And it gives me the right to call upon God in my troubles, being certain that these come from outside myself and are not merely the inevitable consequence of my own perversity.

155   The wicked are far from salvation,
      for they have not sought your statutes.

WICKED

The word "wicked" is so extreme in describing persons or their behavior that it is sometimes used jocosely. But the reality is no laughing matter. To the extent that wickedness exists those who embrace it will be stained by the association. However, references to "the wicked" occur relatively rarely in the narrative texts of the Bible, although there is ample enough evidence of wickedness. Mostly the word is found in the Psalms and in wisdom literature—which may indicate that it is more like a poetic abstraction than a label that can be attached to particular people.

In the psalms the wicked are identified as the godless. They say in their hearts, "There is no God." As a result of their alienation from the spiritual world they are strangers to the righteousness that follows devotion to God's self-revelation; the wicked do not seek to understand God's statutes. Whatever their beliefs, their actions show them to be practical atheists. They are the enemies of the good and persecutors of the powerless. Their prosperity and immunity from punishment often pose a puzzle for the righteous, who ask the same question as Jeremiah: "Why does the way of the wicked prosper?" (Jer 12:1). Yet there is a quiet assurance that ultimately God will reverse matters and the wicked will perish and be remembered no more. "The way of the wicked goes nowhere" (Ps 1:6).

Psalm 37, in particular, has much to say on this topic. The wicked seem to be flourishing and triumphant (35). They borrow without repaying (22). They hatch evil schemes (7, 12) and plot violence against the righteous and the afflicted (14), watching for an occasion to kill them (32). But the time of reversal will come. Their power will be broken (15), they will wither like grass (2), they will vanish like smoke (20), they will perish (9-10, 20), and be destroyed (22, 36, 38), wiped out forever and their children destroyed (28). The lesson the psalm seeks to impart is similar to that found in Psalm 73: the prosperity and ease of the godless is illusory and impermanent. Ecclesiastes would say it is "vanity." A day of reckoning will come when the righteous will be rewarded and those who have lived without God will come to nothing.

Righteousness is no guarantee of earthly prosperity. It certainly relieves us of the anguish occasioned by living a life that is out of harmony with our nature, but it is not necessarily a promise of wealth, status or worldly power. These visible benefits are highly esteemed and sought by many, but they are not necessarily signs of goodness or humanity. In a sense, righteousness is its own reward because it forms in us a kind of detachment from worldly goods and accomplishments, and stabilizes our lives by taking the faithfulness of God as our principal point of reference.

The binary picture posed by the psalm is perhaps poetic and exaggerated. Absolute heinousness is not so common; we are all mixtures of good and evil, and the bad things we do are not always dramatic. Perhaps we practice wickedness more often by omission; by failing to do the good the opens up before us, not from malice but from slackness.

❧

156   Great is your compassion, Lord,
      according to your judgments, give me life

TENDERNESS

It seems fairly unusual for religious people to speak of God's tenderness. Those with a compulsive bent toward moralizing portray God as one who is absolutely upright, and who demands of us that we, in our own limited way, follow this example. Of course, it is impossible, and so we go through life burdened with a sense of our inadequacy. We cannot match God's expectations of us; we represent some kind of cosmic failure. Those who decide that this is no way to live simply blot out any awareness of the spiritual world and pursue their lives as if there were no God.

When these people deny the existence of an overbearing and tyrannical God they are perfectly correct. Such a God is a mere figment of the moralizing imagination, suitable for frightening children, but lacking any basis in sound reasoning or divine revelation.

The God that has been revealed to us by many voices and at different times is a God characterized by great mercy and compassion. This is hard for many of us to believe—perhaps because of our own childhood experiences. God who knows the dust of which we are made does not expect us to perform like minor deities—that was the delusory suggestion made by the serpent to Adam and Eve. As humans, we are a curious mixture of humus and divine imagehood; there will always be a tug of war within us, whether we bend low toward the earth or look upward to heaven. We will not always choose to follow our highest gifts or realize our highest potential; too often we will follow the easier path and let our lower tendencies prevail. However, the fact that we are often disappointed in ourselves does not mean that God is disappointed in us, or inclined to abandon us to our own self-chosen misery.

When we speak of the great compassion of God we are not merely envisaging a merciful tolerance of our failures. There is more. The greater the mess we make of our lives the more God is active: not to punish us for our aberrations, but to repair the damage we have wrought on ourselves. God looks on our situation more to pity than to blame. We are never rejected as being beyond any hope of redemption. We are lost, but a way of restoration exists. Just as there is no point on the planet from which a straight line cannot be drawn to any other point, so, there is always a road that leads from present misery to a more abundant life.

God's life-giving judgments are a lamp for our feet and a light for our path. It does not matter what kind of life-threatening morass into which we have plunged, by exposing our lives to God's compassionate word, we will begin to find solutions. Not necessarily immediately. Sometimes we have to be painfully purged of false premises before we can begin to see a point of light toward which to move. And sometimes the path is rocky and steep, and demands effort. But always gazing on God's word and taking it to heart will open a way before us and endow us with the resources needed to follow it. Such is the great compassion of our God.

157   Many are my pursuers and enemies,
 but I have not turned aside from your testimonies.

MEDIOCRITY

To live in accordance with God's self-revelation usually involves incurring the displeasure of those who have chosen a different path. Sometimes this hostility may be overt and lethal, more often it will be polite and underhanded. Plans and propositions may be negated by passive aggression, suggestions resisted with a smirk, and actions deliberately misinterpreted. To be open to God's word and to be obedient to it means that human authority has less than total persuasive power for us. Because human authority is not implicitly convincing it needs to be coercive if its injunctions are to be put into practice.

It is curious that the effort to remain faithful to God's plan for humanity should provoke such antipathy. There is a fair amount of tolerance for those whose lives are patently immoral, and for those who are bemired in lifelong inertia, but those who try to practice everyday goodness are often scorned and rejected. Like the prophets, they are seen to be a living rebuke to those around them. Mediocrity is the norm; those who try to do better than that are subjected to ridicule, or worse.

To remain faithful to the gift of God's self-revelation and to walk according to its light will inevitably bring us into conflict with the powers of darkness. There is no escaping this. Faith in God's word will not bring us prosperity and worldly esteem; it is far more likely to be a source of trouble and harassment. Even in groups that are supposedly religious, the challenge to operate on the basis of other-worldly standards is often too great. Higher beliefs and values give way before the prevailing customs of secular society, especially in matters that are judged to be of minor importance—forgetting that the way to apostasy begins with small steps.

If we are going to base our life on God's word we need to recognize that this requires a cool-headed acceptance that our fidelity will not win us applause or popularity. It is more likely to squeeze us out of the inner circle into the margins. Few organizations are able to maintain their initial high standards for long; compromise with prevailing social attitudes soon sets in. Those who continue to proclaim the primitive ideals are effectively reduced to silence or are hounded out of active membership. Most of us prefer to live without being admonished by prophets.

Sometimes active persecution forces people to make a decision about the direction of their lives. To the extent that it renders compromise impossible, it can lead to an increase in fervor. What most of us face is far more insidious: the slow erosion of basic values and the gradual rationalization of behavior that was once considered unacceptable. We don't depart and slam the door on what we once believed, we simply drift off into an isolated corner where we can be untouched by any challenge. We lose the specificity of our beliefs and values and allow ourselves to become conformed to whatever is undemanding. We are not wicked; just weak.

158   I look with disgust on those who break faith,
        for they do not keep your utterance.

BREAKING FAITH

The essential element in faithfulness is its permanence. Those who are faithful remain steadfast in their commitment—notably when hard times come. Usually commitments are made in joy and generosity; there is an aspirational quality about them. But, as we all know, times change; storm clouds gather and sometimes we are caught in a downpour of negativity which demands more of us than lighthearted promises. We have to remain steadfast against contrary forces which threaten to divert us away from the noble course we had intended. A changed situation, a harsh word, an unforeseen difficulty, can make it difficult for us to continue as we had planned. We discover to our dismay that fidelity comes at a cost.

Perhaps it is true that we live in a time in which words have become trivialized. We say things but we do not really mean them; we make promises easily and just as easily forget them. As a result, one of the important bonds by which society as a whole is held together loses its tenacity. The same is true of other groups, communities and families. If we cannot trust others to be faithful to the words they have spoken, credibility is lost and solidarity is weakened. If we cannot trust others we are left relying only on ourselves. On the other hand, if I am known to mean what I say, then others can construct a meaningful response, whether they agree with me or not. If my words lack substance they are simply a puff of air that is rightly dismissed.

To break faith is to undermine the foundation of human relations. In Henry Purcell's opera *Dido and Aeneas*, Dido sings to her wavering lover: "O feckless man, it is enough whate'er thou now decree, that thou once thought of leaving me." The verse seems to suggest that even an errant thought is enough to destroy that mutual trust which enables a relationship to flourish. By how much more do actions that are inconsistent with protestations of affection estrange and alienate. The closer the relationship, the less there is room for compromise. There is almost nothing that may be regarded as too small to worry about.

If infidelity damages relationships, it is especially destructive for the one guilty of it. To turn one's back on a commitment is to act dishonorably. It would have been better not to have made the commitment than to hold it so loosely that it is dropped when more attractive possibilities appear. To commit oneself is to be bound; in an enthusiastic gesture of love, one has freely chosen not to be free. To cast off that attachment is to demean oneself and to signal that one's solemn word lacks substance.

Human fidelity is supported by an attachment to the revealing word of the God of all faithfulness. By keeping God's word, we add solidity and strength to our own. By abiding in our willingness to be shaped by the divine self-revelation we begin to share the permanence of God. Our word becomes steadfast: able to endure all the vicissitudes that life brings, solid in its commitments, undeviating in its values, and unshakeable in its love.

159   See how I love your precepts,
      Lord, in your kindness give me life.

FULFILMENT

When we consider our response to precepts and commandments we usually think in terms of obligation and obedience. We are constrained to do what otherwise we would have left undone. Whether this is the result of a sense of duty or under the influence of coercion, it involves acting in a way that is not of our own choosing. Reluctance and resistance may be repressed, but living in accordance with God's commandments often seems to demand of us something that is foreign to our natural inclinations. However, the truth is different.

Inasmuch as we are created in God's image and likeness, our way of living should mirror the inherent nobility of our nature. To be like God is not only our privilege, it is our calling. We are expected to reflect the glory of God in the choices that we make and in the form that we give to our life. We are most ourselves when we act like God, and we know how to act like God by conforming ourselves to God's self-revelation. That is why we love God's precepts. They are not alien impositions, but directives that point the way to a more authentic existence. The word of God shows us the way to become more fully ourselves; to bring to realization the potential inherent in us from the moment of our creation.

What is demanded of us is that we allow God's beneficent providence to shape and reshape us so that what is true, noble and honorable in us expands, and whatever degrades us is gradually expelled. This process takes a lifetime and it works its magic through many twists and turns of fortune—beyond what we can understand or appreciate. We need boundless trust in the efficacy of an invisible hand that guides all that befalls us; not losing heart when we fail to see where events are leading us or when everything seems to conspire to our ruin. Devotion to the Scriptures teaches us to accept God's ultimate governance over all that happens in our world.

Yet we are not entirely passive. While it is true that sometimes—and even often—we have simply to endure contrary incursions into our lives, it is also true that sometimes—and even often—we are called upon to change the course of events by conscious choices. In these circumstances, creative outcomes depend on our capacity to determine what is truly life-giving. This demands of us the capacity for discernment: the ability to step back from immediate impressions and to consider the deeper implications of the alternatives that confront us. We have to activate our conscience to allow it to throw light on the various possibilities. This presupposes that our consciences are living and active, that they have been formed by long exposure to God's word so that they are able to intuit what is from God and leads to life.

Obedience to the divine precepts is not oppressive or alienating, but exposes us more fully to God's kindness, and this radiation of the divine glory is life-giving for us. It causes us to grow so that we become what we were made to be: the image and reflection of God.

160   Truth is the foundation of your word,
    and all your judgments are forever righteous.

TRUTH-TELLING

The importance of foundations is not always obvious; they are hidden away from sight. Viewers may admire the architectural wizardry of a noble edifice, but nobody bothers much with the foundations. Yet, if the basis of a building is not solid, the whole structure is liable to collapse when subjected to unexpected stress.

God's word to us is built on truth, understood not merely as intellectual content but as an attitude that can be relied on. God is committed to truth-telling. God's word will not lead us astray, because the divine revelation is faithful not only to itself but also to us. There is no ambiguity in what is communicated: God's loving kindness is unqualified and unconditional. Nothing that happens in the world of space and time can impugn the reliability of this word which is both comfort and challenge. Comfort because God's love endures for ever. Challenge because this love calls on us to respond: to reciprocate by a return of love, expressed not only by words but also by actions.

Responding appropriately to God's word allows us to live in accordance with the truth of our being. We are who and what we are meant to be when we are singing in harmony with the message we have received. We are living in the truth. This is the service that God's word renders—to show us how to become in reality what we are by nature. Perhaps we read the same inspired texts that others read, yet what impacts on us is quite distinctive. God's word echoes in the chamber of our heart with a unique resonance: judging us, correcting us, directing us, guiding us, consoling us, encouraging us, empowering us. It is uniquely formed to respond to what is most intimate in us, modifying itself to suit our needs as we pass through the various changes and challenges that life's journey encounters. Our interrelationship with God is fundamentally real; there is no scope for regret about past failures or dread about future defaults. God remains an eternal presence in our lives whatever happens; the foundations of the relationship are solid.

When we affirm that God's judgements are righteous, we are not evoking a judge of such rigorous integrity that all are abashed in his presence. The righteousness of God is not something that creates a distance between us. It is an active, contagious righteousness that renders righteous all that it touches. God's undeviating goodness means that the more that we are in contact with it, the more we are suffused with its character. We become good by mingling with ultimate goodness. Not so much by trying to be good and making stern efforts to practice goodness in all that we do. Such virtue is the effect of goodness, not its cause. Our efforts are not primary. What changes us is what God does in us. God's indwelling self-revelation and self-communication constitute an abiding presence that is on our lips and in our hearts awaiting a response. The God who is forever righteous, is forever making us righteous—to the extent that we allow ourselves to be transformed. The word that God utters tells us who and what we are, and it truthfully points to who and what we shall become.

161   Princes oppressed me without cause,
      yet my heart is in awe of your word.

IMMUNITY

The great of this world habitually surround themselves with external pomp and circumstance in an attempt to persuade ordinary people that they are not like the rest of humankind. They are superior or, at least, they want us to think that. It is a great gift to be unimpressed by such claims. The baubles used to present an attractive public face aim at disguising the privilege, corruption and oppression that often accompany the possession of power, especially when it is unconstrained. The rhetoric of authority as service is often no more than a cloak to conceal the personal advantages accrued by those in power.

To be skeptical of the integrity of the powerful—not to accept it unquestioningly as absolute—is to incur their wrath, and oppression will likely follow. This does not always take the form of overt persecution; there are subtler ways of making another's life miserable. The most usual of these is the denial of privileges. Those who give unqualified support to a prince's claims to superiority will find their way through life eased through all kinds of collateral benefits; those who have reservations will be excluded from these.

To resist princely claims of absolute authority usually means that we have reserved our obedience for a less visible power: conscience, Scripture, God. This is a conscious choice that we have made: to give our allegiance to the spiritual world above all the demands that worldly princelings might seek to enforce. It is a consistent preference for the unseen over what is visible, for what is eternal over that which has hegemony merely over a brief span of time, for what is divine over all the enticements of the created universe.

This is more a matter of consistently saying "Yes" to God than of merely refusing to attribute absolute authority to earthly powers. The affirmation of God's authority is not something that is once given and then forgotten. It is an everyday reality. It involves exposing our life to God's self-revelation in the Scriptures, pondering the word and applying it to our particular situation, allowing it to shape the choices that we make. Attachment to God's word enables us to discern the most life-giving path, not only rejecting what is patently wrong, but more especially choosing among several good options what will lead to the best outcome. This is what is meant by the frequent assertion that divine revelation is life-giving. God's word is also a judgement. It teaches us to be self-critical when we have made the wrong choices, and enables us to stumble back to a way that is less harmful.

When we give priority to the word of God we develop a kind of immunity from the pressure to conform to the wishes of the powerful. The word of princes is not absolute. One who is filled with awe at the presence of the unseen God and who accepts the authority of God's word stands back from the submissive throng and commits only to obedience to God, even though it leads to a loss of privileges and even to oppression: "The instruction from your mouth is better for me than thousands in silver and gold" (Ps 119:72).

162   I rejoiced over your utterances,
     like one finding great plunder.

GRATUITY

The reason God's word becomes a source of joy for us is that it is unmerited. It speaks to us out of silence and interrupts whatever we are doing in order to point us in the direction of a more abounding life. At the time, perhaps, we do not always recognize its inherent graciousness; it may seem more like an unwelcome interruption to our plans. Yet, years later, looking back on our lives, we may begin to appreciate that, on many occasions, divine providence has gratuitously provided us with sufficient guidance to reshape our lives for the better.

The image of finding treasure that we may claim for our own without any entitlement on our part, is a good illustration of the undeserved concern that God permanently exercises on our behalf. Unless we have a deep appreciation of the gratuitousness of God's interventions in our life, we put ourselves in danger of thinking that, in some way, we have earned our good fortune by our upright lives and pious service. Not so. We are not chosen because we are good; rather we are chosen in order that we may become a little better. The people of Israel had to be reminded of this. "It was not because you were more numerous than all other peoples that the Lord was concerned for you and chose you, for you were the least of all other peoples" (Deut 7:7).

The gratuity of God's gifts is an indication that human reason is not able fully to comprehend the meaning of what happens by divine intervention in our world of space and time. When Ecclesiastes proclaims that everything is enveloped in fog, he is not denying its intrinsic meaning but reminding us of our inability to grasp very much of the divine purpose. Part of wisdom consists in appreciating the limits of human intelligence. When it comes to cosmic mysteries we are not very bright. This means that the ordering of the universe is best left to God. Confidence that God's loving concern is somehow expressed in everything that happens is built up only by meditating on the record of God's dealings with humanity and the undeviating attachment shown by God even to the nation that repeatedly contravened the terms of the covenant. Opening our hearts to God's self-revelation helps us to understand God's attitude to us and leads us into a state of wonderment at the magnanimity and generosity of the Creator.

God's gifts to us are not rewards for hard work and sustained effort, but an expression of loving kindness toward creatures destined for a noble calling, but unable to live up to their high destiny.

God is constantly helping us on the way to a more abundant life which eye has not seen nor the human heart conceived. It is not a matter of someone working hard or accomplishing much, but of God showing mercy. Everything falls into the sphere of grace. Understanding something of this is a relief from much anxiety and a wellspring of happiness. Gratuity always provokes a response of gratitude, and gratitude is always seasoned with joy.

163   I hate and abhor falsehood,
      but I love your instruction.

PARTIALITY

We are told that the prophet Elijah slaughtered in a single day more false claimants than ever there were genuine prophets (1 Kgs 18:20-40). Perhaps this incident may serve as a warning against being too credulous in accepting unsubstantiated statements from unaccredited sources. We are naïve if we do not recognize that there are also many purveyors of falsity in today's world—the difference being that they have ampler means of disseminating untruth than did the prophets of Baal.

The fact that there is much in this world of space and time that transcends rational comprehension opens the door to non-rational explanations. It seems that we are more likely to accept what is stated clearly and simply than that which preserves intact the mystery of the universe. Bold binary propositions are easier to swallow than nuanced considerations; the headlines of tabloid media attest to this. Opinion becomes confused with knowledge and distorted information leads to a progressive loss of intelligence. There are many for whom the convenience of a black-and-white world is preferable to the harrowing complexity of reality.

There is, however, a subtler and more dangerous form of falsehood that consists in partial truth. This involves selecting a part of the whole and inflating its importance—for example, rigorously observing one of the Ten Commandments and ignoring the others, as if condemning murder and condoning adultery represents a reasonable application of covenant obligations.

More often than not, controversy erupts about conflicting interpretations of complex truths. In a sense, what each party asserts is true, but it is not the whole truth. The resolution usually consists in seeking common ground and building a degree of consensus upon it. Polarizing never leads to truth but only perpetuates division.

We are all prone to seeing only part of the whole because the whole is beyond our powers of perception. We can represent the whole by poetry or art or story or by prophetic gesture, but we cannot englobe its full possibilities. The first stage of wisdom is to recognize our intellectual limitations. Then, in a state of creative self-doubt, we can look for reliable means of ascertaining the validity of our conclusions. This usually means embracing a more collaborative vision of reality and accepting certain foundational principles.

For people of faith this broader view includes not only the notional acceptance of the validity of God's self-revealing word, but the willingness to adopt its implementation. The full meaning of revelation is encountered only when it is freely put into practice. Words—even sacred words—by themselves are just words. Words reverenced, embraced, internalized, and embodied in behavior gradually unfold something of the hidden mystery of reality. A harmony results with creation and with its Creator that is a source of profound contentment. Taking God's word as a light for our path and a code of conduct displaces the Ego as the primary source of our beliefs and values. And it is the ultimate protection against all forms of delusion and falsehood.

164   Seven times in the day I have praised you
       for your righteous judgments.

REGULARITY

What happens in our world of space and time is often confusing and sometimes troubling. We are unable to comprehend the total meaning of events and, as a result, we often lack an accurate perspective in assessing them. This is why it pays to step back regularly from active involvement in issues to try to view matters in a broader context. In doing this we protect ourselves from compounding our problems by restricting our attention to dealing with a single matter even though this may involve neglecting to notice the effects of our actions in another area.

For people of faith, it is easy to reduce religion to a single department of our life with the result that it is effectively barred from having an influence on many of our everyday choices. We say a few prayers and then live the rest of our day as if there were no God. In this way, religious activity is regarded as one activity among many and can be often sidelined by the urgency of things to be dealt with or displaced by the more gratifying possibilities that offer themselves. This is why those who publicly practice their religion leave themselves open to special ridicule when other aspects of their conduct are reprehensible. Most of us have little patience with those who do not practice what they seem to preach, perhaps forgetting that we ourselves could be targets for similar reproaches.

Perhaps religion is better understood not as a stand-alone activity alongside everything else, but a seasoning that adds a special flavor to everything we do. The moral quality of an action is largely determined by the intention with which the action is performed. An act of kindness done to impress a television audience is likely less noble than one done unobtrusively from inner goodness. Dissonance of heart and external action is frequently the object of prophetic denunciation, because authentic religion is concerned chiefly with inner disposition. As such genuine religion has the capacity to enhance the moral quality of whatever is done, irrespective of the objective importance of the action performed. A cup of cold water given in love has more power to produce a good effect than a larger gift bestowed with indifference.

Trying constantly to remember God's self-revelation, as Deuteronomy frequently admonishes us, is easier said than done. Even the most assiduous efforts to remain conscious of the requirements consequent upon divine instruction do not easily percolate into everything we do. We will easily be lulled into a fog of forgetfulness unless we resolve to step back from our activities on a regular basis and to lift up our hearts and minds to God and the spiritual world. This is a practice recommended by many religious traditions at morning, noon and night—at least.

Regularity does not necessarily imply routine. It simply introduces an element of rhythm into our day. At fixed moments, we stop and take stock of our situation—looking upwards to see whether what we are doing contributes to the goal we have set before ourselves and, when necessary, re-orienting our course. Like an ocean traveler plotting a course by the stars.

165   There is much peace for those who love your instruction
    and no occasion for stumbling.

STUMBLING

Probably no human life is without the occasional stumble— usually caused by inattention. When our thoughts are directed elsewhere we fail to observe what is under our feet and, as a result, we trip over an unnoticed obstacle. Our journey through life has its share of stumbles. We may be inclined to attribute these to the unevenness of the path on which we tread, but distraction is the real cause of most of our mishaps. The obvious solution is to concentrate more on the track over which we are passing.

Our cult of efficiency often leads us to attempt to do several things at once. The more activities we try to juggle, the less the quantity and quality of attention given to each. For example, we may be so preoccupied with what has happened in the past or what might happen in the future that we fail to notice elements of the present. Importantly, when our commitment to a particular course of action is diminished, the satisfaction we derive from it is reduced and, as a result, we are less inclined to invest further energies in doing it well. An uncreative cycle of mediocrity ensues.

Some degree of clarity about our ultimate goal in life provides us with a means of assessing the relative value of any particular course of action that presents itself. If most of our choices are directed toward attaining that goal, it is likely that our progress will be more consistent, with less energy expended on bootless detours. Knowing where we are going and how best to reach our destination provides a foundation for a meaningful and contented life.

This long psalm often reminds us of the utility of taking frequent sightings on our journey through life. "Your word is a lamp for my feet and a light for my path" (Ps 119:105). Contact with the Scriptures helps us to identify potential obstacles to our progress and shows us how to avoid them. Our life will never be without such stumbling blocks—or scandals—but constantly refreshing our spirits through contact with the word of God will preemptively help us remain on our feet and moving forward. The obscurity of the world around us will not be a problem. "Darkness is not dark for you; the night shines forth like the day" (Ps 139:12).

Allowing ourselves to be guided by the Scriptures is more than a practice of diligently consulting the text when a particular dilemma dawns. It is more a matter of choosing to live in the context of God's word, by ensuring that, through constant meditation and application, the beliefs and values of the Bible are somehow embedded in our heart, ready to rise to the surface of consciousness when needed. This awareness brings with it a profound sense of peacefulness that empowers us to face difficulties with equanimity, being assured that whatever issues arise, we "remain under the shelter of the Most High and rest in the shade of the Almighty" (Ps 91:1).

166   O Lord I looked forward to your salvation
      and I fulfilled your commandments.

EXPECTATION

The confident expectation that all will be well is one of the fruits of dedication to God's word. From constant meditation on God's self-revelation we begin to form an impression of a God who is totally supportive of human life in all its variety, and whose ongoing creative activity includes bringing everything to its intended fulfilment. This truth is not always easy to perceive, especially when it seems that we—and the whole human race—have made a mess of our lives. However, what God intended by creating humanity according to the divine image and likeness will, by the power of God, be brought to a glorious conclusion.

It is important that we appreciate what is meant by the word "salvation." To be saved is not something that we achieve by our own efforts. It is not our work; it is accomplished by a savior. Just as a drowning person is pulled from the surf entirely due to the activity of another, so we are brought to our personal and corporate fulfilment only by the gracious intervention of God. God is not disconnected from human history. What the Bible insists on is that God is constantly at work—sometimes through human agencies—to bring into reality what has been promised.

The sense of being saved inevitably brings with it a sense of exuberance. The problem is, however, that in our achievement-oriented culture we then begin unconsciously to attribute our joy to our own merits: we are happy because we are successful in receiving salvation, and we are successful because we have been good. Instead of being grateful for a gift gratuitously given, we congratulate ourselves on having received it. In seeking to convince ourselves that we are somehow worthy of salvation, we diminish the glory that is due to the generous and forgiving benevolence of God.

Salvation is at work in our lives through everything that happens and through everything that influences the choices that we make. The providence of God is not reserved to those who are, by temperament, law-abiding. It is all-embracing. It is probably true that those who are imaginative and adventurous will more often make mistakes than those who placidly accept to be governed by a mass of detailed regulations, but this does not mean that the mavericks are outside the range of God's loving concern. Sometimes we are allowed to fall away in order to come to an appreciation of what we have lost, and a greater gratitude when it is freely returned to us. "Your apostasy will instruct you" (Jer 2:19). God is as able to accomplish good through our sinfulness as through our piety. It seems that God never intended to create a world of unbroken blandness, but made provision for the interplay of light and darkness. "I am the Lord, and there is none other. I form the light, and create darkness: I make peace, and create evil: I the Lord do all these things" (Isa 45:5-7).

As we experience more of life we begin to appreciate that the Torah is not only a map for the progress of the godly, but also an incentive and guide home for those who wander. We fulfil the commandments not only by judicious observance but also by repentant return.

167   My soul keeps your testimonies
       and loves them very much.

COMPLIANCE

Two people in love often exchange preferences. He wants to do what will please her and she wants to do what pleases him. This mutual deference is based on affection and is a source of joy to both parties. By contrast, wage-earners do what another wants because they hope to be paid for their service. And slaves and those who are tyrannized by detailed regulations do what they are commanded for fear that non-compliance will be punished.

When the psalmist describes his response to God's self-revelation as one of love, he is locating religion at a level that is far above legal obligation or the hope of reward. When love is the motivation, obeying the divine precepts is an act with deep inner resonances that may be far weightier than the external action. It is a case where quantitative judgments may be awry; it is the quality of the action that give it a value.

Why does the psalmist cherish the testimonies of God? Because they provide the basis for meaningful living. God the Creator has established an order in the universe, which guarantees that, in the mind of God, a cosmic harmony exists. The fact that we ourselves are unable to perceive this indicates only that we are alienated from the mind of God. As a result, many things seem meaningless. To operate within the context of God's self-revelation brings with it a sense of harmony with the universe.

More than that, God's word is our assurance that we are loved by God and have a place within the totality. The experience of being loved provokes in us a return of love and with it comes the desire to approach ever closer to God by ensuring that our thoughts and words and actions are singing in harmony with the music God has implanted in our hearts and in the world. This is more than slavish conformity or obedience based on the hope of a reward. It is a matter of recognizing the intrinsic truth of divine revelation not only in itself but also as it concerns us. In setting forth a plan for humankind to fulfil their role in the scheme of things, God has also revealed to each of us a path of ultimate self-realization.

The love for God we experience gradually extends to all that God's providence allows to happen in our lives—even though we still have to grapple with the throes of incomprehension. We are convinced that the more we allow God's word to enter our consciousness and to remain there, the more meaningful even the most puzzling circumstances will become. Loving the Lord God with all our heart and soul and strength, as Deuteronomy enjoins, is a mandate that can be fulfilled only from within. We cannot be compelled to love; it requires free choice. We love God because, somehow, we have perceived God's lovability and our response is inevitable. But for this to happen we need to freely open ourselves to the revelation and that involves the grateful acceptance that leads us to affirm: "The instruction from your mouth is better for me than thousands in silver and gold" (Ps 119:72).

168　I keep your precepts and your testimonies
　　　since all my ways are before you.

FUTURE

One of the convictions that keep us attached to God's word is the belief that we are intimately known to God. "LORD, you have searched me and you know me, you know when I sit and when I rise; from afar you perceive my thoughts" (Ps 139:1-2). If God knows us better than we know ourselves, it is not surprising that a diligent reading of the Scriptures may well reveal something of God's plans for us that would otherwise escape our attention.

How do the Scriptures manifest my personal way forward when they were written thousands of years ago? Objectively they are merely a record of the faith of our spiritual ancestors but, nevertheless, they can convey a personal message for each one of us. For this to happen we have to allow the sacred text not only to provide matter for mental processes; we must allow them to impact on our consciences. To serve as a mirror by which we may come to know ourselves better, understanding the meaning of our past experiences, becoming aware of the full implications of the present moment, providing pointers for the most life-giving path ahead. This is more than an exercise in biblical exegesis—valuable though that may be—it is an attempt to correspond with the injunction: "If today you hear the voice of God, do not harden your hearts" (Ps 95:7-8).

When the prophet is commanded to "speak to the heart of Jerusalem" (Isa 40:2), he is being mandated not to provide information to the exiles, but to offer consolation by reminding them of the potential for a brilliant future. A prospect beyond the imagination of even the most optimistic, granted the dire situation in which they found themselves. The prophet is not merely drawing inevitable consequences from the present, but exploding rational logic by pointing to something utterly beyond the realm of human possibility. "See, the former things have come to pass, and new things I now declare; before they spring forth, I tell you of them" (Isa 42:9). "I am about to do something new; now it springs forth, do you not perceive it?" (Isa 43:19). "From this time forward I make you hear new things, hidden so that you have not known them. They are created now, not long ago; before today you have never heard of them, so that you could not say, 'I already knew them'" (48:6-7). Each time we open the Scriptures we expose ourselves to the possibility that we might be drawn into an unexpected future. "My ways are not your ways—it is the LORD speaking. As the sky is high above the earth so are my ways above your ways, my thoughts above your thoughts" (Isa 55:8-9). No doubt this is why those who welcome the promise of salvation are admonished to sing a new song (Isa 42:10).

To allow God's word to interact with our conscience to create a harmony allows us to live in concordance with our deepest aspirations and to throw off the alienating effects of being socialized in a culture which is becoming progressively more dehumanized. The revelation of God points the way to what we may become. And it is not merely an affirmation of a glorious future, but a promise to make it a reality.

169   May my cry come before you O Lord,
         by your word give me understanding.

OUTCRY

There are many events in life which challenge both our understanding and our acceptance. For example, when we are struck by personal tragedy or when what is happening around us leads us to exclaim with the prophet Jeremiah: "Why do the ways of the wicked prosper?" (Jer 12:1). Our relationship with God is such that we do not have to hide our dismay or indignation. Like Job, it is healthy to vent our negativity in the presence of God. Spontaneous expression of our feelings helps us to avoid repressing them. It is not as though God needs to be informed of our reaction to what is happening in our lives, but we need to ensure that from our end the communication is truthful.

We do not have to dissimulate when we speak to God—to pretend that all is well when we are laid low by distress. This is to cover ourselves with fig-leaves and to take flight from the gaze of God. Prayer that is merely the performance of ritual gestures and the recitation of prescribed words is condemned by the prophets as empty show. We are meant to appear before God as we are. Since God knows even what is hidden in the heart, it is useless to try to project an image of ourselves that differs from reality.

Since human life will always contain elements of struggle (Job 7:1), we can use our difficulties as a starting point for our prayer. "Out of the depths I cry to you Lord, Lord hear my voice" (Ps 130:1-2). A willingness to approach God mindful of our own weakness, blindness and malice, indicates that we have some perception of the magnanimity of God, whose loving concern for us is not diminished by the mess we seem to have made of our lives. In fact, it is probably true that prayer rising out of difficult circumstances is sincerer and more intense than the casual prayer flipped in the direction of God when life is good. The depth of our pain dispels some of our delusions and opens the way to a more transparent relationship. We come before God as we are.

When we are somewhat ashamed of having distanced ourselves from God, it takes courage to return. This is where we need to be reassured that God is willing to receive us. "To the LORD in my distress, I cried and was answered" (Ps 120:1). The unlimited availability of God means that we are able to lift up our hearts whatever be our situation. There are no preliminary protocols to be observed. No ante-chambers to delay our entrance. It may well be that God does not always respond to our requests in the precise manner we had desired or as expeditiously as we had hoped. But there is always a response and an intervention, although we sometimes appreciate what has transpired only in hindsight.

We cannot pray without receiving some response from God. Often that response will be the gift of a better understanding of our situation, particularly of its life-enhancing character. We can sometimes be led to conclude that what we perceived as threatening was so only because it was an invitation to grow.

170   Let my supplication come before your face;
deliver me according to your utterance.

DELIVERANCE

The self-revelation of God makes possible a relationship that is more than the rendering of obligatory service. Although human beings cannot look upon God face to face, the covenant relationship promises that God constantly looks upon us and is present throughout all the twists and turns of our journey through life. This sense of the presence of God is the source of great assurance and in times of difficulty offers us a possibility of relief. This is the theme that we find often in the psalms: "Hasten to answer me, O LORD, for my spirit is fainting. Do not hide your face from me, or I will become as those who descend into the pit" (Ps 143:7).

God does not only hear our pleas for assistance, but responds and brings us deliverance.

There is a truth revealed in such prayers: we are not self-sufficient. We will sometimes find ourselves in situations with which we cannot cope and we are in need, not only of human solidarity and help but of divine intervention. "O God help me. Lord hasten to my aid" (Ps 70:2). At certain points in our journey we may conclude that without God our life will veer toward shipwreck—whether we are prepared fully to acknowledge this or not.

The timely help of God is not limited to saving us from external dangers; it also helps us to recover when we have allowed our integrity to be violated by rash or wrong choices. Even though we may choose to turn our backs on God, there is always the possibility of reversing our self-destructive choices. "Restore us, O God; let your face shine on us and we will be saved" (Ps 80:4). God is not only the lover of innocence but, by a process beyond our comprehension, is able to restore that which had been lost. Since God is beyond change, the relationship with us initiated at our creation remains constant in the divine mind. We may turn aside from it, but not God. This plan for us is not static it is active. By the operation of Providence God is always working to bring us back to that from which we strayed. To restore us.

The first step in this return is when we become aware that we are lost. If there is still a glimmer of faith within us, a memory of the benignity of God then, in our desperation, we will be drawn to call out for help. As we experience our prayer as being answered the spark of faith begins to flare and our relationship with God re-asserts itself—perhaps against our resistance.

The way God works to bring us back to our senses is by re-attaching us to the inspired teaching of the Scriptures, enkindling in us the desire to be instructed by them and to become more responsive to the divine presence. "Let your face shine on your servant, and teach me your testimonies" (Ps 119:135). What began as a cry for help becomes prayer for greater closeness to the source of our being and the ultimate object of all our desiring.

171   Let my lips utter praise
      because you teach me your statutes.

PRAISE

In the 150 psalms which constitute the Psalter, we are often encouraged to praise God. In Hebrew the book is simply entitled *tehillim*, praises. And often we are given cause to praise God, especially for all the wonderful works that have been accomplished for our benefit. Yet it is striking that about a third of the psalms included in the Psalter are songs of lament. It is as though the intensity of our praise of God is commensurate with our sense of having been protected from harm and delivered from hardship.

Perhaps it is useful to understand the diverse kinds of praise so as to appreciate in what conditions praise of God is appropriate.

Tactical praise is offered when we wish to confirm someone in the work they are doing. Sometimes it is merely task-oriented, but often it flows over into a more general approbation of the doer of the task. Unconsciously such praise can be used as a means of control. Receiving praise feels good and cements the relationship, but it also implies a threat that praise will be withheld if performance declines. Approbation of the person is conditional; it depends on the quality of the work done.

Spontaneous praise occurs when someone is overwhelmed by beauty. A landscape, a piece of music, a work of art can often provoke a gasp of wonderment that no words can fully express. It is as though there has been a sudden glimpse of a world beyond the present that has caused a sharp spasm of admiration that momentarily eclipses the concerns of everyday life. We are taken beyond ourselves. Such moments cannot be manufactured; they come upon us suddenly and surprise us and leave us with a pervasive sense of privilege.

Reflective praise rises in us when we allow ourselves to ruminate. When we make time to ponder events and to penetrate deeper into their meaning. We have to step back from making choices and engaging in activities and allow ourselves to look at reality from different angles and to view it against different backgrounds. Not everything that happens makes sense immediately. Precipitate judgment often leads to wrong conclusions. It is only when we consider matters from a broader context that what has happened begin to make sense. This is a process that goes beyond the gathering of factual information; it is the working of wisdom. When we step back we perceive that something that has occurred is worthy of praise.

The praise that is enjoined in the psalms is reflective praise. We are admonished to consider the admirable accomplishments of God and what they communicate about God's attitude to us both in the past and today. They ask us to see behind the works of creation and redemption an ongoing concern for our welfare which is not diminished by our repeated infidelities. Yes, we are instructed to praise God because, as Psalm 136 reminds us, "God's kindness is without limits."

172   My tongue sings of your utterances,
     because all your commandments are righteous.

CONTAGIOUS

Virtue in other people is not always attractive; sometimes it is oppressive. It is easy to forget the axiom of classical philosophy that virtue stands in the middle ground; both too much and too little of anything are to be avoided. It is the same lesson that Ecclesiastes taught: "Do not be over-righteous or over-wise" (Eccl 7:16). Our experience of our own compromised integrity makes us suspicious of one who presents as having only good qualities. To our way of thinking a virtuous person is one who overcomes strong contrary tendencies, not one for whom goodness has no competition.

Our human experience of the façades used by self-righteousness to protect its secrets, makes it hard for us to comprehend the unambiguous righteousness of God. It is sheer goodness, without a trace of malice. And God's righteousness is unreservedly attractive. To the extent that our spirits are unblemished by sin, we cannot help being drawn to the ultimate goodness of God. It is for this we were created and nothing else quite satisfies our inner yearning.

God's righteousness stamps itself on all that God does. This means that the perceptive soul is able to penetrate the divine works and find there footprints that trace the path back to God. "The heavens narrate the glory of God and the firmament announces the work of God's hands" (Ps 19:2). But among all the works of divine self-revelation the inspired content of the Scriptures is preeminent. Not so much for the bald recital of the facts of sacred history but for the gradual unveiling of the heart of God for those who approach the text in faith and openness of spirit.

To the one who responds to the invitation to "taste and see that the LORD is good" (Ps 34:8), a progressive familiarity with God develops, with the unexpected result that more time is somehow found to be in the presence of the Lord. More surprisingly, a mysterious affinity with the spiritual world and with God develops. God is not only good and attractive, but also contagious. Without any external fanfare, the fervent believer passes from glory to glory and is slowly—very slowly—transformed in an ever-closer likeness to God.

Every utterance from the mouth of God overflows with divine righteousness and has the capacity to change us for the better, to lead us toward a more abundant life. The commandments of God are not merely external prescriptions intended to impose on us an unyielding conformity. They act on us through delight. To the extent that we are charmed by what we glimpse of the divine righteousness we are drawn to embrace the behavioral paths described by the Scriptures as appropriate for the service of God. It is not an imposition. It is a choice, made in love and celebration. That is why "my tongue sings of your utterances, because all your commandments are righteous."

173   Let your hand be my help,
          for I have chosen your precepts.

HELP

The plea for help is frequent in the psalms. A cynic might observe that really sincere prayer is only generated by dire conditions. When all is well, we are inclined to forget God and to manage on our own. When things begin to go awry, suddenly we remember God and call out for help. There is probably some truth in this, but believers ask for God's help even when nothing extraordinary is threatening. The opening verse of Psalm 70 can be used in any circumstance: "O God, save me; Lord hasten to help me."

When we call out for help we are abandoning the delusion of total self-sufficiency. We recognize that we may not comprehend all the elements that comprise the situation, or that we are too weak to respond appropriately. Furthermore, in many cases, what is appropriately asked for and appropriately given results in increased solidarity. The relationship between helper and helped is strengthened.

The help that God gives comes in different forms and arrives through different channels. Sometimes it seems a matter of happenstance, at others, it comes about through the agency and good will of others. Perhaps God inspires us to draw what is needed from within. It may be the unforeseen provision of material resources which enables us to complete the task. Maybe guidance is given concerning a possible pathway to progress. It may be by triggering memories which motivate us to apply ourselves to the work with greater determination. Sometimes it is sincere encouragement and approbation that give a boost to our flagging energies. There are many ways in which God can help us to do what, at first sight, seemed impossible. The key to the effectiveness of such intervention is our willingness to accept help; and this willingness is best indicated by our asking for help.

Prayer is always—at least implicitly—a cry for help. To the extent that we realize that living in accordance with the divine self-revelation is a challenge, we will often find ourselves asking God for assistance in following the path that leads to a more fulfilled life. This is not an endeavor that comes naturally to us; it is inspired and prompted by God's word yet, to our everyday manner of thinking, it is beyond our meagre resources. And so we pray. We pray that God will enlighten us and strengthen us to live in fidelity to what has been commanded. The work is God's and so must be the resources to complete it.

From this we could perhaps deduce the supposition that the purpose of the commandments is not so much that we accomplish them, but that we come to the realization that it is impossible for us, on the basis of our own resources, to fulfil what we have been commanded. The commandments are intended to reveal our powerlessness, our radical need for God. It is our inability to obey what God has commanded that is the essential trigger of our prayer. We pray because we realize that our position is precarious. Not from a position of strength or self-congratulation, but because we know that without God's help all is lost.

174   Lord, I long for your salvation;
      your instruction is my delight.

LONGING

Longing is desire that is both acute and chronic. It is acute because—whatever its external stimulants—its roots are embedded very deeply within us. It is chronic because it endures for years, sometimes for a lifetime. In some cases yearning may become the primary shaper of a person's life. They become lifelong seekers—somewhat detached from the more obvious enticements and inducements of the world around them.

A profound desire that has as its object something beyond the world of space and time is not uncommon—though it requires a good level of spiritual literacy to be able to name it. Such yearning derives its energy from the intuitive side of the brain and so is unconvincing to the brain's rational functions, which give priority to processing data gained through the senses. Many people are conscious of occasional "intimations of immortality," though only a few are able to incorporate them fully into a personal philosophy or lifestyle.

To have caught sight, even momentarily, of the reality of the spiritual world robs what happens in this world of space and time of any claim to absolute value. It invests all reality with an aura of mystery. We can perceive that portion of reality that presently impinges on our senses, but we cannot perceive what is beyond our range of sight and hearing. Nor can we comprehend the relationship of the visible parts to the invisible whole.

Something is missing if we limit our notion of the nature of religion to its organizational aspects, its beliefs, values, rituals and social structures. These expressions of interior faith are important and even essential, but they are not everything. Indeed, as the prophets often affirm, the externals are merely hollow simulacra unless they are fortified with interior sentiment. "This people honors me with their lips but their hearts are far distant from me" (Isa 29:13). Desire to enter more fully into the transcendent reality of God is at the heart of all genuine religion—external beliefs and rituals do no more than approximate the yearning that is the mysterious driving force behind the religious impulse.

There is some benefit to be gained by seeking a more explicit awareness of the desire for God that is often hidden beneath louder and more mundane ambitions. To search within our own experience to rediscover what started us on the road of spiritual searching. To enter into this primal experience and—as it were—to reanimate it. Bringing it into line with our present circumstances and giving it a voice in our choice of options. And then, using the familiar texts of the psalms, to allow this inner desire to speak out and be heard. "My soul longs for your salvation, I hope in your word. My eyes yearn for your utterances, saying: When will you console me?" (Ps 119:81-82). This then becomes a prayer not only of the lips, but also of the heart.

175 My soul lives and praises you,
   for your judgments are my help.

LIFE

When the spiritual world opens up before us and we begin to catch glimmers of the divinity, we also move toward a more comprehensive notion of the boundless extent of reality and a truer picture of our place within the totality. This transformative vision gradually imprints on our hearts and minds a view of reality that does not coincide with that generally acceptable in the world around us. We begin to see ourselves in terms of a much broader reality. We belong not only to our local tribe; we are citizens of the universe.

In ordinary usage life is considered in a binary context as the opposite of death. This may be convenient in arriving at clinical conclusions, but it scarcely does justice to richness implicit in the reality that is life. If we think of life in terms of vitality it is obvious that there are almost infinite quantitative and qualitative gradations possible in the notion of being alive, from the smallest slug to the towering intellectual. When the word of God is said to be life-giving, this is to be understood as increasing our vitality, making us more fully alive and lively. It does this by affirming us, giving us guidance, providing motivation for right conduct, and encouraging us to persevere in the path toward a fuller life when the going becomes difficult.

Everything that I am is God's gift to me; this is the lesson I learn from the Scriptures. The more I allow God's word to circulate through my thoughts and imagination, the more I become convinced that—in one way or another—my life and all my vitality are not my own creation, but come from God through the working of divine providence. The enrichment of my soul through ongoing influence from God's word means that my whole life becomes a hymn of praise to the munificent creativity of God. It is not just my voice that sings. When I open my mouth to glorify God what comes out is the glory with which God has graced me throughout my life. When my soul sings praise, it is God's gift that sings. As is often quoted: "The glory of God is the fully alive human being."

The various ways in which God is manifested to us are all designed to show us the path to a fuller life. They help us to become what we are meant to be. They are not external impositions designed to force us into a pre-formed mold, but invitations and incitements to be more fully ourselves. Constancy in reading Scripture is not rote learning of regulations in search of conformity, but the adventure of discovering who we are in the sight of God. This endeavor is not only a source of necessary comfort; it also contains a constant note of challenge, demanding that we abandon the narrowness of our fixed perspectives and routines, and venture into new territory. We praise God best by growing beyond our narrow confines and allowing ourselves to be constantly re-formed by the ever-creative word of divine self-revelation.

176 I wandered like a lost sheep, seek your servant
   for I have not forgotten your commandments.

LOST

One of the biblical images for sin is being lost. Being lost means not knowing where we are and not knowing how to head toward our intended destination. To the extent that we allow ourselves to wander away from God our lives lose purpose, and we begin to meander around in circles. Losing our bearings quickly leads to mental and emotional disorientation. Our choices become increasingly erratic. We are making no progress yet we keep thinking the same thoughts. Our minds are often filled with the recycling of the same grievances and resentments, so that any hope of moving on into a more gratifying future quickly fades.

Less dramatic than finding ourselves in an alien environment, but having similar effects, is the state of aimlessness. This comes about when we deliberately abandon any notion of having a clear goal in favor of a general fuzziness, in which our choices are made willy-nilly according to whatever momentary advantage presents itself to us. We have no ultimate ambition in life, but are content to swim around in circles; aimlessly, like a goldfish in a bowl. A seemingly harmless kind of existence, but hugely unsatisfying.

What must be for us all a source of great assurance is that God does not intend us to remain lost forever; that is why we implore God to seek and find us. God intervenes in our life. Sometimes this happens through the workings of Providence, by the impact of events or the agency of other people. Sometimes disaster explodes our complacency. Sometimes our re-orientation can come about through our interaction with the Scriptures. Our ongoing contact with God's self-revelation provides us with guidance for a more fulfilling life. Sometimes by helping us to move in a different general direction. Sometimes—amazingly—by seeming to address itself to the particularities of our present situation. Although its prescriptions seem to limit our freedom, this is only because they envisage long-term benefits. We do not always perceive the implications inherent in the choices we make, and sometimes the exigencies of the present obscure what is needed for a more creative future. Having a point of reference outside our immediate circumstances is a useful corrective for our moral myopia.

Remembering the commandments, as Deuteronomy frequently advises us, helps us to overcome our tendency to drift away from God, but it also provides us with a means of finding a way out of the morass our foolishness has created. It provides us with a vantage point that transcends the demands of the present moment and gives us confidence that there is meaning to be found even in the ups and downs that characterize every human life.

Sometimes being lost is a good thing because it offers the opportunity for rejoicing when the lost one is found. Beyond that, wandering off the track sometimes gives a chance of seeing what would otherwise be passed by unnoticed. We see reality from a different angle and, perhaps, come to appreciate our expanded vision. They say that the shortest distance between two points is a straight line. This may well be true, but the shortest distance is not necessarily the most interesting. Living according to the strict demands of sequential logic may seem like an efficient way of arriving at our destination—except more often than not its practitioners suffer burnout before arriving at their goal. Perhaps a limited amount of wandering is needed if we are to attain our full humanity, if it is true that "to err is human." Within the universal providence of God our going off the track sometimes may turn out to be an enrichment not only for ourselves but also for others.

In a certain sense, this long psalm could be seen as an example of creative wandering. It has but a single theme, but yet has formulated 176 different ways of celebrating the life-enhancing role of God's self-revelation. Spending time wandering with the psalmist perhaps will lead us to appreciate the gift that we have received and to allow God's word to play a significant role in our lives. If this happens the text will become not merely a psalm to be sung but also a pattern and a program to be followed.

Notes

1. Thus Leopold Sabourin, *The Psalms: Their Origin and Meaning* (New York: Alba House, 1972), 381. "Tedious repetitions, poor thought sequence, apparent lack of inspiration reflect the artificiality of the composition."

2. An alphabetic acrostic is a device in which the first letter of each literary unit follows alphabetic order. Using the whole alphabet can be taken as an indicator of completeness. Ps 119 is composed on 22 stanzas of 8 verses, each corresponding to a letter of the Hebrew alphabet, in which each verse of the stanza begins with a word starting with the same letter. Ronald Knox attempted to reproduce this schema in his English version, but the result was not good. For a detailed description of the psalm's poetic dynamics, see David Noel Freedman, *Psalm 119: The Exaltation of Torah* (Winona Lake: Eisenbrauns, 1999).

3. Thus in Gen 12:6-7, the Lord appears to Abram at the terebinth of Moreh, the teacher's terebinth, the tree often favored as a place of revelation. See Deut 11:30.

4. Thus, Georg Fohrer, art. "*Sophia*," in TDNT VII, p. 476. He writes, "The common translation 'wise,' 'wisdom' is unfortunate and to a large extent inexact. It does justice neither to the broad range of the Hebrew terms nor to their precise meaning. If knowledge is presupposed in detail, this is not so much a deeper knowledge in the theoretical mastery of the questions of life and universe as a solution of a practical kind on the basis of concrete demands."

5. Exod 20:2-17; Deut 5:6-21; Exod 34:10-26. See Michael Coogan, *The Ten Commandments: A Short History of an Ancient Text* (New Haven: Yale University Press, 2014), ix–xiii.

6. The series includes both prescriptions and prohibitions. With the cessation of temple worship, many of them were no longer relevant. For a listing see, among other references, www.chabad.org.

7. Thus, *Pirke Aboth* 1.1: "Moses received the Law from Sinai and committed it to Joshua, and Joshua to the elders, and the elders to the Prophets, and the Prophets committed it to the men of the Great Synagogue. They said three things: Be deliberate in judgement, raise up many disciples, and *make a fence around the law*" (emphasis added). Translation by Herbert Danby in *The Mishnah: Translated from the Hebrew with Introduction and Brief Explanatory Notes* (Oxford: University Press, reprinted 1972), 446.

8. This prescriptive nuance was, of course, emphasized in Latin translations with the use of the harsh monosyllable *lex*, possibly derived from the Sanskrit root for binding, as indicated by the related word "ligature."

9. "It is an old idea that morality binds us by our own will, but law binds us from without, by reference to an extraneous will. In morality, humans are autonomous, acting as a law unto themselves. In law, they are heteronomous, subjected to the will of some governing authority, even if that be a democratic form of legislature. This distinction, if well-founded, points to a–perhaps to the–fundamental conceptual distinction of morality and law. It points to the distinction between autonomous and heteronomous normative order. Here, it will be argued that the contrast is well-founded, but not absolute. Law is not heteronomous *sans phrase*, but only relatively heteronomous. It is, however, this relative heteronomy of law that differentiates law from morality." Neil MacCormick, "The Relative Heteronomy of Law" (first published April 1995), accessed November 10, 2018, at https://doi.org/10.1111/j.1468-0378.1995.tb00040.x.

10. For a discussion of the issues, see S. Bengler, "Der langste Psalm—Anthologie oder Liturgie," *Vetus Testamentum* 29 (1979): 257–88.

11. Freedman, *Psalm 119*, 25.

12. Timothy Lloyd Wilt, "Alphabetic Acrostics: perhaps the form can be represented," *The Bible Translator* 44.2 (April 1993): 207.

13. Saint Ambrose, *Expositio in psalmum CXVIII* 1.2; PL 15, 1264a.

14. T. S. Eliot, *Murder in the Cathedral* (1935).

15. Saint Augustine, *In Psalmum CXVIII Enarratio* 4.1; CCL 40, 1674.

16. Saint Bernard, *On Precept and Dispensation* §16; SBOp III, 264.

17. Augustine, *In Ps CXVIII* 5.1, 1676.

18. Ambrose, *In Ps CXVIII*, 1.8; 1267A.

19. Augustine, *In Ps CXVIII* 7.4; 1684.

20. On the meaning of these terms see M. Casey, *The Promise of Deliverance: Reading Second Isaiah* (New York: Orbis Books, 2021), 63–69.

21. Hans-Joachim Kraus, *Theology of the Psalms* (Minneapolis: Augsburg, 1986), 148.

22. Bernard, *Letter* 18.1; SBOp 7, 67.

23. Saint Benedict, *Rule*, 1.9.

24. Aelred, S. 128.13; IIC, 275.

25. *Tehillat Hashem* (Brooklyn: Merkos L'Inyonei Chinuch, 1982), 336–38.

26. Augustine, *In Ps CXVIII* 10.6; 1695: *dilectione et delectatione iustitiae dilatemur.*

27. Aurelius Cassiodorus, *Expositio in Psalterium* (Psalm 118:18), PL 70, 842D.

28. *The Divine Liturgy of Our Holy Father John Chrysostom* (Pittsburgh: Byzantium Seminary Press, 2006), 52.

29. Ambrose, *In Ps CXVIII*, 3.46; 1306B.

30. Augustine, *In Ps CXVIII*, 18.31; 1724.

31. Bernard, Ep 18.1; SBOp 7, 67.

32. Augustine, *In Ps CXVIII*, 31.4; 1771.

33. *The Seven Modes of Love*, 347–53; in *Cistercian Studies Quarterly* 54.1 (2019): 93.

34. See Casey, *The Promise of Deliverance*, 63–66.

35. Ambrose, *In Ps CXVIII*, 9.16; 1396B.

36. Bernard, Adv 2.5; SBOp 4.363.

37. Bernard, *On the Song of Songs* 54.8; SBOp 2,107.

38. *Troylus* I, 102.

39. Charlton T. Lewis, *A Latin Dictionary* (Oxford: University Press, 1966), 165.

40. According to the maxim of Paul Ricoeur: *Le symbole donne à penser.*

41. Fyodor Dostoyevsky, *The Idiot* (Harmondsworth: Penguin, 1965), 465.